DATE DUE

DE2 0 00			
JE 11 03			

DEMCO 38-296

College for Sale

Knowledge, Identity and School Life Series

Editors: Professor Philip Wexler, Graduate School of Education and
Human Development, University of Rochester, New York, NY 14627,
USA and
Professor Ivor Goodson, Faculty of Education, University of Western
Ontario, Canada.

College for Sale:
A Critique of the Commodification of Higher Education

Wesley Shumar

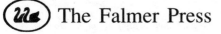 The Falmer Press

(A member of the Taylor & Francis Group)
London • Washington, D.C.

wder Square, London, EC4A 3DE
& Francis Inc., 1900 Frost Road, Suite 101,

First published in 1997

A catalogue record for this book is available from the British Library

**Library of Congress Cataloging-in-Publication Data are available
on request**

ISBN 0 7507 0410 1 cased
ISBN 0 7507 0411 X paper

Jacket design by Caroline Archer

Typeset in 10/12pt Times by
Graphicraft Typesetters Ltd., Hong Kong.

Printed in Great Britain by Biddles Ltd, Guildford and King's Lynn on paper
which has a specified pH value on final paper manufacture of not less than
7.5 and is therefore 'acid free'.

Every effort has been made to contact copyright holders for their permission
to reprint material in this book. The publishers would be gateful to hear
from any copyright holder who is not here acknowledged and will undertake
to rectify any errors or omissions in future editions of this book.

Contents

Acknowledgments

Like most research projects, this work has developed and changed over many years. It began with my dissertation work and so I must first thank the members of my dissertation committee. I benefited in many ways from years of guidance and input by these mentors; it was their teaching which sparked my interest in the political, epistemological and ethical implications of turning the anthropological lens on the institutions of knowledge production. My mentors fostered an innovative and creative approach to the doing of anthropological research as well as habits of critical reflection upon the nature of participant observation and results. From them I learned to think through the local and its relationship to larger political, economic and historical forces.

I also owe a debt of gratitude to other colleagues and to my informants, several of whom wore both hats. Together we explored the ironies of an ethnographer-informant model that assumes a gulf of social, geographical and temporal distance between the two: in this study, ethnographers and informants share a world, and their hats. Their willingness to share their stories and criticize my work made possible my understanding of the complex transformations occurring in American universities. Further, their insight into my own stories created a genuinely dialogic process of data production and analysis. What insights exist in this work are due to that collaborative process in which I learned to think about my life as well as the lives of others. The limitations of expression of these insights are, of course, wholly mine.

I am grateful to the following for permission to reproduce material published elsewhere: Table 3, 'Phases of productivity growth (GDP per man-hour) 1870–1987' from *Dynamic Forces in Capitalist Development*, p. 51, by Angus Maddison, Oxford University Press, © 1991; Table 5, 'Percent of families' with low, middle, and high relative income, by region, 1969–1989', p. 320, and Table 4, 'The shrinking Federal Student Aid Grant, school years beginning in 1977–1989 (1991 Dollars)', p. 366, from *The State of Working America, 1992–93*, by Lawrence Mishel and Jared Bernstein, Economic Policy Institute Series, M.E. Sharpe, Inc. © 1993; Table 7, 'Percentage changes in faculty compensation by rank in public and private institutions of higher education by AAUP category, 1971–72 to 1978–79 (in current and constant [1967] dollars)', from *Three Thousand Futures: The Next Twenty Years for Higher Education*, p. 300, by The Carnegie Council on Policy Studies in Higher Education, published by The Carnegie Foundation for the Advancement of Teaching and Jossey-Bass, Inc. © 1980, also originally from

'Coping with adversity: The economic status of the profession, 1971' *AAUP Bulletin*, June 1972, and 'An era of continuing decline: Annual report on the economic status of the profession, 1978–79', *Academe*, Bulletin of the AAUP, Sept. 1979; and Table 8, 'Number of faculty collective bargaining agreements by bargaining agent (1975 to 1987)' from 'A professoriate in trouble: And hardly anyone recognizes it', by Dennis McGrath and Martin B. Spear, in *Change: The Magazine of Higher Learning* **20**, 1, January/February, p. 30, 1988, reprinted with permission of the Helen Dwight Reid Educational Foundation, published by Heldref Publications, 1319 Eighteenth St., N.W., Washington, D.C. 20036–1802, copyright © 1988.

I would like to thank Annette Lareau and Philip Wexler for their interest in this project at its early stages; their support and guidance helped me get the project off the ground and their advice and thorough criticism sustained and improved the work. My thanks as well to the editors and staff at Falmer Press who are enormously supportive and understanding of the trials of writing in an era of academic downsizing and job insecurity Finally, I would like to thank Marnie Whelan. Without her ideas, as well as her intellectual, emotional and editorial support, this work would not have been possible.

Introduction

... doing research is a similar exercise to going on a voyage of discovery, and that we undertake scholarly studies to make the familiar strange. In Flecker's poem merchants, poets and pilgrims set out for Samarkand, each with their own mission. The pilgrims search for knowledge, the merchants for trade, the poet tells stories. Qualitative research involves the same three goals. Researchers seek enlightenment and understanding, tell stories about them, and finally exchange that knowledge for good (the PhD, a job, publications, royalties). (Delamont, 1992, p. vii)

Position in the classification struggle depends upon position in the class structure; and social subjects — including intellectuals, who are not those best placed to grasp that which defines the limits of their thought of the social world, that is, the illusion of the absence of limits — are perhaps never less likely to transcend 'the limits of their minds' than the representation they have and give of their position, which defines those limits. (Bourdieu, 1984, p. 484)

Personal Beginnings

This work grows from several personal and intellectual commitments and dilemmas. I am trained as a cultural anthropologist, and I see the discourses of culture and ethnography as central to my concerns with higher education. But while my field's methodology of participant observation and its notions of culture have both recently been much drawn upon in educational research, particularly in the discourses around politics of identity (for example, multiculturalism, afrocentrism, cultural literacy), nevertheless I have come to see that ethnography, participant observation and culture are all contradictorily constituted discursive loci from which forms of power are disseminated. Cultures do not so much exist in their own right as they are imagined into being by various discursive apparatuses; sometimes by the state for political reasons, or by participants in ideological struggle or one kind or another; but also, I believe, through the legitimating influence of ethnography as it is generated in the supposedly innocent and disinterested arena of intellectual inquiry.

Ethnography makes a strong claim to legitimacy. Through the phenomenological conceit of participant observation, the ethnographer claims to know the people because s/he has been there. In literal terms, being there is how we all learn to know people and places and things; 'I saw it with my own eyes' is difficult to question; impossible to deny. And I do not wish to belittle that 'being there', because I, as many anthropologists, believe it to be a powerful form of knowledge and potentially valuable contribution to understanding and tolerance between groups of people. I do wish to problematize 'being there', or rather its ideologically constructed variant, participant observation. An ethnographer not only comes to a deep knowledge and appreciation of a group of people, but s/he invents that group for the purpose of considering it and sharing the subsequent information. Willis's Lads, Eckert's Burnouts, or MacLeod's Hallway Hangers, did not exist before being invented by Willis, Eckert and MacLeod. The members of each may have seen themselves in relation to one another, as they doubtless saw themselves in relation to others, but they did not constitute a group entity before the act of naming gave externally-recognized shape to a seemingly self-identified group. There are ways in which groups exist before naming but not in the self-conscious and referential way that the ethnographer brings to the text. Ethnographies constitute objects.

Peter Rigby (1985), an anthropologist who studies East African pastoralists, was very aware of this dilemma of participant observation when he wrote:

> The very term 'participant observation' implies the false ontological objectivity, derived from the natural sciences, which I have been trying so strenuously to dismantle. In the sociological context, it allows the logical possibility of being an 'observer' without being a 'participant' or a 'participant' while not being an 'observer'; both postulates are patently absurd. (p. 31)

We all participate in and observe social life. People under study are participant observers as much as the ethnographer is. The distinction between the two is found in the forms of discourse deployed by each group. The discourse of the ethnographer is often that of powerful outsider to a social group, who uses that position to constitute and define the group. (Bourdieu, 1977) in making an ethnography, an object, a 'social group', is brought into being, enhancing the ethnographer's professional reputation and very possibly creating a reification later to be used by bureaucratic apparatuses in deploying forms of social control (for example, state policies, welfare programs, etc.).

The issue is ethical as well as scientific. Partly because of the difficulties I see as inherent in participant observation, 'ethnography' in the traditional sense is too limited a term to describe my approach in the present work. As a graduate student in anthropology I consciously decided against both the study of small foreign communities or of poor, ethnic, marginalized communities in the US; the traditional objects of anthropological study. I chose to follow the advise of Laura Nader (1972) and 'study up' by looking at the institutions of higher education and the centers of knowledge production in the United States. This decision had the advantage of giving me a kind of insider status, and allowing me to think both about what Bourdieu calls the objective structure of the social and subjective strategies of actors. However, my position in this complex field was, and remains, a very marginalized one. Marginality, being on one hand an insider but on the periphery of successful academic life and so in some ways an outsider, gives shape to the theoretical and empirical perspective of this work.

In anthropology as well as in education, it has become popular to discuss both marginal groups and the way they are constituted through marginalizing discourses from centers of power. It has also become popular to talk about how these margins do not constitute whole cultures and whole identities but fragmented and contradictory identities and cultures. These discursively constituted lines of force and the ways they mark out distinct groups, make groups invisible, or, ironically both; have attracted the intent interest of much recent ethnographic work. (Tsing, 1994; Rosaldo, 1989; Giroux, 1993). While this work is very important there is a danger of falling into a 'false ontological objectivity'. The new others are fragmentary and contradictorily constituted products of global transnational economic forces, but others nonetheless. And these new others still play the traditional role of the other. They are temporally and spatially removed from us (Fabian, 1983) and serve as a foil for the definition of intellectuals and society at the center. They can be the symptom of our crisis of identity. What is not recognized is the operation of power by Western institutions and systems of power and the internal fissures and contradictions of these institutions and systems. In other words, we — the intellectuals, the speakers, the creators of social groups — remain invisible to the analysis (Rosaldo, 1989, pp. 206–7).

In practical terms this book is about myself, my friends, the people I work with and institutions that I am part of. We are affected by the same global forces that impact the life of peasants in Malaysia, data processors in Barbados, industrial workers in the midwest. As Rosaldo states:

> All of us inhabit an interdependent late-twentieth-century world marked
> by borrowing and lending across porous national and cultural boundaries
> that are saturated with inequality, power and domination. (*ibid.*, p. 217)

I take the kind of interpenetration that Rosaldo discusses seriously. The tradition of ethnographizing the other is transformed in the present text to studying the self, becoming other to myself. This doubling is theoretical, political and strategic. Theoretically my effort is to take the notion of commodification and analyze the implications this process has had on intellectuals and university life in the United States. What I am calling the commodification of culture is part of the global explosion of transnational corporations and their power to define (and encourage others to define) everything, all aspects of social life, in instrumental economic terms. This process with its myriad implications produces the contradictions and fissures which inexorably marginalize people all over the world by limiting them to part-time or temporary work.

Politically, I believe we need to define the workings of power and the ways in which more and more people are being marginalized because it is clear that this is not only a question of our personal futures but what kind of world we will share with our colleagues and the subjects of our studies. In that pursuit, it is easy to get distracted by fashionable new ethnographic objects or by what Gavin Smith (1991) calls 'a narcissistic preoccupation of the new ethnographic writers with the way they themselves perform cultural production' (p. 213). And it is hard to recognize the operation of power on one's own doorstep; easier and more comfortable to think about how the global economy is affecting itinerant fruit pickers or unemployed steel workers someplace else. And then many younger university intellectuals and their marginalization are made invisible by their own strategies of survival. They resist and deny being identified as temporary, part-time or flexible, because it delegitimates them. This denial helps to maintain the illusion that fragmentation goes on always elsewhere; in the field, at smaller universities, in the Third World; not at the center, not here, not at my university, in my department. Neither the older generation, still benefiting from the remnants of an older and more gracious (to university professors anyway) past; nor the younger one, shut out and struggling, wants to consider the implications of this political process that we are inevitably part of. Who could blame us?

Strategically, I am the voice of the margin making a place to speak from within the center and using the resulting platform as a vantage from which to view larger social and political processes. I am an exile at the center of the institutions of culture and the legitimating power they wield. It is the very working of that power that makes me invisible; just as invisible as it makes millions of even more marginalized others. My strategy is not unlike that of a marginalized forager in the rainforest or ghetto dweller in an American city. I am driven to seek visibility and legitimacy through the fissures in the constructions of power, to fall through the cracks wherever I can.

I think that Rosaldo's (1989) claim that anthropologists deny the power of their society by denying their own culture and the way that culture has made itself transparent is a very important claim (p. 202). Rosaldo argues for voices that recognize a shared world between anthropologist and informants; is one of those voices, but that is not enough (*ibid.*, p. 217). The operation of power privileges critical voices like Edward Said and Renato Rosaldo as it denies the many marginalized intellectual voices in their midst. To really understand how power operates we must not only share a world with our informants but recognize that the same processes of fragmentation, marginalization and invisibility operate at Stanford and Columbia as in the rainforests of the Philippines.

The work that follows is not therefore an ethnography but something more. It is ethnographic, confessional, theoretical. It attempts to map two different but related spaces; the subjective space of consciousness, individual and collective as found in the discourses of colleges and universities, and the shifting space of an immense global capitalist economic system that has by now normalized crisis; in fact made crisis its *raison d'être* the way God was reason and justifying principle for the nineteenth century Protestant Bourgeoisie.

The next three sections briefly outline the notions of commodification, a semiotic framework to analyze advanced capitalism and what I like to call the quantum sociology of Pierre Bourdieu. Following that is a brief outline of the book by chapter.

The Commodification of Culture

On the surface, the idea of commodification of culture is a simple one. Social activities, such as writing, painting, teaching, learning; which may in the past have been done to glorify God or for personal fulfillment, are increasingly directly in the service of the marketplace. These activities and the things they produce come to be valued in terms of their ability to be translated into cash or merchandise, and not in any other ways, such as aesthetic or recreational pleasure. Eventually the idea that there are other kinds of value is lost. In higher education, this historical process has resulted in education's becoming valued for technological innovations that create new, saleable products or for providing skills that a worker can sell in the marketplace. This has already happened. One of the goals of the current work is a political/economic analysis to look at this historic process of commodification of university education during the twentieth century, particularly post-World War II.

At a deeper level the notion of commodification is very complex. I will argue that the movement of late capitalist economic logic draws higher education, as it draws other arenas of culture and society, into the center of economic activity as a way to deal with contradictions of capitalist production and this produces new contradictions for institutions of higher learning to face. Universities and colleges have been used by corporate interests to develop products, train labor and foster new research into technologies of consumption. As education is largely an institution linked to the State (Althusser, 1971; Barrow, 1990) this contradictory process is one the State is part of in late twentieth century capitalism. The State is used by capital to advance its needs, develop products and markets and train laborers, with the cost accruing to the State. As David Harvey (1989) has argued, capitalism is an expansionary process, one that must continue to define more of the social as commodities (p. 344).

The process of drawing culture in general and education in particular into the circuit of commodity production (Johnson, 1987, p. 47) has a discursive impact on institutions; on the ways rules, procedures and regulations are articulated; as well as having an impact on the social products of higher learning and on how people talk about what they are doing and what their doing does. In each of these discursive arenas the force of the signifiers produced is to ultimately see all meaning in terms of what can be bought, sold or made profitable. Education has increasingly little meaning outside a system of market relations.

I would like to relate three illustrative tales. The first is a story about an arboretum which serves as an educational outreach to the community, schools and colleges in its area. The second is a personal story of my realization that I was a migrant worker and the last is a sort of report from the front: young anthropologists talking about how to sell themselves in the academic marketplace. In each of these instances the talk shows constraint by commodifying forces, and meaning is clearly seen in instrumental economic terms.

The Hay Ride

I participated in a hay ride at a local arboretum two summers ago. This arboretum has an education outreach program, providing environmental education programs for school children from pre-school to high school as well as curriculum and training for teachers in local schools. Beyond the educational program the arboretum provides trails for hiking and guided nature walks for the public. The hay ride I was on was part of a summer festival put together to raise money. It was a beautiful, warm and sunny summer day, and it was wonderful to be in this place on such a nice day. As I sat on a hay wagon being pulled by a tractor over the grounds of the arboretum, there was a self-consciousness among the adults on the ride and discomfort with the artifice, mitigated only by the pleasure of the children, who were a lot more interested in playing with straw than the ride itself.

One of the arboretum's directors was on the ride and was talking to his companion about the financial plight of the arboretum. Local government funds were drying up, he said, and the arboretum was having to cut back on its services to the community. At first his conversation was very pessimistic, but after he repeated several times that times difficult he said there was a silver lining. After all, he said, the arboretum was supposed to be of service to the community and it was good in a way that these hard times had forced them to tailor their service to a buying public. His discussion was full of metaphors of the marketplace. He talked about needing to give the customer what s/he wanted, and being more competitive, providing better products. The crisis of state funding and the decline of resources was recast by him, as I listened, as an opportunity to become more competitive in the market for recreational services. It was an odd place to hear this kind of talk. The director, clearly no business expert, was simply repeating the rhetoric that many people in non-profit organizations have begun to use. I found it interesting that in his discourse were several hidden assumptions — that it was wrong to ask the state to provide for the welfare of citizens, that states should economize and not waste money on recreation, and perhaps most tellingly, his naive and by no means unique assumption that the market will determine what the public need and want.

When I began this research, few people thought about the notion of the commodification of culture. Now in the 1990s not only are we aware of the impact of commodification but hear it being touted in Washington as a solution to social ills. So familiar an idea has it become that we don't question this logic but accept it as the way things have always been. We have a very short memory. We have collapsed the past with the world of the present. In our remembering that there have always been financial crises and market pressures, we forget that the world that we strove for in the past was different.

The structure and logic of institutions does more than provide for individual needs. They also structure how those needs are perceived and how valuable they are. They have our help in this. Every conversational reference to the value of market forces for state government, public TV, social welfare helps to build that world. We speak it into existence and give it a kind of solidity that we imagine it has.

Hidden beneath this continuing commodifying discourse are the most pressing economic problems of our age. At the end of World War II, the federal government began performing a regulating function, smoothing out the basic crises of capitalism. The state provided the jobs, money and financial regulation that made possible a unique period in American economic history. But by the time the post war boom gave way to the 70s the resources of the Federal government were heavily overextended and there was a fiscal crisis of the state. That fiscal crisis was passed on to local governments and public institutions in the 80s. As a result and ever since the already heavy tax burden on ordinary people has grown and created the present great crisis of civic life and public welfare. In this crisis, the daily rhetoric of commodification has been used as a way to forget the past and re-imagine it as a failure to see the strength of the market when in fact the current fiscal crisis is a symptom of the contradictions of the market. In this study we will not only look at how higher education has been pressed into market service over a long period of time and how higher education is drawn into the current fiscal crisis of the state, we will also see how contemporary cultural conflicts, over such things as the use of resources, the value of teaching, what ideas are being taught; in general the whole range of assaults universities and colleges currently face; are all symptomatic of the contradictions in late-twentieth century capitalism and the tendency toward commodification of culture.

Driving and Flexible Accumulation

I live about twenty miles south of a large East Coast city. One night, I was driving home on a crowded interstate highway, reflecting on my day. That morning, I had been fifty miles north of the city teaching an anthropology class in a small private college. Now I was driving home after 9.00 at night from a class at a branch campus of a comprehensive university in the suburbs. In-between I had taught and done some research in the city during the afternoon.

My thoughts on this drive were with dissertation research. I had been concerned for months about the prospect of doing fieldwork in a foreign country among a peasant or tribal group of people, which appeared to me on the face of it a purely exploitative venture. My personal interest in getting a PhD seemed impossible to reconcile with the concerns of the people I might study. The thought of doing research among a poor and disenfranchised group in the US seemed little better. How could field work be anything but a voyeuristic, self-serving activity? It was, of course, possible to fantasize about making a long-term commitment to a group of people and remaining involved, perhaps eventually giving something back to them in exchange for what they gave me, but I could readily see that this rarely happens. Paul Rabinow said that when he was in graduate school there were two kinds of anthropologists; the ones who had done field work among the 'other' and those who hadn't, and he remembered that the ones who didn't had less of a claim to the status of anthropologist. Rabinow is one of the few overt expressions of this phenomenological conceit; that living among the other, 'being there', is a rite of passage allowing claim to certain forms of knowledge and kinds of status available in no other way. Roland Barthes said 'language is a fascist', and 'to name and classify is to dominate symbolically'. I felt trapped between the rock of my reluctance to exploit and the hard place of needing to do field work among the 'other' in order to justify my professional life. Barthes further said the goal is to abjure, to shift ground, to be neither a dominator or one of the dominated. Was it possible to bring these ethical ideas to bear on my ambivalence toward fieldwork?

Part of the desire to classify the other is to avoid the realities of one's own classification, but it did dawn on me, traveling up the interstate in my car on a dark rainy night after a long day, that I was in fact a migrant worker. There is a long tradition in the West of using the other to define the self, a form of symbolic exploitation often paired with material and political domination. The other is both inferior (for example, the primitive) and definitive of the self (man in a state of nature and as Fabian (1983) has shown man in the past). I thought perhaps the route out of my own ethical dilemma was to understand the self and the sets of social, political and economic constraints in which I found myself and my colleagues, through a reflection on the producers of knowledge and the institutions which constrain them.

Johannes Fabian (1983) has shown that part of the discursive tradition of anthropology has been to deny coevalness with the Other. While ethnographic fieldwork involves a sharing of time and space with a group of people, the process of ethnographic writing involves a temporal distancing in order to classify and reify the Other. Fabian refers specifically to the Western tendency to classify the primitive and allocate them an atemporal classification. Fabian's work is valid for much ethnographic research in education as well. Ethnographers relegate disempowered groups, such as students, minorities and in some instances teachers, to atemporal classifications through their writing. One of Fabian's suggestions for the critique of ethnography is to 'conceive a theory of praxis' (*ibid.*, p. 157). Concern for praxis also motivates the work of Pierre Bourdieu, who when he saw how ethnographic work being done in Algeria served colonial goals, decided to become a sociologist. Bourdieu (1977, pp. 72–6) very interestingly argues that the anthropologist, seeing him/herself an outsider to a culture, makes that weakness a virtue by assuming the outsider's ability to model the society, (Bourdieu's methodological objectivism), is superior to the natives' own knowledge. Bourdieu does not deny the power of objective models but shows clearly that without knowledge of subjective strategies, the ethnographer has no way of knowing what is really going on with the other. In a different way from Fabian, Bourdieu too argues for a theory of practice, a probabilistic rendering of the strategies engendered by habitus.

My contribution to Fabian's call for a model of praxis is to locate myself and the university workers around me in the larger contradictions of global capitalism as it affects the work force in the university sector of the economy. Not surprisingly, the effects of these forces on university workers are similar to those on other workers in the United States. I have also attempted to look at the particular crises that universities face as a result of economic restructuring, demographic changes, and changing ideas about the role of universities in the United States. Further, I have attempted to assess the strategies of my colleagues and co-workers as well as the changing consciousness of university professors as the ivory tower is dismantled. In so far as it is possible, I have become other to myself, using what C. Wright Mills (1959) calls the 'sociological imagination' (p. 5). My decision on the highway to label myself a 'migrant worker' and, using this conceit to think about the structure of the university and the forces brought to bear on it and on my peers and me, sent me on a journey of discovery. The university where I was getting my degree not only taught half of its own courses with graduate students and part-time labor but, as a large public research university, was also supplier of part-time and temporary college professors to colleges and universities throughout the metropolitan area. The lower cost of teaching their courses was useful to institutions scrambling to cut costs and find new *products to sell* to attract more new students; all efforts to deal with fiscal shortfalls soon amounting to crisis. My study of commodification began with objectifying my position within the productive capacities of universities and the emerging patterns of labor in the 1980s.

Fabian's discussion of the denial of coevalness and Bourdieu's reflexive sociology have several implications for me. First, theoretical models of local ethnographic site and global forces are used to talk about peasants in Malaysia and the Caribbean (Comaroff, 1985; Scott, 1985; Ong, 1987; Freeman, 1993) or underclass students in urban schools (Willis, 1981; Foley, 1990; MacLeod, 1987), but there is clearly reluctance use them at the centers of power. University professors have not been looked at through this lens. My position in the field has enabled me to see ways in which an entire younger generation of university workers is marginalized while only a very few of their rank are successful. These successes (and failures) are often spoken of in terms of quality of work or political savvy, and are rarely seen to be the inevitable result of restructuring on a global scale of work and capital. We — university professionals whose studies include people and their lives — have simply not seen ourselves as subject to the same sets of forces as the other peoples of the world and as a result we have privileged the analysis of the 'other' while allowing our own culture to remain opaque (Rosaldo, 1989, pp. 202–3).

The denial of coevalness leaves us with no way to respond to commodifying discourse addressed to us on a daily basis. University faculty are by and large not engaged with the political processes that are transforming the universities where they work. The depolitization of college faculty has a long history (Barrow, 1990, p. 198), and has important implications in the present. Without either involvement in the process or intellectual tools to critique our own position, university intellectuals are increasingly trapped by the relentless logic of commodification. This logic tells me I can buy a sports car, establish my own press or create a new market niche as a way to survive. It militates against my addressing basic questions about the status of education, the nature of knowledge and the quality of my future by simply making these things unprofitable, and therefore meaningless.

Hot Commodities

'The Caribbean has arrived', declared a recent PhD in anthropology to a group of colleagues. We were sitting in the lobby of a large hotel at an academic meeting, and as usual the conversation had turned to jobs. This was in the 90s — in the 1980s up-and-coming academia, like everybody else in America, believed the dream. The dream was that if you worked hard, made the right connections, published and managed to be in the right place at the right time, you got a tenure-track job in the university. But by the time I had joined 500 recent PhDs crowding around the fifty jobs being advertised at the meetings, the dream gave way to despair and then, paradoxically, relief. Despair because the future for the university work for which we had all trained and committed to looked unremittingly bleak. It was a relief — at meetings, anyway — to realize that we were all in this together, and not individual failures.

We were having this 90s discussion in a space appropriate to our mood, sitting in a post-modern bar located somewhere near the bottom of a fifty-storey beehive. Instead of the simple traditional lobby space, a large open area from which it is possible to go up or out, the interior of this hotel was a hollowed-out cylinder with a central post and lighted glass elevators sliding up and down a vast vertical space. The floors, visible above our heads, were open to the central core and had ivy growing down over a rail so that each level looked both organic and geometric, sort of a computer-generated rainforest. The space was a temple to our late twentieth century post-industrial world; grand and alive with geometric machine life. People subjugated to the technologies they've produced, extensions of computers and mechanical processes, as Neil Postman suggests in *Technopoly*. In this shrine to the 'new world order' my colleague, a specialist in Caribbean cultures, went on discussing the irony of having not one but several job interviews to go to; an almost unheard-of problem 'Several years ago', she went on, 'the Caribbean was considered a place where true culture didn't exist. The people were part-modern, part indigenous and so somehow culturally impure, tainted by the West. Now thanks to transnationalism and interest in fragmented identities the Caribbean is hot.' Many of us who work in the United States and Europe have had many fewer job interviews and so we listened with envy and fascination.

Even as anthropology moved beyond notions of cultural purity and an Other radically separated from the modern self, new objects began to be invented, and we began to talk of the multicultural Other. This new Other is more contemporary. Part modern and part tribal, it's more confused about identity, at the moment that identity has become an academically fashionable concept. At first glance this new other might seem to share time and space with the anthropologist. But true coevalness is still denied and the other is still reified in that THEY are fragmented; but we are not. Global fragmentation is reserved for the other by the ethnographer in the university. This denial is important because the new other is not only a new way to talk about culture but is itself, as my Caribbean-expert friend can attest, a commodity to be sold in the marketplace of books, articles, and academic jobs. The exchange value of Caribbean identity was at the heart of my colleague's ironic claim — 'It's hot!' Anthropologists who could lay claim to possessing knowledge of *this* other were being courted with the promise of elusive jobs. And not just by universities seeking to add fashionable panache to their departments. In the world of transnational corporations and expanding global markets, cultural hybrids and fragmented identities are both the products of global forces and their raw material, in the form of labor and consumers. It is necessary for the anthropologist to not only acknowledge our cultural participation in these global processes (Rouse, 1995) and acknowledge the other's analysis of us (Rosaldo, 1989), but also to perform an analysis of the fragmenting and dissociating processes in institutions here, particularly in universities and publishing, sites of intellectual practice. Denial of power makes it possible to participate in a commodifying processes unconsciously. I believe those processes must be brought to consciousness.

Commodification and Semiotic Analysis

I have tried to preview above some of the ways in which the process of commodification has changed public institutions and affected individuals at those sites. As we have seen in the examples, this commodification takes place in conversation and collegial interaction, but it is also voiced by university rules, procedures and governance. Finally and possibly most effectively, commodification takes the form of commodity signs. Everything and everyone in every arena; can be thought of, and increasingly is, as a commodity for sale on the marketplace. Universities are busily developing and putting to work technologies of consumption; developing ways to get people to *buy* courses, programs, degrees, certificates and ideas.

Each of these three interrelated processes — talk, governance, and products — is a semiotic process. The examples above show how talk reflects and produces a 'commoditized apprehension of reality' (Taussig, 1980, p. 10). In the amazing process of marketing the university, other, self, articles, books, students and faculty all become signs in a rapidly circulating system of commodity signs. It is impossible to think about late twentieth century capitalism and what has happened in universities and to intellectuals without thinking of semiotics. Many who have discussed the semiotics of late twentieth century capitalism have talked about a loss of the real (Agger, 1989; Baudrillard, 1983). A traditional political/economic analysis is not adequate for study of the commodification of education because while the model Marx sets forth is valuable for seeing how higher education has been drawn into the contradictions of capitalist production, it does not adequately deal with the rise of consumption technologies and the vast mass culture industry upon which so much consumption rests.

In the brave new world the symbol functions not only to produce desire for goods, the symbol becomes the good itself while referring to something other. In late twentieth century capitalism everything both refers to something other and is itself a commodity in an endless chain of signification. Baudrillard sees this semiotic giving way to what he calls simulation; the map before the real, where symbols don't represent realities, they simulate them. Agger describes the same process by saying that the distance between text and reality has collapsed in what he calls 'fast capitalism'. Agger argues that we no longer see urban design, a social statistics, and positivist science and money as texts, we see these things as reality and as they cease to be texts it becomes increasingly difficult for critique to be leveled at these approaches to the world. So Agger (1989, pp. 20–1) says critical theory is no longer a critique of the dominant ideological texts in a powerful culture, but has been reduced to a fashionable commodity itself. So Adorno, Agger, Habermas all become commodities rather than scholars exercising a political practice in a particular culture. People who employ these signs make claims to the same set of commodity signs — I can sell *myself* as a 'hot commodity' in 'the marketplace of ideas' (Solomon and Solomon, 1993, pp. 28–9). The need and desire to do so masks the operation of power in expressions like 'critical theory is hot' or 'the marketplace of ideas'.

Just as in the larger economy, where technologies of consumption began at the turn of the century to need to guarantee consumption for large vertically integrating industries (Barrow, 1990; Ohmann, 1987), we can trace how universities and colleges have been economically pressured into seeing their social product in terms of consumption. This process is historical. Over time universities responded to various crises, i.e.; over-enrollment, under-enrollment, their role in the larger military industrial complex; with economic logic. This led to the process of marketing the university and the products of the university. Clearly universities are not alone in the use of market metaphor and equally clearly they have been and continue to be affected by decisions in corporation, especially publishing, and the government.

Finally, the contradictory and increasingly untenable position of the university and intellectuals during the development of a vast vertically integrated corporate capitalism with increasingly more ubiquitous technologies of consumption has led to various crises within the university. The university has responded with an array of new procedures; rules and regulation, faculty unions, collective bargaining agreements, and court precedents. In the proliferation of this bureaucratic discourse the legal and administrative imaginings of the university is marked out. The official discourse articulates what the university has been, what it has become, and what it will become in the future.

I have drawn on the work of Richard Johnson (1987) in discussing these three realms of semiotic analysis, interactional commodity signs (technologies of consumption) and the administrative/bureaucratic technologies of social control. Johnson argues that different theories in cultural studies tend to deal well with one aspect of what he called the 'circuit of cultural production.' Inasmuch as culture tends to be commodified in modern societies, a product for purchase in the marketplace; perhaps some of the disagreement among theorists is due to the partial nature of their culture analysis, the fact that they look at only one aspect of the production or consumption of cultural signs. In a similar vein I have attempted to look at the circuit of educational production. These different semiotic arenas, and their attendant theories are not my stab at eclecticism but an effort to provide a holistic analysis of what I am calling the commodifying process. The overall plan of the book attempts to complete this circuit by looking at all aspects of the commodification of education and its historical development.

Chapter 1 will develop the model of commodification, drawing on the literature in education, anthropology and critical theory. I will show that the model of commodification allows us to see how the university has been made part of the state and how as a state apparatus it has functioned to deal with the contradictions of a capitalist economy. Further, as the economy and state have undergone crises these crises have changed universities and the people who work for them.

In the second chapter I will look at the lives of marginalized intellectual workers in the sweatshops of knowledge by examining several stories and vignettes. The main story is about the invisibility of marginalized faculty part-time, and temporary teachers and their struggle to define themselves in terms of place; struggle over offices, filing cabinets, listings in phone books, and participation in university events like commencement. Other vignettes will look at university faculties' contradictory consciousness of being a professional vs. being a worker and the ways administrators and some faculty imagine the university and the way that image fits with dominant images in corporate culture. Finally the chapter will comment on the attitude of students as they grow more apathetic in this environment where education loses substance and becomes the sign of legitimacy or skill.

Chapter 3 focuses on particular changes in higher education since the sixties. The history traces the expansion of higher education in the sixties, and the emphasis on a democratic culture. It then moves to the contractions of the seventies and eighties and increased focus on career and the instrumental functions of education and on to the late eighties and early nineties as higher education has faced its own financial problems and developed a more instrumental approach to education. At each step of this history the emphasis will be on impact on the way individuals in the academic system think about themselves.

The political economy of higher education is discussed in chapter 4. I will discuss the value of a Marxian political economy for understanding the events that have taken place in the last thirty years and education's place in the US economy in general. The chapter will then move on to a critique of political economy. I will suggest that the emphasis on production limits political economy and that we need to look at the way universities have responded to the need to increase consumption in order to see how they have changed. It is the focus on consumption that has led universities to hire more administrators while decreasing faculty. The chapter will address issues of post-modernism and situate faculties of American universities in the global economy. The chapter will also look to the ethnographic data to see how faculty are understanding these larger social forces.

Chapter 5 will look at the Yeshiva decision and examine how the 'factory of knowledge' and 'community of scholars' model were codified into law. This important legal opinion is built on the social discourse around the transformation of the university and its effects on faculty. The chapter will draw on the political and economic work of the previous chapter to show that legal decisions codify ideological struggle and become the basis for future understandings of the university.

Chapter 6 draws on several ethnographic cases. The first will look at the organization of a union and also at several strikes at a large urban university. I will discuss the general confusion and disagreement among faculty about their status as workers or professionals. The chapter discusses faculty involved in the creation and development of a part-time union. Here issues of marginalization, inadequate benefits, and invisibility will be explored. Finally we will look at attempts on the part of graduate students to realize they are exploited workers and create a union of their own.

Chapter 7 will focus on the development of marketing, planning and advertising in the university. Administrations have grown into modern corporations as they have taken on more of these market functions and higher education has become more organized around consumption. I will look at the transformation of college materials and catalogs, and at issues of education consumers' rights.

Chapter 8 deals with a number of symbolic struggles over political correctness, multiculturalism, cultural literacy and fears about the decline of Western culture. These struggles have been influenced by the forces of commoditization. The chapter will discuss the difference between producers' rights and consumer rights and shows that in re-imagining students as consumers the university as a democratic institution empowering people to produce knowledge is lost. Passive consumption raises new issues; should there be lots of designer education for specific markets? What effect does this have?

Chapter 9 returns to the lives of faculty as they face problems created by pressures of the marketplace higher education has become. The chapter will deal with the new stratification of the work force. Part-time faculty face being institutionally invisible and the lack of job security and benefits. Full-time faculty have been stratified into researchers and teachers and teaching is increasingly stigmatized. Faculty have less and less control over their work; a complex process I will analyze. Finally the chapter will deal with issues of consciousness; how faculty members understand themselves and the others around them, and how they understand these larger social forces that shape their world.

The conclusion binds the theoretical threads woven through the book. Commoditization is the logic of the marketplace moving into more and more arenas. That movement is promoted by the basic contradictions in a capitalist system. Contradictions in the larger infrastructure have moved our economy toward what has been called a post-modern moment. Relationships between large social forces and the actions, decisions and consciousness of individuals, (in this case university faculty) is explored and summarized.

Chapter 1

Commodification

I have chosen the concept of commodification as a central organizing theme for the changes going on within the institutions where I work, and for the changes going on in education and other arenas of social life in general. The term has been used by a number of scholars working in education from a sociological perspective, and it has also been used by many anthropologists to describe the relationship of more traditional communities to encroaching capitalist development.

In this chapter I will develop my notion of commodification and why I think it is an important tool for understanding recent changes in higher education. I will draw on the development of the idea to show that the history of sociological ideas in the study of education; ideas like reproduction, resistance, contradiction, and cultural capital, do not have to be seen as antagonistic frameworks but can be ways of focusing on different aspects of the commodification process[1]. Finally, I will draw on the anthropological tradition of the concept of commodification in order to talk about issues of subjectivity and consciousness. I will address how university workers and students see themselves and their activities differently through what Michael Taussig (1980) has called a 'commoditized apprehension of reality' (p. 10).

Central to my goal is to develop a model to analyze the social processes that people who work in universities have experienced. Because we have experienced these processes we think we know them. All of us have experienced the elements of this model: The increased use of part-time labor, the tendency for administrations to act like corporate management, we have caught ourselves calling students consumers. Examples of talking about the university as a business can be found as early as the beginning of the twentieth century and perhaps even before. The familiar feel of this set of social conditions lulls us into the belief that we understand them, especially since we can label them with terms like student apathy, bureaucratic management, even commodification. Familiarity with a set of conditions coupled with a label often leads us to assume that we have an understanding of larger social processes.[2]

There is another reason labeling a process leads us to thinking we know that process. That reason has to do with Marx's notion of use-value and exchange value. Marx pointed out that in the system of commodity production, where goods and services are produced for sale, a given commodity has two values, the value of its utility, (what I can do with this commodity) and its value for exchange, or how much money I can get for it. This fact of capitalist economics means that there is a tendency on the part of producers to think about the appearance of a product separately from its substantive use. Appearances are important (Haug, 1986, p. 17) because they affect whether the good will be purchased or not.[3] Part of the 'commoditized apprehension of reality' is to fetishize labels, whether they be clothing labels, or analytic terms. This is an idea Ben Agger discusses in his work *Fast Capitalism*. For Agger the circulation of signs and labels has reached such an amazing speed that there is no longer time to ponder, or any distance from an object enabling us to reflect on it. The label has come to substitute for analysis and all of us who write and what we write are pressured to become empty signs (Agger, 1989, pp. 23 and 26–7).

These ideas make it clear that we need a notion of commodification to think about what has happened in the university, to education, knowledge, and writing. We need to theorize that notion of commodification, to slow down and pose an analysis of the penetration of the economic into all aspects of social life. Higher education is clearly a very important arena of this economic hegemony, as the very ideas and terms we use to understand and analyze the world are influenced by the pressure to be traded, turned into capital, bought and sold in the marketplace of ideas and for the scarce positions in the academy.

Structural Marxism

I will turn now to the development of commodification in the sociological, historical, and anthropological literature on education. A dramatic shift away from the functionalist and positivist dominated research on education began with Louis Althusser's (1971) article 'Ideology and ideological state apparatuses'. Althusser, taking the structuralist ideas of Lacan and combining them with a Marxist political economy, theorizes in this article the reproduction of capitalist relations. The question of how a class-based exploited work force is reproduced stably is an important one and one that Marx himself only partly addressed. With new social science ideas Althusser is able to add a new dimension to the study of ideology in society and hence how consciousness is produced.

For our purposes there are three aspects of Althusser's argument significant to the development of an understanding of commodification. First, Althusser argues that the reproduction of the work force is a main concern of any society, and is a role taken up by the state. The state's larger role is the reproduction and legitimation of the society. This role is carried out, according to Althusser, both by repressive apparatuses, like police, military etc., and ideological apparatuses, like the family, church, and school. I will discuss the work of Bowles and Gintis, Pierre Bourdieu, and Basil Bernstein as these scholars have taken up the ideas of reproduction in education.

Second, Althusser see schools as central institutions of the ideological state apparatus in modern capitalism. Althusser argues that the family-school coupling has replaced the older family-church coupling of pre-capitalist European society. This means that schools play a significant role in modern capitalist society in the reproduction of the work force. Althusser (*ibid.*, p. 132) points out that this reproduction is not just training for skills but also training of students to 'submit to the rules of the established order.' This is the beginning of the formulation of a more modern notion of the hidden curriculum.

Finally, in the most far-reaching part of his article, Althusser writes that ideology constitutes the individual as subject; 'ideology interpellates individuals as subjects' (*ibid.*, p. 173). Drawing on the psychoanalytic ideas of Lacan (the ideas are also relevant to the social psychological tradition growing out of Mead and Goffman) Althusser sees that the subject is constituted by ideology and it is through that ideology that the subject knows the social world. The subject's subjugation to the system of domination is a pre-condition for knowing oneself as subject.

Althusser certainly appreciated a notion of struggle, but the structuralism of Lacan lent his semiotic constructions a sort of despairing seamlessness. There is no outside to his system of ideological dominance. With Althusser it is hard to imagine struggle and change, though he was deeply committed to it.

Contemporary thinking on ideology owes a great deal to Althusser, although the debt is often negatively acknowledged if at all. Current constructions make more room for conflict and contradiction. Peter McLaren (1988), for example, discussing the ideas of Henry Giroux, argues that Giroux, by placing emphasis on power and meaning can create a more open model (p. 170). Individuals are pressured by the dominant culture and the meanings it produces; however the openness of these semiotic systems means that individuals and groups can constitute new and heterodox meanings.

Althusser's structural Marxism opened up a number of new and important areas, his work, although now often dismissed or discredited, set up the terms for a great deal of thinking about the relationship of educational institutions to capitalist economies. Althusser's effort opened up two new horizons, the reproduction of workers through ideological state apparatuses which give workers skills and train them to be subordinate to the existing rules of order, and the role ideology plays in constituting subjects and their world views. While these new research concerns are not what I would call commodification, they are important background to seeing the development of the commodification of education.

Social and Cultural Reproduction

There have been by now a number of excellent attempts to assess the development of social and cultural reproductionist perspectives, for example, Weiler (1988), Aronowitz and Giroux (1985), MacLeod (1987). It is not my point to add to the list of reviews but to use points from this literature ito build a larger perspective on commodification.

Reproduction theories begin with the most basic aspect discussed by Althusser, the reproduction of the work force. Many point to Bowles and Gintis as their work in education attempted to point out the ways in which schools discipline children for different social class positions differently. That disciplining of the work force made sure that working class kids were trained for working class jobs and middle class kids were trained for middle class jobs. Bowles and Gintis focus on Althusser's

notion of the ideological state apparatus inculcating the student into the established rules of order, and moreover doing so differently for children of different
class positions. Their emphasis was on the discipline of the hidden curriculum. For
instance, in some community colleges bells ring to indicate the start of classes and
a late bell rings to indicate student lateness, while in a more affluent four-year
colleges there are usually no bells at all. Bowles and Gintis might suggest that there
is a 'correspondence' between bells that time-discipline the community college
students and the clock-punching, time-disciplined jobs that these graduates will get.

Jean Anyon (1980) illustrates this principle nicely in her article 'Social class
and the hidden curriculum of work'. Anyon's study looked at five schools and
attempted to categorize the student body by social class background. She found that
for each school there was a different approach to knowledge. The working class
school approached knowledge as a rote task that needed to be completed, the
middle class school approached knowledge as something that needs to be understood conceptually but it was still done in a rote fashion, the upper middle class
school emphasized creativity in thinking about knowledge, and the elite school
focused on larger abstract principles. Anyon argues that each of these emphases
'correspond' to the ways work is handled by each of the class groups.

There has been much criticism of basic social reproductionist approach but I
will summarize a few of the points. Like the criticisms of Althusser and structuralism in general, the emphasis on social control makes these processes appear
seamless, without any potential for change. Students are seen as passive vessels to
be filled up with an ideological world-view and then sent into the work force like
automatons. No agency, in short. Apple (1982a, pp. 43–4) and Aronowitz and
Giroux (1985, pp. 74–9) have pointed out that while the social reproductionist
approach does not share the functionalist's desire for social solidarity, the model is
functionalist-like. It demonstrates that the capitalist system reproduces itself and
ignores change. While these criticisms are valid and valuable there is a risk of
throwing out the baby with the bath water. Current research fashion perhaps over-
valorizes and overemphasizes agency. Bourdieu has said that while it is true that
reproductionism tends to emphasize determination over agency, there does seem
to be a lot more determination than social change.

In Althusser's 'Ideology and the ideological state apparatuses', the social
reproduction approach is nicely illustrated. Althusser's point is that the school-
family coupling has played a major institutional role in the reproduction of the
social relations of production. We may see a dynamic tension in the civic and
economic roles of the school, but most would agree today that schools play an
important role in the reproduction of the economic system. The economic role is
there and growing in importance (Bowles and Gintis, 1987, p. 208).

Where the social reproductionists fall short of the model that Althusser set
forth is in accounting for the workings of an ideology that 'interpellates' the subject, and the way subject formation operates through educational institutions. It
is my contention that the process of subject formation will be influenced by the
market. The economy produces subjects (*ibid.*, p. 131) and educational institutions
both cooperate in the process of creating Homo economicus and are also changed

by it. They must produce a product that economically rational students can consume. But how is it that these processes operate? They need to include agency and slippage while at the same time showing a general pattern.

What social scientists who have focused on agency and the resistance of students to school and capitalist oppression have failed to fully consider (Willis, 1981 and 1990; Aronowitz and Giroux, 1985) is that the market economy needs a subject imbued with agency as well as trained for a role. Capitalism needs a subject who passively accepts his subjugation but acts as a free agent in the marketplace. Both resistance to capitalism and subjugation to capitalism require agency, and so there needs not only to be inculcation in schools, but the production of free agents, 'the individual is interpellated as a (free) subject in order that he shall submit freely to the commandments of the Subject . . .' (Althusser, 1971, p. 182).

In Althusser's example the capital 'S' Subject is God but we could substitute the market as the Subject in the modern secular world. Ironic that the ability to reinvent symbols and engage in political resistance comes through the same social process that produces subjects who freely accept their subjugation. While Althusser sets the theoretical ground for this ideological process I believe he errs on the side of emphasizing subjugation even when his goal is emancipation. I will return to these points later but for now I move to a discussion of efforts to understand the cultural processes of subject formation in the family and education.

The models of cultural reproduction put forth by researchers in the sociology of education; particularly Bernstein (1971 and 1982) and Bourdieu (1977 and 1984), Bourdieu and Passeron (1977), Bourdieu and Boltanski (1978) represent a significant addition to the social reproduction theories discussed above. Bernstein and Bourdieu discuss more symbolic mechanisms that allow students from different class background to be educated differentially and to perform differentially.

Bernstein (1971 and 1982) articulated a model of class-based cultures which were learned through language and interaction carried out in the sites of home/ work/school. Bernstein articulated what he called linguistic codes, styles of interaction which tended to fall into ideal types which he called restricted and elaborated. Bernstein's argument is a complex one, involving the tendency of class-based cultures produce particular styles of interaction and ways of viewing that interaction. These interaction styles represent an entire world view which is articulated in the home, carried to the school and later informs the work environment.

Restricted code interactions tend to be more concrete, external to the individual and require an authoritarian logic for enforcement. For example, the act of giving a child a directive can be done in a concrete way (preventing the child physically from running into the street) without the child's involvement. Elaborated code interactions tend to be more abstract, and to rely on individually internalized mechanisms of control. A directive of this kind to a child in this way would encourage the child to set his/her own agenda for achieving a goal and would encourage the child to feel good about the achievement of that goal. Bernstein argued that these interactional styles tend to put elaborated code children at an advantage in school because schools operate through an elaborated code and the elaborated code child will internalize the goal of the institution while the restricted code child will not.

Pierre Bourdieu (1977), drawing on the work of Bernstein, Goffman and others, takes these ideas even further. Bourdieu breaks with the more objectivist notions of reproduction and argues that in order to understand the reproduction of social class groups one needs to not only understand the objective structure but also the subjective strategies and practices of groups of individuals. Bourdieu calls for a 'theory of practice' and in an effort to develop such a theory comes up with the central concept of the habitus. Much current criticism of Bourdieu tends to misread him and fail to appreciate his break with objectivism. That criticism fails to see the central role habitus has in Bourdieu's thought (Bourdieu, 1990a, p. 107). The habitus is a structure and structuring principle which Bourdieu uses to break away from the traditional dichotomy in the social sciences of either subjective, for example, phenomenological, hermeneutic approaches; or objective, structuralist, Marxist, positivist approaches.

Bourdieu (1977, pp. 26–7) explains his position in *Outline of a Theory of Practice* by focusing on a critique of structuralism. The notion of science and its construction of objective structures is necessarily timeless. In order that the structure have a constant form it must lie outside of time, and so we see culture as the rule-bound, normative concepts that are elicited from natives when questioned about their practices. These practices, do, however, develop over time. Objectivism indicates the limitations of the analysts' understanding rather than the reality of the natives' social world. Because we are necessarily always outside the informal practices of members of a community we have made a virtue out of a weakness, to paraphrase Bourdieu. The normative and the rules only reflect the ideological system of the native. This is only one aspect of the system of connections which make up the society. In order to complete the idea of structure we must have a structuring principle, and rather than an implicit theory of practice which would be naive, we consciously strive to formulate a theory of practice. For Bourdieu, this is found in the notion of the habitus. The habitus is:

> . . . systems of durable, transposable **dispositions** structured structures predisposed to function as structuring structures, that is, as principles of the generation and structuring of practices and representations which van be objectively 'regulated' and 'regular' without in any way being the product of obedience to rules . . . (*ibid.*, 72)

Habitus is not consciously acquired but rather 'inculcated' through the practice of corporeal discipline, 'meaning-made-body'. The focus of analysis then, is the informal practices and networks of relationships which exist and how these practices are then produced through the structuring action of the habitus and also how they further shape and affect the structure of the habitus. We move beyond the realism of a modeling objectivizing science and toward a 'dialectic of the internalization of externality and the externalization of internality' (*ibid.*, p. 72). How, specifically, does Bourdieu model the notion of the habitus? Social identity, he states, is perceived through difference. Habitus is the mechanism by which the individual not only structures the world, through a process of selection and taste, but it is also a structured structure where everything already has its place. It is because the habitus is inculcated through childhood, further transformed by the educational process, that the actor does not need to consciously reflect on his/her activities. The strategies of individuals and groups with similar inculcation is the strategy of a structuring structure. Habitus produces taste which then actively restructures the world through the practices of everyday political interaction, whether through the competition of games of reciprocity, or games of status and taste selection within 'advanced society'.

Bourdieu is led from these ideas on the habitus to the notion of cultural capital. Taking from economics the idea of knowledges, technologies and practices that become part of a group's human capital, Bourdieu argues that the accumulation of cultural capital in advanced societies represents one of the main strategies of upward social mobility as direct access to Capital is blocked.

Education becomes an important route to the accumulation of cultural capital and mechanisms of exclusion in educational institutions are often based on the cultural practices of particular groups. Habitus sets the precondition for taste and Bourdieu has shown that taste in music, art and literature is shaped by habitus and social class background. Educational institutions draw on tastes and even orientation to knowledge and the world in order to sanction some and to discourage others. Bourdieu (1984, pp. 23 and 291; 1985, pp. 732–6) refers to these practices of symbolic dominance as symbolic violence.

The importance of Bourdieu's analysis is that there are external mechanisms of exclusion; that is, tests which show that lower-class students have not assimilated enough of the right kinds of information, or that their mode of thought lacks subtlety, and there are mechanisms of selection whereby students self-exclude themselves on similar grounds. In other words, lower-class students make choices and decisions that limit their access to cultural capital and educational credentials.

Because of habitus, habitual patterns of acting, (dispositions) middle and upper-middle class students often have more of the right kinds of knowledge and modes of discourse and they engage in less self-exclusion. Of course these are probabilities, tendencies which in any real context might produce counter-examples and counter-trajectories. Bourdieu's sociology is what I have called quantum sociology, he has modeled sociology on important principles borrowed from modern natural sciences; the need for reflexivity, the location of the analysis and the probabilistic nature of data; but these are tendencies and patterns, not rules.

Bourdieu has taken us a long way toward understanding some of the particular ways 'ideology interpellates the subject'. We can see that actors are engaged in an active strategy, within a given field, where there are limits to access of resources and limits to what can be done in that field. The actor is by necessity a player in that field, that is the precondition for being a 'subject', a person. And the actor is not always conscious of how a particular strategy works to his/her advantage or disadvantage. It allows the illusion of democratic competition, because we don't calculate the advantages or disadvantages that come with different concentrations of cultural capital and differing habituses.

There have been a number of criticisms of Bourdieu's work, most concentrating on his view of reproduction. Bourdieu has been accused of seeing too much structural determination and not enough agency. I tend to agree with Bourdieu that his critics fail to appreciate his model. Willis' (1981) criticism of Bourdieu is that sometimes active resistance produces the reproduction and that actors can partially see through their own domination but then guarantee that domination through other limiting ideologies like racism and sexism.

I would suggest that there is nothing in principle in *Learning to Labor* not accounted for in Bourdieu's theory of practice. Willis' ethnography is an example of habitus in action. I do, however, agree that much of Bourdieu's work is of theoretical nature and that ethnographic detail is often missing. Willis' ethnography and others that focus on resistance (MacLeod, 1987; McRobbie, 1978; Hebdige, 1979) offer a lot more detail about the processes of subjective tastes and orientations and how the struggle with symbolic domination goes on. Further, Willis creates the possibility that this is not a closed system; that one might potentially escape domination and bring about real change; a point that critical theorists after him draw upon (Giroux, 1983; Weiler, 1988).

There is another idea in Willis' ethnography that furthers the model of commodification I am building. Willis, in his analysis of the lads' culture, engages in a discussion of theory and practice. Willis points out that the lads don't value a book learning cut off from the experience of everyday life. Book knowledge is pointless for them because it is not connected to the pains and pleasures of life (Willis, 1981, pp. 13–5).

When I was a graduate student I did some painting and carpentry to pay my rent and among carpenters there are many wonderful stories about the stupidity of architects. Stories about how architects forgot closets and bathrooms in the designs of the buildings. Often the things architects fail to consider, according to the carpenters, were things that had to do with the body and everyday life. Architects, according to the laborers a few rungs down from them, were disconnected, living in a world of theory separated from practice. These carpenters often saw themselves as the ones who corrected the failings of intellectual superiors. They were the ones who had 'real knowledge'.

My experience with builders seems very much to echo the working-class sentiments of the lads. Willis points out that the lads are right. In a perfect world theory separated from practice is worthless. However in capitalism that is not so. The theory is valuable in and of itself. It is a sign, a tag that represents superior knowledge and technical skills and can be traded in for cash, whether the skills are superior or not (*ibid.*, pp. 126–9). This is part of what Bourdieu means by cultural capital.

In capitalism, knowledge and the markers of knowledge, degrees, certificates, professional associations, etc., are commodities themselves and circulate as commodities. This brings us back to Bourdieu, who says that it is through mechanisms of symbolic dominance that certain educational tags take on more value than others and have greater ease of circulation. A carpenter can have great architectural skills but without the legitimated tag s/he cannot trade those skills for cash.

I have taught many students in adult evening education and there is an interesting

irony in some of their lives. One of my students had been promoted to
required a bachelor's degree. He worked for a steel company. The company ac
to let him keep the promotion as long as he remained in school and made progres.
toward the degree. The student pointed out that he will work this job for eight years
before he has the requirements for the job. I asked him how important the degree
was for doing his job and he replied that it was not important at all, but that the
company wanted him to have the degree.

Apple (1982a, p. 41) takes these ideas further and suggests that the commodification of education involves both the reproduction of a work force, making
sure workers have the requisite skills dispositions and values; and schools to produce 'particular kinds of knowledge forms required by an unequal society'. Apple
shows that the knowledge produced by schools is not just a sign to be exchanged
in the marketplace, but that schools produce 'technical knowledges' to suit the
needs of a corporate ruling class. These knowledges, which attempt to produce new
products and thereby gain greater control over the social processes of production,
are limited by the same corporate interests that go into promoting their production
(*ibid.*, p. 25).

Apple echoes David Noble (1977) arguing that the state through educational
institutions has taken a hand in the production of the technical and administrative
knowledges, subsidizing the training of a work force and the research and development that goes into the production of new products (Apple, 1982a, p. 54). Further, this process puts schools and the state in general into a contradictory position.
On the one hand the school plays to the corporate interests in the production of
knowledge and the smooth reproduction of the work force, on the other hand it
must play to the interests of citizens and to ideas of democracy and equal opportunity (*ibid.*, p. 58). This is an idea which is also taken up in Bowles and Gintis'
(1987) more recent work.

Commodification in Higher Education

We are now in a position to define the term commodification and discuss its
application to education in general and higher education in particular. Commodification is a theoretical notion. It is a way of modeling certain changes that have
taken place in social life. These changes are ones that have occurred in the infrastructure of society, particularly the economy. But economic changes have political
consequences that are struggled over and they also have an impact on the way
people see themselves and their world.

Jean Baudrillard (1983) in *Simulations* suggests that capitalism has become
a dizzyingly self-contradictory system where the only meaning is the concept of
profit, itself an illusory and empty sign. In a more complex fashion Ben Agger
(1989, p. 16) talks about collapse of the boundary between text and the world. For
Agger, names of scholars, for example, Theodore Adorno, names of books, ideas,
concepts; even my notion of commodification, are becoming commodity signs, or
things to be circulated and exchanged for the value of their appearance, not for

substance. Or, the importance has shifted from what an author or an idea conveys to one's ability to convert it into capital.

Most basically commodification is a model to discuss the process by which the economic overtakes other institutions and aspects of social life. I would suggest that this is one of the most important aspects of 'late capitalism' and that there are structural reasons for this commodifying process.

As much as we may argue about specific aspects of Marx's thinking on capitalism, one idea at the core of Marx's thought remains a central contribution to thinking about capitalism. Capitalism is an unstable social system 'structured in contradiction' as Althusser would put it. Crisis is at the core of capitalist society, and the contradictions in capitalism, which produce crises also give capitalism its dynamism, for example, overproduction, cycles of economic depression, monopolization, etc.

Crisis and instability drive the search for new markets, new products, and cheaper productive processes. Much current work looking at the 'globalization of production' and the 'new international division of labor' demonstrates how the global economy is being forged out of these ongoing crises. One lesson to be learned from capitalism is that the crisis is never over. Crisis is the norm and is part of the meaning of the system. Crisis is the anxiety over the search for larger profits, which are themselves the only thing that has any meaning in a capitalist social system.

It is this crisis structure to capitalism as an economic system that Apple and Noble argue makes education an important institution. Without the drive for new technologies and greater social control, education's value to the economy would be much less. But these economic pressures on education not only shape students and the kinds of knowledges schools produce and disseminate, they also bring crisis to education. The crisis structure becomes part of the educational institution. The response to educational crisis is often a rational[4] one, one that attempts to solve problems and deal with issues through the rationality of the marketplace.

To summarize, the ideas that go into the notion of commodification, particularly as it relates to higher education, involve the transformation of the social activity of education due to a series of crises. These crises are produced by the needs of a capitalist economy, the reproduction of a work force, the guarantee of new products and new markets, and the use of state apparatuses to manage people in the society and the overall social system. The rest of this work will show that over the course of the entire twentieth century, but particularly since World War II, there have been a number of economic pressures directly affecting the structure of institutions of higher education in the United States. These economic pressures have produced contradictory results with the university increasingly being used by capital to provide research and the training of labor, without fully paying for these services. As a result there have been a series of fiscal crises in the university that have forced universities to see themselves as businesses providing a product to a market.

The above-mentioned process of transformation involves not just rearrangements in institutional structure, but changes in how education is viewed and changes in the subjectivities of the actors involved; students, teachers, and administrators. In anthropology and critical theory there has been a theoretical discussion to elaborate the idea of commodification which has taken into consideration these issues of consciousness. The anthropological discourse has attempted to bridge the notion of subjectivity, culture, and the large structures of the political economy.

Anthropological Theories

Anthropologists increasingly have used the terms commoditization and commodification to label processes they observe in developing parts of the world and in institutions in developed nations, particularly the United States (Taussig, 1980; Appadurai, 1988; Kopytoff, 1988; Comaroff and Comaroff, 1990). While there has been widespread use of these terms, only recently have anthropologists attempted to theorize them. I will look at another example of commoditization in higher education in the United States. In order to analyze the current state of higher education and the events that have led to the present situation, I will argue that the concept of commoditization is central to posing a thorough analysis of the system. Present debate around intellectuals, education, and cultural literacy have been clouded by the smoke-screen of partial analysis, partisan politics, lack of a theoretical base, and a failure to look at the overall historical picture. The concept of commoditization allows an analysis of the system of higher education which has up to this point not been possible.

It is necessary therefore to define this term commoditization rather than just use it as a label for processes we experience but don't fully understand. The best discussion of commoditization is in Taussig's (1980, pp. 23–38) work *The Devil and Commodity Fetishism in South America*. A close look at Taussig's analysis suggests that Marx's idea of commodity fetishism might be a good way to explain the behavior of tin miners in Bolivia and plantation workers in Columbia. The peasants in these South American countries, when working as wage laborers under difficult conditions, practice a form of devil worship. The devil (Tio) is said by them to have control of the mines. If offerings are not made to Tio, then miners are likely to die in the mines; Tio will eat them (Nash, 1987; Taussig, 1980). In contrast to Taussig's analysis, which follows below, June Nash's account of devil worship includes descriptions of miners who claim to have seen Tio in the mines. When Tio is described, he is usually seen as a white person with red beard, boots, helmet; the image of the northern employers. Nash's (1987, p. 256) understanding of this phenomenon is simply that the belief provides a little symbolic mastery over difficult and dangerous conditions. It is a bit like Malinowski's ideas on magic; that it gives a measure of control over an aspect of life over which no real control is possible. It is also therefore, while perhaps necessary, false consciousness.

Taussig on the other hand attempts to pose a different analysis and avoids categories which force him to refer to the peasants' beliefs as false consciousness. False consciousness is a concept often used by Marxists to suggest that there is a true economic reality which is the genesis of all super-structural phenomena. Therefore culture and human understanding is always dependent on this base economic reality and is derived from it. Taussig wants to avoid this pitfall; he doesn't really want to suggest that there is some economic reality all things can be reduced to and from which all reality can be developed. Such economic determinism is something Marx himself was careful to avoid.

With commodity fetishism, Taussig sees Marx's more sophisticated attempts to grapple with the ideas of consciousness and understanding and their relationship to the economic reality of especially capitalism as workers are exploited by owners in a system where there is little justice and little hope. Commodity fetishism is the way Marx explains our way of understanding how the world grows out of the materially-produced social relationships and institutions which have developed in a capitalist social formation.

Commodity Fetishism

Let us look at two extended passages from Marx's *The German Ideology* in order to build a picture of the notion of commodity fetishism. Marx and Engels (1974) states:

> The production of ideas, of conceptions, of consciousness, is at first dir-
> ectly interwoven with the material activity and the material intercourse of
> men, the language of real life. Conceiving, thinking, the mental intercourse
> of men, appear at this stage as the direct efflux of their material behavior.
> The same applies to mental production as expressed in the language of
> politics, laws, morality, religion, metaphysics, etc. of a people. Men are
> the producers of their conceptions, ideas, etc. real, active men, as they are
> conditioned by a definite development of their productive forces and of the
> intercourse corresponding to these, up to its furthest forms. Consciousness
> can never be anything else than conscious existence, and the existence of
> men is their actual life-process. If in all ideology men and their circum-
> stances appear upside-down as in a camera obscura, this phenomenon arises
> just as much from their historical life-process as the inversion of objects
> on the retina does from their physical life-process. (p. 47)

There are, of course, a lot of important, well-discussed ideas in this passage. For the moment I wish to skip over the image of the camera obscura, an image much discussed (Mitchell, 1986), and look instead at some other ideas in this passage. A lot of abstract discussion about materialism or economic determinism has been based on this passage and others like it but, practically, what Marx (1967, p. 80) is saying is that it makes more sense to think about the structure and process of life, out of which ideas and codified discourse have come, as emanating from real life situations; i.e., particular configuration of the productive forces, the real competition of groups, the concrete issues of a particular moment. Out of these material conditions flow legislation, laws, court decisions, art, music, min-iseries, etc. We, as individuals in society always look at ideas and the products of 'consciousness' after the fact, and after some distance from the material conditions that went into the 'symbolic struggles' (to borrow Bourdieu's term) that framed the development of ideas and ways of looking at the world. It appears that these conceptions and discourses have a life of their own, independent of the context from which they came (*ibid.*, 75).

This is historical materialism, or one important component of it; looking at history from a particular vantage point. It is a powerful interpretive scheme because it allows us some distance from familiar ideas. It makes the familiar strange, in the words of the surrealists (Clifford, 1988). Marx says the thinking, conceiving and mental interactions of people flow out of their material behavior. This material behavior is itself a structured whole. It is not some reductive concept of economy or subsistence but the whole structure of society which goes into the production and reproduction of life. So then what appears as independent, a new idea, with Marx's hermeneutic can be looked at as something which has come from a complex set of historical circumstance.

If we now turn to *Capital, Vol. 1* and look at the section on commodity fetishism, Marx implies that the political economists of the nineteenth century, by failing to look at the historical circumstances out of which commodity production has come, are mystified by the objects themselves and fetishize the commodity. They give the commodity a life and will of its own. By failing to separate the ideas of exchange value and use value, they see value (exchange value) as being intrinsic to the object rather than seeing it as being a product of human labor and activity which it more properly is. Use value and exchange value are the products of human labor and social activity in particular historical circumstances and within particular social formations (Marx, 1967, p. 83); this perspective allows the analyst to focus on the human laboring activity and the mechanisms of human exploitation rather than seeing wealth and poverty as effects of the goods themselves.

We turn back now to Taussig, who will make a very important analysis based on these ideas of Marx. By denying the primacy of human relationships in the production of value, through a collapsing or condensing of exchange value and use value, a capitalist system produces the illusion that value emanates from the object itself. It appears the commodity circulates of its own accord, subject to the demands of the market, and people appear to be passive victims of market forces. Commodities move people around. Further, this fetishized relationship to commodities and all the elements of this relationship appear timeless, ahistorical; part of human nature. We see our categories, which were produced through history, from the vantage point of a immovable set of concepts and institutions. Time, efficiency, accumulation, profit; all seem natural categories of life and ones that should apply to all humanity. This process of making seemingly natural categories out of historical relationships is what Taussig (1980, p. 5) calls reification. He uses the example of time as a category. Citing work by Evans-Pritchard on the Nuer, he quotes Evans-Pritchard reflecting upon the fact that the Nuer have no conception of time. They simply perform their daily tasks. Taussig points out time is nothing more than a way of measuring or defining human relationships. In capitalism, because we sell our labor according to a rationalized production system we sell labor time, and specifically agreed-upon segments of our lives. From the specific historical circumstances of the invention of the steam engine, the moving of factories to the cities and the advent of gas lighting; come things like shift work, around-the-clock productivity, the idea that an ideal factory is making money because producing commodities is the way to realize profit, and as a result, time becomes a thing. Further, it becomes a thing controlling us. We worry about running out of time, say we are short of time, that time is getting away from us, etc. Reification is a process specific to capitalist (and perhaps other advanced) societies. Things become more important than people. Our understanding of the world shifts from social values created by people, to one which is pre-given. We forget that the notion of property has been part of a long struggle in Western history; now we take it as a given reification that suggests that our notions of ontology and epistemology are greatly distorted because of our failure to see the ways in which people create the institutions and struggles which then in turn produce them.

Taussig suggests that the implications of this truth are immense. In order to historicize our concepts it is necessary to reflect upon all positions from which ideas and social relationships come. All the categories of science, economics, even history are produced through particular historical relationships and struggles and in a capitalist society take on the appearance of finished products. Scientific categories are based upon natural-appearing categories like time, space, land, labor, all of which are reified social relationships, or elements of the exploitative history of a capitalist society. Nothing short of a complete analysis of the concepts we use and the data we pore over will do when attempting a critique of the institutions within a capitalist society or the influence of those institutions on people in other societies, Taussig summarizes:

> Conditioned by history and society, the human eye assumes its perceptions to be real. It cannot, without great effort, contemplate its perception as a movement of thought that ratifies the signs through which history expresses itself ... Certain human realities become clearer at the periphery of the capitalist system, making it easier for us to brush aside the commoditized apprehension of reality. (*ibid.*, p. 10)

Taussig will use this analysis to suggest that the practice of devil worship among peasants in Bolivia and Colombia is an understandable response, and a sophisticated attempt to interpret a set of social relationships that come with capitalist production, that seem not only strange but completely unnatural.

By comparing the overall structure of life in peasant communities with that of capitalist communities Taussig is able to show that the concepts upon which we base our understanding of reality, for example, the free alienated individual, competition, capital accumulation etc., are specific to our social formation, and most social formations, including medieval Europe, have found these concepts alien. With this analysis it becomes possible to think of capitalism, rather than the 'primitive', as being strange or backward for failing to see the social basis of commodities and commodity relations and instead fetishizing those relations.

Because Taussig is comparing pre-capitalist societies to Western society, he tends to see commodity fetishism as a static, *fait accompli* instead of an active continuing historical process. Hence he says . . . 'commoditized apprehension of reality', implying that commoditization of social life in Western capitalist countries is complete. It is certainly not my point here to find fault with Taussig's excellent and important analysis of the way in which pre-capitalist groups make sense out of capitalist exploitation, but we can see that every object of analysis tends to impose limits on the categories used in that analysis. Taussig's commoditization is in fact itself a reified category. The capitalist societies have it, the pre-capitalist ones do not. However, we are concerned in this text with the institutions of higher education within the United States. For our object of analysis it becomes much more important to attempt to re-theorize the notion of commoditization and emphasize its processual character.

Rethinking Commodity Fetishism

Mitchell (1986) and Amariglio and Callari (1989) examine commodity fetishism as a way to think about Marx's analysis of capitalism and the theory of the subject which grows out of it, rather than directly taking a stand on the issue of class. In this way they hope to avoid the economic reductionism which is the tendency of those who emphasize the position of the working class in the transformation of capitalism.

Mitchell (1986, p. 162) argues that the 'camera obscura' and the fetish in Marx are images used to extend through metaphor a scientific field of analysis. These images have an interesting tension between them. The 'camera obscura' produces precise replications of reality but the image has no substance; it is a phantom; while the fetish is a mystification of reality but is a concrete material object. Mitchell goes on to show that Marx has taken powerful images from his time and used them in a rhetorical strategy to explain the operation of capitalism. Let's look at how Mitchell discusses the fetish.

Marx takes the notion of the fetish from the text of nineteenth century anthropology. The anthropologists bringing back the religious fetishes of non-Western peoples allowed Europeans to think of themselves as more enlightened than the so called 'primitives'. In 'primitive' religion the fetish was an object that had power and therefore it was an object which could motivate behavior. In their smugness the educated Europeans saw themselves as much more rational beings who could not be moved to act by an object which when looked at scientifically, clearly had no power.

As we saw in Taussig's work earlier, Marx shows how in capitalism, a subject makes a fetish out of commodities and sees behavior motivated by the commodity object. This is the myth of the hidden hand of the market. He even commodifies his own life with the notions of time and money, and sells his labor power on the market. Marx uses the image of the fetish to turn scientific reason back on itself. Western man is not more rational and enlightened. He too finds himself moved to act by a fetishized object — the commodity fetish.

For Mitchell this is a rhetorical move on the part of Marx. By using the image of fetishism in comparison, Marx can bring to light a general property of capitalism. Mitchell's point is that by not remaining historical and dialectical many contemporary Marxists 'have made a fetish out of fetishism'.

> But I also have a critical aim, which is to show how these concrete concepts have to a certain extent crippled Marxist thought even as they have enabled it. This disabling, I will argue, arises from the neglect of the concreteness- and particularly the historical specificity-of ideology and fetishism, a tendency to treat them as reified and separable abstractions instead of dialectical images. One might put it more simply by saying that ideology and fetishism have taken a sort of revenge on Marxist criticism, insofar as it has made a fetish out of the concept of fetishism, and treated 'ideology' as the occasion for the elaboration of a new idealism. (Mitchell, 1986, p. 163)

Amariglio and Callari (1989, pp. 35 and 43–4), in their analysis of Marx's theory of value, go on to argue similarly to Mitchell. Their point is that Marx was arguing against the economic determinism of the nineteenth century political economists. The labor theory of value is not itself an ontologizing of the primacy of the economic, but again (as Mitchell would say) a way of posing an analysis which is historical and dialectical. It is in this way that Marx is able to pose a critique of capitalism.

What I argue is that over two important moments of capitalism, ones we could call, along with others, the moment of modernism, (located by theorists like John Berger (1969) at the turn of the century); and the moment of post-modernism, which might be located by David Harvey (1989) after 1973. These two points in the history of capitalism are important because they are points at which the system of accumulation shifts or begins to respond to crisis produced by the systemic crises of production and consumption which are inherently part of capitalism.

The 'commoditized apprehension of life', as Taussig calls it, also changes over these two periods. Richard Ohmann (1987, pp. 143–51) shows in his *Politics of Letters* that advertising played an important role at the turn of the century in the guarantee of an existing market for products. This influenced the creation of brand names and the creation of monopolies of production and consumption.

Harvey (1989, pp. 125–9) calls this the beginning of the Fordist system of accumulation which he sees as only succeeding to smooth operation after World War II. Of course with the beginning of advertising and mass marketing and brand products and national magazines as the vehicle of this semiotic system, much of the way life is perceived changed. As advertisers invent an image of social life playing to domestic patterns, themselves in the process of changing, they created stereotypes and visions of the future. These advertisers (not knowing that they were paraphrasing Bourdieu) changed the way people lived and saw the world. So commoditization is a process in capitalism which itself is always changing. As a process it is possible to locate general principles like the principle of reification discussed by Taussig, but it is a dynamic process, one which imposes changes on that reified view of the world. Primarily, commoditization is a term to describe the way in which institutions and systems of thought change as the dynamic infrastructure of capitalism moves to deal with its internal contradictions. These internal contradictions are part of the structure of capitalism. Marx himself noted that the labor theory of value leads directly to an understanding of the tendency of capitalism to produce crises of overproduction. Workers were not paid enough to have discretionary income and therefore there were never enough consumers to buy goods. Fordism as a system was not just large-scale industrial labor, but a system to try and produce leisure time and discretionary income for consumption as well. We will see that Fordism has its own contradictions and therefore had to change as well.

Secondly commoditization is a process which effects institutions in capitalist society differentially. In general in a capitalist society there is movement to see all relationships as ones that can be presented in terms of exchange. Capitalism moves to see everything in terms of 'economic rationality'. This economic reason brings us a way of seeing everything in terms of buying and selling, profit and loss. But this movement is a process as well. As capitalism responds to the various crises over its history different institutions are rethought in terms of buying and selling. For example, at the turn of the century professors complained that college was a place where schools sold degrees to students. At this point the use of market terminology was metaphorical. It was a way of seeing the process. By 1990, which is the substance of this text, it is no longer a metaphor. In large part because of capitalism's response to the crises of accumulation, higher education has become institutionally rearranged on a model of capitalist accumulation. While the university does not produce a commodity in the traditional sense, the service it provides is taken as product and the institution uses capitalist institutional arrangements to produce it. This for me is the commoditization of higher education, the evolution of a vision of education as, not just a product to be bought and sold (which is itself a semiotic in the process of change and very important), but the entire institutional rearrangement of higher education into a productive industry. I will return to this in more detail in the subsequent chapters, but for the moment I return to the theoretical discussion of commoditization.

Recently theorists looking at Marx's notion of commodity fetishism have been emphasizing its strategic importance for Marx as an image or metaphor to make clear the hidden assumptions of the classical political economist's work on capitalism (Amariglio and Callari, 1989; Jameson, 1981; Mitchell, 1986). For these theorists commodity fetishism and the labor theory of value are not timeless truths but rhetorical moves to both analyze a moment of the structure of the capitalist system, and to show the political position of the classical political economists in the justification of a capitalist system of exploitation. These moves on the part of current theorists are both an attempt to move beyond the debate around economic determinism in Marxist theory and also an attempt to deal with the transformations in the capitalist system; what Mandel might call the three moments or periods of capitalist accumulation (Jameson, 1981 and 1989; Mandel, 1975).

However the emphasis on the rhetorical use of images like the 'camera obscura' and the 'fetish' skirt the difficult issue of Marx's emphasis on class as the model for the production of a true history. We must look at some of the current thinking around class and how changes in the class structure have forced Marxists to rethink ideas on class.

Class Theory

A problem in Marxist theory has been the position of class and particularly the place of the working class in Marx's theory of history. Marx of course from his position at the rise of industrialism gave a very important position to the working class in the transformation of capitalism. They are the group where much of the tensions in the capitalist system concentrate. They are also the most exploited group and stand to gain the most from a redistribution of wealth. Throughout the twentieth century as Fordism/Keynesianism became the stabilizing forces in capitalism a large organized industrial working class was part of the compromise of that system. If it is true that capitalism is moving toward what Jameson (1989) would call an international, post-modern, more complex form of organization, or what Harvey (1989) more clearly calls 'flexible accumulation', then it is also clear that the working class as an organized group is becoming more divided. There are still some unionized industrial laborers, but there is a move to more flexible time workers as well, part-timers, piece labor, sub-contractors. This picture is further complicated by the technological and historical shifts which have allowed corporations to exploit these different groups of laborers in different countries and parts of the world. The organized working class of Marx's vision is becoming more and more fragmented.

Further, mass consumption, as one of the strategies of resolving the crisis of capitalist accumulation (Ohmann, 1987), has produced a subject that differentiates itself from other consumers by consumer choice (Bourdieu, 1984). Late capitalism has also produced more and more specified and fragmented markets where the consumer is presently encouraged not to think of him/herself as one subject but many characters all who need different commodities to play the different personas. This characteristic of late capitalism Deleuze and Guattari (1977) have referred to as schizophrenic or schizo-culture.

The rearrangement of production and consumption have forced theorists to question the role of class in the transformation of society. Will it in fact be the working class that overthrows capitalism? Baudrillard (1975 and 1981), Laclau and Mouffe (1985 and 1987) and others think it will not be the working class coming to consciousness and organizing a revolution. Other Marxists, like Wood (1986) and Geras (1987), still think class is central.

If we remain focused on the commodity fetish it is possible to see that while capitalism has become much more complex the process of exploitation and appropriation of surplus value are still central to the accumulation of wealth in capitalism. People are still hurt in the process and end up suffering. But the means of that suffering is more difficult to theorize about. Surplus value can now be extracted in many ways in many places for the same industry. There are factory workers in Brazil and pieceworkers in the Midwest of the United States making cars for the same manufacturer. Ironically, this is also the moment when an international workers movement is really needed, but practically, it has to be asked how could such a movement could organize and imagine itself (Anderson, 1991) as one group. These questions cause theorists to either abandon class or move to new ways to think about its position in the global capitalist system. Funnily, while much capitalist production is moving to third-world countries and/or returning to household and by-the-piece production, the university in America is turning into a factory. University professors are one of our remaining models of the industrial worker. These new structures of labor in global capitalism are a very important part of the 'conditions of post-modernity' (Harvey, 1989) and therefore any analysis of commoditization must deal with aspects of the post-modern.

The Discourse of Post-modernism

Much of the debate in post-modernism attempts to deal with the transformations of late capitalism and the shifts that the process of commoditization have brought to the 'social world' and the human subject. One of the most famous and flamboyant spokespersons of post-modernism is Jean Baudrillard. Baudrillard suggests that because of the institutions of mass media and the technologies that have transformed media, computers, fiber optics, video, etc., have really led to an end of the social and the death of the 'real': all things now are simulated (Baudrillard, 1983).

While Baudrillard is capable of realizing that the 'real' in the past was socially constructed, his point is well-taken that it was quite different from contemporary conditions. In the contemporary world, capital has been released from its industrial moorings and allowed to spin off in all directions, creating new and more dizzying spectacles which produce no real substance such as junk bonds, media spectaculars and Disneyworld. For these reasons Baudrillard, like many of his contemporaries, breaks with Marx. For them, Marx is too much caught up in the production metaphor of the nineteenth century. The production metaphor is just that, a 'mirror of production' which may have reflected some of the organization of capitalism in the nineteenth century but is no longer useful as a way of describing late twentieth century capitalism. I will return to a critique of these ideas but for the moment I want to pursue some of the important positive implications of Baudrillard's work for an understanding of contemporary marketing and advertising, of what I will call technologies of consumption.

Market Segmentation

Throughout the history of capitalism and into the present, the 'crisis of overproduction' has been a serious problem of capitalism. This is one of the important insights of Marx, and of course later commentators have discussed this issue too. In capitalism the goal is the production of exchange value. Under industrial capitalism, commodities are produced as cheaply as possible to be sold for a profit.

There are moments of crisis in the history of capitalism where the goods produced cannot be sold. Not that there is no need for the goods, but there are not enough consumers with the money to buy goods. The condition of the housing market in the United States today is a good example. At the moment when homelessness is reaching an all time high, there is a slowdown in the housing market. Developers have 'overproduced' housing and now they can't sell. The solution to this apparent contradiction is simple. Builders build high income housing because there is more profit to be made than in low income housing. The developers and builders compete with each other in the high income market until they produce a glut. Then there is a situation like the present one where people live on the streets and luxury houses sit empty.

There have also been throughout the history of capitalism different attempts to solve this 'crisis of overproduction'. At various points in time capitalists have sought overseas markets, for new consumers to take up the slack and buy goods. War and the threat of war have sometimes been good ways to solve this problem. Government can buy the goods and use them up in a war, or they buy more and more high technology to prepare for war, which needs to constantly be renewed because the technologies obsolesce. This behavior led to the so called 'military industrial complex', as the government becomes the guarantor of a market.

Richard Ohmann (1987, p. 152) points out that at the turn of the century capitalists needed a more guaranteed market. The cost of production was becoming too high for them to depend on a free market. And what these turn-of-the-century capitalists hit upon was advertising. Advertising changes the face of the capitalist world and it changes the subject from a citizen into a consumer.

Ohmann follows the history of the development of national magazines, the process of generating revenue for the circulation of the media through advertising and the ability of the advertising itself to persuade a buying public. Advertising has learned to imagine social life, putting a brand name in the midst of that imagination. With that power, the capitalist no longer had to rely on the merchant to sell the merits of his product to the buying public; he could rely on the public to come in asking for brand names and world-view advertising had linked with it. Ohmann argues that the rise of mass culture is inextricably linked to the development of advertising as a solution to the production problems in capitalism.

Advertising also ushered in a fundamental change in the capitalist system which coincided with the rise of what we call 'modernism'. The complex machinery which is the hallmark of modernism (Berger, 1969) was also the reason for the need of a more guaranteed consumer. Industrial production became too expensive to rely on the free absent hand of the market. Advertising not only smoothed this transition, it allowed capitalism to exaggerate a tendency already there; the emphasis of appearance over substance. W.F. Haug (1986) does an excellent job of describing this tendency in capitalism. For the capitalist, use-value is of definitely secondary concern, only inasmuch as it helps sell his product, which is to say, only as an idea to be implied or promised. The capitalist is far more concerned with exchange value. Exchange-value is enhanced if you make the product look more appealing. Advertising can create an appealing fantasy world that convinces potential consumers their identities are tied up with this product, that they need it. Further, shiny and colorful packaging can appeal to infantile sexual nature and further enhance buying behavior. It is easy to see Baudrillard's simulation originate here in the center of capitalist production, an easy solution to some of the contradictions of capitalism. Less obviously, it also began to change the way people led their lives, saw themselves, and most importantly, it changed the infrastructure of capitalism itself as a substantial portion of capital came to be dedicated to the production of advertising images alone. These images were at the time still dependent images, they relied on the real product behind them to give them their meaning, but this was the beginning of the product not as it is but as it is imagined. Later, Baudrillard was to argue that the sign function of the product was all there ever was and the Marxian separation between use-value and exchange-value was specious (Baudrillard, 1983).

As momentous as these solutions of the early twentieth century were, they still did not get rid of the 'crisis of overproduction' they set out to address. It was still possible to produce more than people could or would consume. Another important shift came when producers begn to see consumers as more than one consuming being. This ability was called 'market segmentation'. Baudrillard's analysis of this is powerful: As capitalists moved away from seeing the 'real' world as a fixed place it became possible for them to re-imagine the social space. A person once was a citizen; he/she was one — one vote, one job, one house. Capitalism also once was tied to this image of the real. Towns used to have one movie theater. In that theater there would be one movie playing for a week or longer, depending on how well it did. Marketing used to calculate what percentage of the real market they were selling. If you got 70 per cent of the market (which meant people) to go to a particular movie you were doing well.

But 'market segmentation' allowed us to completely change this picture. Now we can imagine markets not as people but as loci of taste. There are the primary markets, as well as the clustering of taste for, for example, horror movies; and then secondary and tertiary markets, those whose tastes who will buy a horror film after some conditions are met. Each person is a complex of many tastes, a fragmented subject who can moreover be encouraged to develop different aspects of his/her nature. So now it became profitable to gut the movie theater and divide it into several small screening rooms, in which to show the several films targeting specific primary markets (taste groups), and sell more than 100 per cent of the market as it was understood in the old sense of citizens in the community. Capitalism now imagines consumers. There are now more consumers than there are people, and the consumers, not the people, are what count. This technology, like advertising at the turn of the century, has changed the nature of human subjects in a fundamental way. People are now 'fragmented' into taste areas. Not only that, but the fragmentation is produced not just by consumption but through the entire rearrangement of the productive sector as will. This brings us back to a critique of Baudrillard's overemphasis on consumption.

Production and Consumption

Baudrillard breaks formally with Marx in the *Mirror of Production* (Kellner, 1989, p. 33). In this work he suggested that Marx could not break away from the metaphor of production. However, in the contemporary world where subjects are shaped by the forces of media and computer technology, consumption is more important in the movement of capitalism. Advertising and marketing have produced greater and greater fragmentation until there can be said to be no longer any social but only simulation as discussed above. Capital is no longer tied to production, but is now a free-wheeling perverse entity which amasses itself and turns all into economic reason.

While Baudrillard's analysis is interesting and important, he fails to make his analysis historical and therefore I believe he makes a number of erroneous assumptions. I have been carefully trying to show that the dizzying effects of late capitalism are attempts in capitalism to solve the 'crises of production'. From Ohmann's analysis of the development of advertising and national magazines as an attempt to rationalize production, and the effects of the creation of 'mass culture' to the more fragmentary effects of 'market segmentation' and the post-modern subject, all are attempts on the part of capitalists to guarantee profit on production. While it is true that looking at production is inadequate in the analysis of late capitalism, Baudrillard assumes that all there is, is consumption; that there is no production. But clearly these complex effects of late capitalism are driven by an interplay between production and consumption.

Bourdieu, in a lecture he gave at the University of Pennsylvania, discusses the problems of an analysis posed from 'the bottom up'. His remarks were aimed at Foucault. While Bourdieu and Foucault were both interested in the minutia of everyday life, Bourdieu insisted that sociology (and anthropology) needed to pose its analysis from the 'top down'. There was a need to look at the structure of positions which produced certain behaviors for Bourdieu, not just the behaviors themselves. While Baudrillard agreed there were structural elements producing the conditions of post-modernism, he argued the fragmenting and perverse nature of these structural conditions ripped the social apart and hence we could only look from 'the bottom up' anymore. However if the production orientation was an effect of a certain stage of capitalism so was the consumption effect. The mistake of idealism was to focus only on the ideas and not look at the institutional arrangements out of which these ideas grow. This refers back to the passage of Marx in *The German Ideology* I began this chapter with. The ideas seem to have a life of their own because we experience them independently of their material conditions. Arjun Appadurai (1988, p. 12) in the introduction to *The Social Life of Things* makes a very interesting analysis of the relationship of Marx and Simmel. While Appadurai saw Marx as still caught up in the nineteenth century 'episteme' of production, he argued that Marx's analysis of capitalism was very complex and perhaps there were more points of contact with Simmel's analysis of the circulation of money than might be seen at first glance. Appadurai correctly argued, in my opinion, that an analysis of economic systems that take into an account the circulation of goods is absolutely necessary, and production may in fact be done simply for the desire to circulate. However Appadurai walked a fine line. He conflated Bourdieu's critique of objectivism in the social sciences with Baudrillard's model of the circulation of signs.

Bourdieu argued that by failing to look at the subjective strategies of actors we have reified 'primitive' systems of exchange into a logic we cannot understand. While their systems of exchange may be different than ours we should be able to understand the strategies of actors trying to improve their positions. This argument of Bourdieu's is very different from Baudrillard who saw all economic systems as sign play. If production was an episteme of the nineteenth century to get caught in, then surely consumption and the notion of the sign was also an episteme to be caught in. We cannot forget that the production orientation of the nineteenth century political economists was not just at the level of concepts but at the level of infrastructural arrangements as well; just as our preoccupation with the sign is due to infrastructural arrangements of the twentieth century.

Bourdieu (1977) and deCerteau (1984) suggested another fruitful avenue of returning to the structural 'top down' analysis. Consumption and production are inextricably related. Bourdieu's notion of habitus is a structure which selects (consumes) according to patterns produced by the 'objective conditions which went into the production of habitus. Taste, style, consumption are not random and incoherent, as Baudrillard might have us believe, but are the products of the 'discipline' of the material conditions of social life. As those material conditions become more complex as they have in late capitalism, we should expect the conditions of habitus to become more complex as well. As there are more class fractions produced by the infrastructure, there will be an increasing array of symbolic expression through consumption.

Consumption is a kind of production (*ibid.*, p. xii). deCerteau argues that there is not only a process of identification that goes on when members of a group consume products as symbols of their nature and identity and values; but there is a differing going on as well. Consumption resists by turning the selection on itself and transforming the meaning of the product from the intended meaning of the producers to a subverted meaning of the consuming group. This, for deCerteau, is where the politics of everyday life becomes very important to the analysis of large social and cultural systems (*ibid.*, p. xiv). Bourdieu and deCerteau allow us to see that there is a dynamic interplay between the large producers in a capitalist system (whether they are commodities, culture, spectacles, etc.), and the consumption and subversion of these products. Unlike Baudrillard who in his later work gave the impression of a gigantic worldwide image producing machine which was, like the terminator, absolutely unstoppable; Bourdieu and especially deCerteau, by looking at the overall process, showed we are not helpless and there is still room for action. That action is constrained but there are clearly cracks in the system. The economist David Gordon (1988), criticizing the 'globalization of production' and 'new international division of labor' hypotheses suggested that while this research is on to important trends, they often make too much of a powerful monolith out of these corporations at the forefront of globalization. While corporations are rich and very powerful, Gordon points out we can't forget they are reacting to crisis themselves and there are weaknesses in the capitalist system.

The failure to tie consumption to the production of late capitalism is responsible for the distorted vision of Baudrillard and some of the other 'post-modernists'. They saw capitalism on the one hand as so complex and fragmented as to be impossible to study and on the other hand to be so powerful and global as to preclude any action. This is part of an ethnocentrism which has developed in left circles in Western countries who fail to accept that the 'third world' was the source of capital for the industrial revolution and it is again the source of capital and goods for the consumption-oriented Western world. I will come back to the analysis of accumulation in late capitalism and pose what Baudrillard fails to, but I would like to suggest another reason for Baudrillard's break with Marxian analysis.

In Europe and France in particular the Communist Party (CP) had become part of the state. After World War II many of the leftists and Communists who were active in the resistance were driven out of the DeGaulle government and not given much of a place in power. One of the effects of this was a very radical left wing, and an important Communist party in France from the end of World War II to 1968. After the 1960s the communist and socialist parties' power grew. This led to the 'mainstreaming' of many left wing intellectuals, as people got jobs in government and research. By the late 1970s anarchism was the only radical critique of the capitalist state because the CP was part of the government. This situation is also part of the German reality and well-portrayed in the film *The Lost Honor of Katrina Blum*. The ultra-left wing movement of the late 1970s in France was a reaction to this situation. It was an attempt to avoid cooption. So people like Foucault were talking about the micropolitics of power, of surveillance and the all pervasiveness of power, because the state had absorbed the left. On this level Perry Anderson is right about the failings of 'Western Marxism'. Baudrillard, I suggest, is also reacting to the position of Marxism in the intellectual discourse in France and rejecting production out of hand because of the political constraints to do so, and also because such strong statements make a better intellectual package to sell on the marketplace of ideas (an idea we'll analyze in the next chapter).

Flexible Accumulation

In chapter 4 I will look in detail at the ideas around the globalization of production, the new international division of labor, the issues of the return of piecework and forms of patriarchal accumulation in capitalist societies, and all the new concerns around the organization of production and consumption in late capitalist societies particularly the United States. Harvey (1989) argued that all these things coming together might be the beginnings of a new structure of accumulation in capitalism he called 'flexible accumulation'. I will look at how these macroeconomic changes are affecting higher education. However, for the moment I want to finish the discussion of commoditization.

Jameson (1989) sees the culture of post-modernism of which Baudrillard is an important spokesperson as being generated by these new conditions of late capitalism. Harvey makes this issue even clearer. Harvey suggests the Fordist/Keynesian system was one where accumulation under capitalism became relatively stable for the years of 1945–73. Capitalism avoided the contradictions of overproduction by organizing large-scale production, paying higher wages which the capitalist agreed to by big government orchestration, new ideas on the circulation of money and a favorable world market condition after the war.

By 1973 this system started to break down as foreign competition increased, the monetary policy began to produce inflation and cash gluts, OPEC put up oil embargos (Bluestone and Harrison, 1982). The scramble after 1973 by corporations wishing to secure profits, plus new computer technology such as: silicon chips, fiber optics and fax technology, was what ushered in flexible accumulation. New technology and an increasingly hostile market allowed capitalists to move production facilities to the Third World. The general goal of capitalists was to cut costs and so the use of simple commodity production in the Third World and at home became more common. New marketing technologies, new ways to take advantage of a global market while at the same time selling not to a mass market but by targeting specialized segments was also part of the strategies of flexible accumulation. It was under these conditions of crisis in late capitalism that we began to see the new forms of commoditization, as new arenas of social life were looked at for their profit-making potential. One tendency of flexible accumulation, Harvey points out, was to produce spectacle, media, services and soft production because the return per unit of input was very good. This led to Baudrillard's vision that the mass media and technologies of image-making beyond mass media were changing the social arena. While this was quite true and the process of subjectification under these new conditions needs to be looked at, they were also inextricably linked to the new productive infrastructure of late capitalism.

As the Fordist/Keynesian system broke down, the shifts in the global productive structure had effects on higher education in the United States. Two immediate effects were, first, the reduction of commitment on the part of the State to the education of citizens. The second was the use of federally-sponsored research by private corporations as a way to subsidize research and development. These macrostructural shifts, along with demographic changes, have produced new crises in higher education which are being dealt with using the same technological innovations that capitalists have developed to respond to their current economic crises.

One of the central points of this work is that there is an isomorphism between the structure of industries and institutions of a profit-making nature in American late capitalism, and the structure of higher education in the United States. Education is being both produced and consumed in new ways which has entailed the transformation of institutional arrangements, people. Explaining this isomorphism and not accepting the common sense idea that this is natural because its going on everywhere, is the goal of the following chapters. The transformation of university employees into producers of education, the creation of educational consumption and the sense that this is all obvious; are all aspects of what I am attempting to theoretically relate to the discourse on commoditization. But finally this process under capitalism is contradictory. As we come to the end of the twentieth century the globalization of capitalism has brought the hope of new markets and the globalization of production with its related local problems of unemployment. The university brings students from diverse backgrounds to not only provide enough paying customers of education to keep the institution going, but also in realization of the globalization of the economy. And this happens at the moment the state funds are drying up for student aid and higher education is seen as a necessity to staying afloat in the global economy. These pressures have made the university a site of national conflict as people struggle with the ideas of the liberal tradition verses multiculturalism and political correctness. These struggles at the level of consciousness are the products of much deeper fractures in the structure of society that will be explored in this book.

Notes

1   Richard Johnson (1988) in an article titled 'What is cultural studies anyway' discusses what he calls 'The circuit of cultural production'. He suggests that culture has been commodified and is literal a commodity for sale in late twentieth century capitalist societies. Social scientists who focus on different aspects of that process of the production, distribution and consumption of cultural commodities tend to use different theories. Johnson suggests in a totalizing vision that we need to find ways to put together what might at first glance seem to be conflicting perspectives in order to understand the overall circuit of cultural production. I draw very much on Johnson's argument. Education is one aspect of this overall cultural production. I would argue that at least some of what colleges and universities produce are cultural commodities.

2   Think, for example, of the tendency of social scientists to use the term 'globalization of production' or 'global assembly line'. These terms give us the impression that we understand a complex and far reaching set of infrastructural changes that are in fact very difficult to imagine or think about. It is certainly valuable to be able to label these complex processes, but we do not want the label to substitute for analysis.

3   We will discuss these ideas in much more detail in chapter 7, where I analyze the impact of marketing, advertising and strategic planning on universities and how education is affected.

4   Foucault argues that the rise of reason is historically connected to growing market and its worldview. In *Madness and Civilization* he argued the definition of mental illness that came out of the enlightenment was an economic notion of functionality. Could a person work and be productive, and the degree to which they could not indicated the seriousness of their malady. Likewise in *Discipline and Punish* he sees the modern technologies for getting individuals to internalize social control also as an outgrowth of the liberal free market ideology developing from the eighteenth century. The economic rationality that Foucault sees developing as part of the modern era has by now become our dominant mode for thinking about reason. I would argue that this is general to our culture but takes on specific importance in late twentieth century capitalism and in institutions like education that have become central to the increasing of markets and new products and the management of the work force of this late twentieth century society.

Chapter 2

Elements of Bureaucratic Identity

North Urban University is a large university situated in a poor, predominantly African-American and Hispanic neighborhood of a large city. Its governance structure includes board members from the State and private sectors, making it a hybrid of a public and private university. This combined structure arose historically when the university was transformed from a private university with a mission to provide educational opportunities for the average person in the city, to a research university within the State system. An important aspect of the institutional identity of North Urban is the contradiction inherent in its dual roles as teaching university offering career mobility people of the inner city and major state university producing research and training professionals. The university, with modest tuition structure for in-state students and fairly non competitive admissions standards, is an important institution of higher learning for working class students of the city attempting to improve their economic opportunities through increased cultural capital. The university also provides opportunities for working people to pursue advanced degrees part-time and at relatively low cost.

Walking across the campus of North Urban University, it is impossible to miss evidence of the rapid expansion in higher education in the 1960s and early 1970s. Many schools built entirely new campuses in the 1960s, sometimes creating a double campus made up of a few nineteenth century buildings surrounded by a new campus of functional modern brick and concrete. On North Urban's campus, there was a flurry of new construction in the late fifties, all of which was finished by the 1970s, and there has been no new construction since then. Unlike many private colleges and universities in the area, where new building and renovation continues into the 90s, North Urban's campus is relatively unchanged since the 1970s. It is a hodgepodge of buildings each seemingly designed without reference to its neighbors; the effect is a chaotic jumble of utilitarian buildings of many styles, all rather ugly. Within its urban landscape of abandoned and collapsing buildings, with thousands of students from dozens of ethnic and social backgrounds streaming from building to building, the campus is striking and energetic; a phoenix rising from the urban ashes, the vision of democratic opportunity and multicultural tolerance. It is a thriving urban space.

To North Urban in the 1970s and 1980s came a group of idealistic young adults who took democratic opportunity for granted and who believed in the power of higher education to break down the last remaining barriers of intolerance and inequality and to create a new society. These graduate students, like many of the time, were filled with the fervor and idealism wrought by the 1960s and at the beginning of their graduate careers they were still living in an economy that seemed to promise limitless professional opportunities. A political scientist I spoke to called 1970s 'a good time for thought', and it was. It was a time when traditions were being rethought, a time when the micro-politics of power and discourse were being explored, and the shape of fields of inquiry was changing. Interdisciplinary programs such as women's studies, Black studies and Native American studies were invented and other new visions of interdisciplinary work were being imagined.

This young group of future scholars came to North Urban with a democratic interdisciplinary vision that was not universally held. During the 1960s and 1970s there was a rapidly increasing number of faculty jobs in the United States; economists of higher education often said at the time that it was difficult for many of the rapidly-growing colleges to find faculty. Many books published in the 1960s talk about the employment crisis in higher education caused by the shortage of faculty. But there was already a kind of *over*production affecting the faculty members in the 1960s and early 1970s. While the comprehensive colleges and state universities were expanding their departments and programs, the expansion of positions in prestigious schools and departments was not keeping up with demand. Ivy league departments were turning out more PhDs than the Ivy league could absorb, so graduates had to 'trade down', to accept less desirable positions. An older faculty member at North Urban who is an Ivy league graduate joked to me while talking about a project she was working on at a more prestigious university across town, 'We haven't heard from Harvard yet. We're still waiting for them to discover us.' There was a note of irony in her voice and a twinkle in her eye. She knew it was nonsense but that didn't mitigate her disappointment at having to 'trade down' from her Ivy league expectations to a mediocre university like North Urban.

Her disappointment is not sympathized with by the younger faculty or graduate students of the 1980s and 1990s. Ever since the mid-1970s universities like North Urban have been experiencing declining federal and state subsidies, actual and imagined enrollment declines and increased operating costs, all combining to create an ongoing state of fiscal crisis. This has produced a leaner vision of higher education, with few new buildings and fewer new academic positions. As the perceived fiscal crisis continues into the 1990s, existing faculty jobs are often eliminated when the professor holding the position retires or changes jobs. If the job is not eliminated, it is opened as a temporary appointment. At North Urban many new faculty positions are called Dean's appointments, one-year positions which the university can renew for a number of years instead of committing itself to a tenure-track position. This means fewer jobs for the graduate students of the 1980s, and in this leaner, meaner market of few jobs and many PhDs competing for each one, a tenure-track job at North Urban looks very good indeed. For many people opportunities are much more limited; to jobs in community colleges, or to a string of temporary positions and juggled part-time work at a number of schools. When these shrinking horizons began to affect even Ivy League graduates, the symbolic value of the position at North Urban increased.[1]

Interestingly, these changes corresponded to a cultural movement that encouraged the rethinking of old boundaries and produced new often interdisciplinary approaches to intellectual and political reality. These new visions, of the university, one's place in it and the relationship between mentors and students, are all important steps in the transition to consciousness of an academic workforce. The data from North Urban holds true for much recent academic experiences, as can be seen by a proliferation of stories in the media. As the graduate student strike at Yale in 1995 (see note 5), demonstrates, even at former bastions of privilege, graduate students have begun to perceive themselves as an exploited workforce, and not — as was the traditional line — initiates enduring a painful internship that would yield a well-paid professional career in the end.

Methodological Concerns

My own relationship to this project — my interest in studying the university — comes out of the consciousness that took shape between 1975 and 1985. As a cultural anthropologist, I am aware that anthropology's particular claim to the production of knowledge relies on a phenomenological conceit. Like other social scientists, anthropologists study people, but 'people' does not include us. The people who are the subject of anthropological study are always the other, the one who is not-me, who can be looked upon with a cool objective eye. Scientists often pretend that it is possible to stand outside and (more accurately) see that which does not involve us. Traditionally, anthropologists are even more devious. Gathering their data in intimate contact with people, they make a conscious attempt to transcend the gulf separating people by sharing their lives and experience, after which they write about the data as if it happened only to someone else.

In the 1960s some anthropologists began to question the contours of this anthropological discourse. In particular they wondered why studying the other nearly always involves members of a powerful group studying the less powerful; often people who have little informed input and no critical access to their own representation. What would it mean, they wondered, to be more honestly and personally involved with a group of people; such that you were not just an observer sharing the pot with stranger only to later separate yourself to produce data. What would it mean to more completely share your life with them, as they do with you?

These questions led me to personally reevaluate some of our suppositions as anthropologists and university workers, and to probe the subtle mental barriers that separated 'us' from 'them'. The other in the Third World or the American ghetto is often seen as profoundly influenced by predatory global forces of colonialism and economic expansion, but we rarely include ourselves in this equation. No one would deny that we are part of these same processes but there is a subtle discursive shift that traditionally denies our presence in a shared world with our informants. One anthropologist, discussing power and forms of resistance with a group of graduate students said: 'If the poor people of color in the urban ghetto would simply refuse to consume, they could cripple the system.' The practical problems in this vision aside — it was offered in an informal discussion; not meant to be taken as a rigorous idea — the locution 'them' by this anthropologist is very interesting. It takes as given that of course *we* (the middle class university-educated) needn't refuse to consume because it's not our issue. We tend to talk about this and other struggles as if they didn't include us, which of course they do.

My decision to turn the ethnographic lens on the university culture I am part of involved a desire to capture a process of knowledge construction in the university — the social sciences in particular — and to see it against the backdrop of the vast ever-changing political and economic conditions of our time, called variously post-modernity, transnationalism and (more recently) globalization. It seemed to me clear that the imagination of the university was changing in both its work processes and in the minds of the people making up the university. But because our own culture (Rosaldo, 1989, pp. 202–3) is often suppressed in the discourse of studying the other, these changes and complex movements, of which we in the university were and are well aware, are going on without a careful analysis of the underlying structures of change.

The habit of what Johannes Fabian (1983) calls denial of coevalness — 'a persistent and systematic tendency to place the referent(s) of anthropology in a time other than the present of the producer of the anthropological discourse' (p. 31) is not overcome by studying one's own culture. Othering is an integral part of the way in which anthropological discourse has been structured historically. The informant is by definition the 'other', rhetorically separated from the self and turned into data. But writing books and articles about the culture are part of the history-making process and are always political acts, not just neutral, static data about some social facts. The ethnographic tradition of going off to a far-away island and temporarily sharing someone else's exotic life before returning home to turn the experience into a book for one's colleagues — never the subjects of the study — to read and admire has to be seen as another of the many ways that we westerners hold ourselves apart from everyone else. It is just one more of the many ways we deny that what goes on in our country, our corporate board rooms, our patterns of consumption; all have a direct impact on other people in the world.

The border is currently a very fashionable intellectual concept. Borders are places where people are forced by economic exigency to live with one foot in two or more different worlds, as for example Mexicans who live in Mexico but must cross the Texas border to find work. Current economic trends of transnational flows of labor and information force more and more marginalized people to work outside the culture in which they live. Recently, Henry Giroux (1993) used the concept of the border in the discourse of multiculturalism in education when he described public school teachers as cultural workers crossing between the borders of students' cultures and the dominant culture as they attempt to negotiate for knowledge and access to power in a society that marginalizes gender and cultural groups (pp. 32–6). University workers work on another kind of border. Not only in the way Giroux has in mind, but also on a border that parts the reimagined and reconstituted university, where marginalized university workers trade in intellectual commodities, from the ivied place of ideas we imagined we would work when we began graduate school.

The denial of a shared world is more subtle but still possible even when the people written about are people who share your everyday world. Writing the other is a process of representation, and through a variety of representational schemes becomes a way in which the ethnographer claims authority for her/his own voice while rendering the informants believable. The conceit is one that could be called ethnographic realism. The subjects of ethnographic study never speak for themselves; when they are quoted in the text the quotes are carefully chosen not as data but as anchors in the real; proof that the ethnographer was *really* there with the subjects and is (therefore) qualified to speak for them. Even the stories we tell each other about fieldwork reinforce this phenomenological conceit. Some anthropologists have become aware that this denial of coevalness begins with the ethnographer's confessions. Confessions of field problems can be a way of establishing ethnographic authority, a way of saying 'I am a real flawed human being who is qualified to speak for the other.'

So as I go on to engage in this very ethnographic practice (telling stories), I remind the reader that they are just my stories. Psychoanalysis speaks to this reflexive theoretical problem I have painted myself into — for the object relationist there are always two objects; the one in mind and the one out in the world. When the object in the head bears little relationship to the object in the world the discourse is called schizoid. The aim of mental health is to develop empathy, a correlation between the person-as-object in your head with the person-as-object in the world. For me ethnographic storytelling is a question of trying to empathize. I hope the people and stories in my head bear a relationship to the objects-in-the-world, but even if I am successful in this, it must be remembered they are my stories, and not the truth of my informants' existence.

Democratic Visions, Flattened Horizons

North Urban was an unusual place in 1978. There were a large number of very talented graduate students with a democratic vision of higher education. Some of these graduate students had transferred to North Urban from more prestigious programs, sometimes in a conscious rejection of elitism. They were also eager to reject traditional notions of pedagogy such as disciplinary borders, functionalist and conservative models, and the hierarchical nature of the production and dissemination of knowledge. These idealistic leanings were shared by students at North Urban for more material reasons, such as not being able to afford more expensive education or the need to pursue a degree part-time due to family or job considerations.

This cohort of highly motivated and politically aware graduate students took an active role in the shaping of intellectual work at North Urban. They lobbied for a voice in hiring and curriculum development. They saw themselves as a group involved with, and invested in, the interests of minorities, well represented in North Urban's undergraduate population of students from a variety of social class and ethnic backgrounds. On this diverse campus, where forms of neo-Marxist theory mixed with post-structuralism and deconstruction, there emerged a utopian vision of the possible; a world where the true revolution — not the traditional Marxist class revolution, but one where everyone would be empowered by knowledge, giving rise to an unquenchable democratic spirit. Power, we believed, would be transformed because people would have information.[2] At the time, I don't think it would have been put in quite this way. The several models discussed included traditional Marxism, a movement looking at the micropolitical context of discourse and the symbolic and some other more traditional functionalist views of people and society that promoted a status quo. Ned Harris, a graduate of North Urban, talking about this period told me that he remembered thinking of the Nicaraguan revolution as our revolution. He said that a Bruce Cockburn song popular at the time, *If I had a Rocket Launcher* (Cockburn, 1984, High Romance Music Ltd.), reveals our imagination of, and emotional investment in, the Sandanistas' struggle against the Samoza regime as a people's struggle for self-determination, as an attempt to wrest control of their economy and society away from a brutal dictator who was the puppet of international corporations. We saw the liberation of this people as iconic, as symbolizing our own liberation from a deadening global system. It became a vision of struggle against rationalized bureaucratic world order run by global corporations and backed by the US military. Needless to say the failure of the Sandanistas, like the failure of peace in Vietnam for an earlier group of idealistic students, created bitter new pessimism.

In a bleak vision of the Vietnam war, Jean Baudrillard (1983) illustrates this view by talking about the ways in which the Vietnamese revolution was a failed one. Referring to Vietnam he observes

> Why didn't the American defeat (the greatest reversal in its history) have any internal repercussions? If it had truly signified a setback in the planetary strategy of the USA, it should have necessarily disturbed the internal balance of the American political system. But no such thing happened. (pp. 66–7)

Baudrillard's answer to his own question is that the war in Vietnam did achieve desired results, though those results were not the US military's stated aims. The Vietnamese had to be brought in line with the world economic system and they were. He goes on to point out that even though the Vietnamese were still communist, communist regimes were more effective than the West in 'liquidating "primitive" precapitalist and antiquated structures' (*ibid.*, p. 68) Both the Vietnamese and Nicaraguan revolutions seem in retrospect to have been very much about the reorganization of social systems; specifically in eliminating or changing those which did not suit the purposes of the rapidly growing transnational corporations.

Baudrillard signals a change in the mood at North Urban. The four or five years around the end of the 1970s was characterized by a kind of democratic optimism, but the political success of Reagan in 1980 and the policies he championed and implemented rapidly ushered in the pessimism that Baudrillard describes in 1983. The people had won the war against a global system in Nicaragua. Then we all watched helplessly as the global system (with American backing) created the contras and effectively crippled the economy. By the end of the Sandinista rule the economic output of Nicaragua was near zero.[3] This mood of pessimism coincides with the beginning of the 'casino society' (Harrison and Bluestone, 1988; Strange, 1986) during which the technical intelligensia (lawyers, MBAs and information managers) grew in social and economic power. At the same time, the role of the humanistic intellectual declined as Federal, State and other funding to universities dried up in consequence of the Reaganomics of the 1980s. The drying up of support left more university professors and graduate students competing for increasingly scarce resources.

In this more suddenly more competitive academic marketplace, graduate students in the humanities and social sciences at North Urban found it increasingly difficult to compete for the scarce jobs and grants that would allow them to continue in the fields they had spent long periods of time training for. Several of the North Urban graduate students applying for funding found out that they were unable to get the grants they needed to do their fieldwork, further the universities office of research saw itself not as an office providing help with the funding process but as a gatekeeper.[4] I suggest that out of this juxtaposition, the democratic optimism of the seventies followed by the crushing reality of the 1980s, a new academic workforce was inculcated. Structurally, real limitations on the academic horizons of this generation were probably well in place early in the 1970s, but the democratic vision didn't give way to the pessimistic despair and careerism until the 1980s. And while graduate students across the United States and even other parts of the world[5] found themselves in the same boat competing for the scarce resources in higher education, North Urban's cohort was particularly hard-hit because so few of the students were connected into networks of scholars, grants and research facilities that make the transition to work and academic positions easier.

During this same period, with fewer job opportunities and greater competition for grant money, the relationship between the graduate students and their teachers came to consist less of the graduate students following their footsteps of their mentors than had previously been the case. Mentors, with the best will in the world, cannot offer their students hope of a job at an institution like North Urban, due both to the scarcity of those jobs in the first place and their own declining influence. As a result, they have less voice in the directions their protégés take professionally. Students typically follow their own interests and opportunities and accept less professional guidance from their mentors. In some instances faculty might even hope their graduate students' work will rescue *them* from academic obscurity, rather as families sometimes pin their upward-mobility dreams on the younger generation. Both the younger and the older generation struggled to understand this situation. One result was that graduate students at North Urban took a long time to complete degrees. It took a long time to get funding and once you did your fieldwork, the prospects of employment were not there to motivate the completion of the degree. While the older generation had to rush off to their first jobs and try to quickly finish their dissertations, this younger generation of scholars seemed to be willing to defer the process. We will see in chapter 9, that being a PhD candidate in a soft job market was in fact more legitimating than having the degree.

The good news, such as it was, was that as we will see the response of colleges and universities generally to the decreases in enrollment after the so-called baby boom had passed college age, coupled with decreased state support, was to begin to hire more part-time and temporary teachers to cope with budget shortfalls. This rising demand for a cheap, flexible workforce which could be hired and let go at a semester's notice, dovetailed neatly with the need of the newly-emerging inter-disciplinary PhD candidates and PhDs for jobs. Or, to make a distinction we discovered at this juncture, *work* (that which pays the rent); not *jobs* offering stability, professional standing and health benefits.

The PhDs of the 80s and 90s at North Urban became, not the junior tier of assorted faculties across the country, but the backbone of a flexible workforce migrating throughout the metropolitan area. As this process began it was perceived by the individuals involved as well as by the colleagues they worked for as evidence of their academic failure. But as the phenomenon continued consciousness around the issue changed and as it moved from less prominent universities like North Urban into the Ivy league the issue has gained national attention.

The Production of Habitus

Following Bourdieu (1973, pp. 494–6 and 1985, p. 196) it is possible to think of the field of cultural production as an economic activity, the accumulation of cultural capital. Increases in cultural capital are the main methods by which individuals strategize personal upward mobility. But Bourdieu (1984, pp. 143–68) also discusses a generation in France which he says was cheated. As the number of college degrees in general and PhDs specifically increased there were inflationary pressures on the cultural credential. It was no longer distinctive to have a degree and the job applicant could not depend on this credential to get the same calibre job. For middle- and upper middle-class students at North Urban there was also a style that involved a fashionable downward mobility. Ned Harris put this idea very eloquently he said that our generation thought we would fight the system, go to North Urban (the people's university), so resisting the prestige system of status accumulation in higher education. We also intended to gain our just middle class rewards eventually. So (we thought) we could do the right thing in undermining the tyranny of meritocracy, make a better world, and still end up public intellectuals in prominent positions. Not only did this imagination die a quick and by no means painless death, as discussed above, but professional status came to be something none of us can take for granted. The inflationary process made fashionable downward mobility backfire. Dressing down is a fashion statement only if you do it out of choice and not necessity. Legitimacy, for intellectuals, used to reside in collegial opinion and depend on ideas and originality, and be lent to the institutions where intellectuals worked. But in the bleak new order of scarcity and paucity of job opportunity this legitimacy has all but disappeared. Everyone began to talk about jobs, the lack of jobs and strategies to get jobs in the early 1980s, rather like the so-called yuppies we liked to be dismissive of. The irony of this was not lost on us. We all had friends and acquaintances doing hugely well in fields like law, real estate and

business and we certainly knew there was little meaningful critique of the bur-
geoning income inequality, but young PhDs at North Urban devoted most of their
energies to simultaneously trying to break into the ever elusive job market while
disguising their perceived professional failure.

The heating up of this job market started credential inflation. At North Urban
in the seventies we were aware that while someone of a previous generation might
have gotten a first tenure-track job while still a PhD candidate, and while this might
still be the case for Ivy University candidates, we had to have degree in hand before
even hoping for a job. We knew, as North Urban graduates, that we needed to
prove our worthiness before being considered. Even the degree might not be enough.
As it got progressively harder to get interviews, PhDs turned to other forms of
credentializing; publications of significant articles or books were seen as essential
to the cv. Ironically, this resulted in some North Urban graduates being better
published than the faculty they hoped would hire them. The process for many North
Urban graduates became quite frustrating. Faculty in less prestigious schools looking to increase their cachet in a buyers market would openly state they were only
hiring people with prestige degrees. Many times a PhD candidate from an Ivy
league institution would be hired over a North Urban graduate even though the
North Urban graduate already had a PhD and perhaps some publications. Further,
as North Urban graduates pressed on in order to impress people they hoped would
hire them they became *too* published, either embarrassing less-published faculty
who were doing the hiring, or limited their chances for hire because their traject-
ories had become so well defined.[6]

The pressures to publish and to be on the cutting edge of intellectual fashion
created a curious situation in the 1980s where young faculty following the academic fashions would publish in progressive areas, but found that university situations were not discussed in any sort of progressive terms. Edward Said (reprinted
from Critical Inquiry #9 in (Foster, 1983, pp. 146–58)) called what was developing
in the 1980s 'literary Marxism', a political radicalism disconnected from the world
of real politics, confined entirely to text. Said believed this was evidence of the
hegemonic power of the Reagan revolution; that there was no material political
opposition to it. Said's critique, however, missed the deeper irony of the time. Neo-
Marxism was very fashionable in the academic world at the time and using Marxist,
deconstructionist and late post-modern theory was sure-fire cachet in the publishing
world. And while these ideas were hot and a good way to interest book publishers,
they were nonetheless politically radical, and there was at the same time a growing
awareness that universities and academic departments were interested in hiring
well-published but less controversial intellectuals. As a result, the intellectual fashion in progressive political agenda began to function more as a commodity sign
than as a political plan in the world. The problem was to be hot enough to arouse
interest from universities, but not too dangerously controversial to get hired for
one of those scarce jobs. The hope was always if one worked hard enough to do
everything exactly right it was possible to beat the intimidating odds.

Increased competition for jobs and academic positions meant those more
institutionally connected to what Bourdieu called social and symbolic capital had

access to opportunities others did not. North Urban PhD candidates knew they were 'less connected' at North Urban, and there was a growing awareness there that to get a grant it was necessary to get letters of reference from prominent researchers and that without these connections funding was unlikely. North Urban, like most large research universities, has many large grants and institutes that raise money in different fields, but many of the social science and humanities faculty were not well funded, and this of course decreased the chances for a graduate student to work on a mentor grant. Without social capital or connections, the world of funding seemed all but unimaginable to us at North Urban. The process of grant writing and receiving involves utilizing a variety of resources: teachers, colleagues, texts, perhaps courses or speakers on the subject; but this was all nearly forgotten in the sheer seeming impossibility of it all. When someone did get a grant it was regarded as a blessing of nearly magical proportions.

Applying for funding and jobs is a highly specialized discursive function and involves cultural knowledge not often directly articulated. It is part of the hidden curriculum of higher education. Graduate students discuss these issues with each other and their mentors, but this usually happens outside of the normal academic discourse, as side-talk and informal chat in a variety of informal settings. A colleague who did her PhD at a prominent public university and a post-doctorate at a prominent private university told me that she and her colleagues constantly talked about career strategy, applying for funding, getting publications, producing a rich meta-discourse about getting ahead in the field that provided her with knowledge and experiences not available in other places. It is part of the symbolic capital that a PhD candidate must accumulate. At North Urban, many graduate students lacked not only the social connections to get grants but also and more crucially the symbolic capital of knowing exactly how it's done. North Urban graduate students simply were not exposed to mentors who could model effective strategies and as a result they did not learn the privileged discourses of grant application and funding. Drawing on the work of Bernstein (1971) Bourdieu (1984) and Goffman (1959), it can be argued that North Urban graduate students were missing two important things in the institutional grant agency connection process. First, they did not have the social capital. Their mentors were not well connected to granting agencies and other colleagues who were doing research and sitting on boards of the various scholarly associations and grant agencies. That lack of social capital is very significant. For one pre-doctoral fellowship program in the late 1980s all but one of the recipients was from a prestigious university. Some of the older faculty at North Urban in fact imagined their students awould bring *them* notoriety. Sam Philips, another graduate from North Urban, was told by several faculty members they were expecting great things from him and that he would bring North Urban the attention it deserved. In these good graduate students the older faculty imagined a kind of institutional upward mobility, similar to the way working-class and middle-class parents imagine the upward mobility of the family through their children. The second thing North Urban graduate students lacked was the vision of how to proceed; how to write a grant application, search all funding avenues, apply for many grants and strategize constantly about how to move ahead. This knowledge as mentioned above is often more a part of the student culture and less something that comes from a mentor. One needs to see and acquire the linguistic competence to master the granting process, which may include calling grant agencies on the phone and running drafts past the administrator of the grant. Most of the North Urban graduate students did not have this cultural knowledge.

In the heated-up academic marketplace, access to two forms of capital — the socially-acquired knowledge how to negotiate funding and connections to prominent researchers in the field — became increasingly more important. Paradoxically, capital lost value in this process. As jobs and resources got scarcer, more and more capital was seen to be needed. This scarce marketplace was experienced in several ways by the people involved. Often the scarcity of jobs and funding was seen as motivation to work harder to get one of those scarce jobs. But sometimes failure to get one felt shameful; a personal failing. A professor I know at another state university in the area used to save up his paychecks and deposit several at once so as to not be embarrassed at the teller with such a small amount of money. While most of the PhD candidates I knew at this time were aware that the situation was not entirely their own fault, most also secretly feared it was because of something they were doing wrong.

It is a powerful fact that many of these PhDs, though trained social science students and professionals, had limited consciousness of the failings in the system. There were critiques, but responses were individualistic . In *Working Class Without Work*, Lois Weis remarks on a similar tendency among Freeway girls. The girls in Freeway High School developed what she calls a 'glimmer of a critique of patriarchy' (Weis, 1990, p. 79) but they responded to it with individual solutions. Weis places no value judgment on this, but she clearly does not include herself in that analysis. In other words, while the 'working-class high school girls' respond to inequality individualistically, the enlightened researcher (she seems to assume), does not. But in my study I found highly educated social scientists, well able to articulate their position in the social field and to discuss their own tendencies to respond to situations in a particular way; capable of a highly rational, self-aware discourse; still were confined to individualistic solutions. The only alternative — political organization — was dangerous, risking the loss of all jobs, even part-time ones, not to mention absolute loss of hope of ever making it in the academic world. Despite this stark truth, political organization has arisen and continues to develop[7], though my informants did not often talk about it as a meaningful personal strategy for dealing with the job market.

Older faculty tended to respond to the new generation of PhD candidates individualistically as well. For one thing, the older generation's legitimacy depended to some extent on the denial of events in the academic marketplace. As resources declined, departments subsidized traditional low teaching loads, sabbaticals and grant leaves for tenured faculty by hiring adjuncts. Adjuncts were plentiful (campuses were thronged with PhDs looking for work), required no employment commitment longer than a semester, and cheap. In the late 1980s in the North Urban area adjuncts were paid between $1500–$2000 per course, on average. There were no retirement, medical or other benefits; only social security tax was usually (though not always) paid by the institution. It's easy to see the advantage to the institution of using adjuncts. A starting full-time tenure-track professor at this time earned about $30,000 and taught anywhere between four-eight courses a year, depending on the institution, making the cost per course taught by a new full-time faculty member between $3750 and $7500 a course, not including the cost of benefits. More senior faculty were of course even more expensive.

The Making of a Flexible Workforce

This tremendous inequality developing in an academic departments required the permanent faculty to find ways of thinking about this inequality. I encountered essentially three different responses among my tenured and established colleagues. The first and most rare was to acknowledge that the structural inequality existed and suggest something ought to be done about it. A much more common rationale was to treat the adjunct member of the faculty as still in training, as doing a lamentably underpaid internship but nonetheless getting valuable teaching experience. The third response was simply to see the adjunct as a failure who would have a job if only s/he were good enough.

As many of North Urban's PhDs began to seek work in the 1980s, they hit the job market at the moment that many colleges and universities were dealing with declining enrollments and budget shortfalls. Those colleges were increasingly using part-time faculty to meet some of their budgetary needs. The use of part-time labor had originally been seen as temporary, but the practice quickly became institutionalized and colleges came to rely on a certain percentage of their courses being taught by part-time faculty even after budget problems had been solved or reduced. One dean in justifying the situation told me that the university had many kinds of part-timers. Most of them (the dean told me) *wanted* to be part-time; very few of them were actually seeking tenure-track jobs, only taking part-time work to make do. No doubt there were and are many kinds of part-time workers, but the graduate student population at North Urban was composed of many graduate students who actively sought academic careers but failed to find tenured positions and who became during the late 1980s a flexible workforce, piecing together enough income to live on only by moving from school to school, earning in the process no stability, benefits or professional standing.

A colleague, discussing these issues, told me some stories about his life. While he was still a PhD candidate, he was legitimate in the eyes of the senior faculty he worked with. As an adjunct in the department he didn't have an office, a phone or usual conveniences but he did feel he was socially accepted. His colleagues liked to talk about his position as if it were a rite of passage; 'we were once the bottom of the pile too, but you'll finish your degree, get a job and move on'. The extent to which this was a polite pretense was revealed, after my colleague received his degree and continued to adjunct-teach with diminishing hopes for a 'real' job. He became conscious that his professional standing was diminished. Older faculty still asked how the dissertation was going — sometimes the very people who had read his vita, knew that the dissertation was finished, because they had hired him to teach part-time — still asked months later how the dissertation was going. The unspoken message was — you don't have a job yet? of course you must still be a student. The subtext — that this was a polite way of avoiding the only other assumption; that if he didn't have a job it must be because he wasn't any good — became increasingly clear as time went on, said my colleague. Many other informants had similar experiences with older mentors and peers.

The dilemma of the inability of a whole generation of scholars to improve their positions is complicated because its understanding requires the unmasking of the ways in which strategies and forms of social inequality operate in the academy itself. It's traditional to think of the academic world as a meritocratic system in which the best researchers and teachers rise to the top. When someone doesn't rise there are only two ways of explaining it. Either there is a structural disadvantage, the system is structured such that unequal access to cultural capital puts some individuals at a distinct disadvantage and the best *don't* necessarily rise to the top, and the traditional assumption is wrong. Or the assumption is right and the academic who fails to rise is a hack. Many senior faculty, even when they were uncomfortable doing so, saw the younger part-time workers as hacks. Discussing 'the Scholastic view', Bourdieu (1990b) has pointed out that university professors have an investment in understanding the world in which they operate as being structured differently than the social fields they analyze professionally. Professors live in a world seemingly disinterested and tend, consciously or calculatedly, to keep their careerist aspirations secret behind a mantle of scholarly cooperation and the dissemination of knowledge and information. If I submit a research article to a prominent journal, officially it must be because I feel the research belongs there or needs to reach a wide audience for other scholarly reasons; my personal career reasons are not supposed to enter into it. Further, different access to prominent individuals and being given special attention because of academic prestige is not supposed to influence the decisions of publishers, granting agencies or perhaps even hiring committees. Self-interest, in the form of self-conscious status accumulation, has no official place in academics and must be relegated to the hidden world of strategy, so senior faculty are caught between compassion and a need to deny what was actually happening. That double bind has led department chairs to offer hope to their temporary and part-time faculty in an instinct of scholarly cooperation and generosity. Not infrequently, the offered hope of benefits or a permanent job or a better contract comes without any assessment of the likelihood of the offer coming through. It is motivated by the desire to give a gift. Ironically, etiquette demands that the temporary or part-time faculty member acknowledge the gift even though s/he knows that it is not likely to come through. The offering carries symbolic weight and to refuse it would be rude, not to say impolitic on the part of someone in an already tenuous position in the department. So the marginal (part-time, temporary and adjuncts) are in an interesting position. Forced to see themselves as hacks because they have failed to accumulate the appropriate symbolic capital to move them to a better position, at times they must deal with the jealousies of their senior colleagues and they must accept the empty gifts offered to make the seniors who are worried about the juniors feel better. All these ironies must be accepted politely no matter how transparent. Being marginal enables one to see the inequity of this situation and further to see that none of the seniors understand the way power and inequality work in the academic department. The senior colleagues still believe in merit as the motivator of careers and the juniors see this as naiveté.

Many of the part-time and temporary faculty have responded to both the shortage of jobs and fears of intellectual and professional inadequacy by being super academics. Their personal imperatives are, teach well, have a reputation for popular courses, do exciting and ground-breaking research, publish a lot; in short, succeed through overkill. Recently Cary Nelson (1995) has written about the interesting ironies of this 'heated-up' marketplace. Nelson suggests that the strategy of recent PhDs to teach and publish more might actually damage a candidate's chances in the job market because by positioning her/himself a candidate doesn't allow the existing faculty to imagine her/him. Nelson talks about the importance of an up-coming younger generation on the ideology of academic merit. Many college departments imagine their future and their influence on the field in terms of the younger generation of faculty they hire. Unlike the hierarchically structured European system of higher education, American schools depend for their unique position and contributions to the field on the work of people in their departments and the new directions they take. For this reason, young new hires are extremely important. They are the way the department defines itself and its goals. This is sometimes expressed in very mundane terms such as, 'we want to move in the direction of geriatric research so let's hire a gerontologist'. Nelson's point is that young faculty, trying to get ahead in a tight job market, who publish books and articles in an effort to bolster their credentials may hurt themselves in this hiring process because their having extensive credits makes it harder for the department to recast them in terms of department needs and wishes. With a record of work behind them, that imagination is eclipsed. This leads to a yet another double bind for junior faculty. Don't publish, and you're a hack, but if you do publish you run the risk of not being viewed as what the faculty wants. Further, in some instances in my research there was embarrassment because a job applicant was much better and more frequently published than many of the members of the department.

Teaching and research have for a long time been antagonistic symbols in the discourse of academic life. Faculty often consider their teaching pulls them away from research. Further, the idea that teaching is a lower-status activity than research is built into the structure of many academic departments and is part of the lived experience of university professors. At one local university, a North Urban graduate in sociology who landed a series of one-year appointments in the sociology department told me that in this department people openly argued about the number of new 'preps' they would have to do. No-one wanted to develop a new course and certainly not more than one; it was simply too much time to devote to teaching. This informant had several semesters in a row of doing three new preps a semester, and this was seen as the normal course of events — as the lowest person in the status hierarchy, he had to teach the most new courses. At another university members of several academic departments openly talked about how much they disliked teaching and shared strategies for getting out of as many courses as possible. Tenured individuals admired one another for how little they were teaching. In both of these institutions the untenured one-year appointments and part-timers did the bulk of the teaching.

Of course many university faculty enjoy teaching and work very hard with their students. It is not my intention to argue that the bulk of university faculty are irresponsible in their duties.[8] But these attitudes about the relative value of teaching and research are omnipresent, even where more subtly and cautiously appraised. Within an academic department there is a commonly sliding status scale with research on top and teaching near the bottom. Many academic departments are aware of the destructiveness of this hierarchy of values and there are many efforts to deny it, true. The denial is itself proof of its existence and power.

This relationship between teaching and research fits also into the meritocratic vision of academics mentioned earlier (the best rises): when you are young, your academic career is more difficult because you must carry a heavier teaching load with more new preps and you have to also do research and publishing to get tenure. But (the scenario goes) your reward for hard work and success is more research time later in your career, with less time teaching. This implicitly makes research a sign of academic success, with teaching only being done by those who must because they are not (yet) successful.

Many of the younger marginalized faculty became very good teachers. They were flexible and creative and often very popular with their students. And they taught a wide range of subjects, because the interdisciplinary thinking of the late 70s and early 80s allowed them to justify teaching a wide range of courses, and many developed expertise in a variety of subjects. The concerns of the late 1970s around interdisciplinary work and intellectual questioning of the politics of disciplines turned into a technique for survival. An anthropologist could teach classes in criminology, deviance, race and ethnic relations, or other things, because there are ways to see all these subjects related to the basic enterprise of cultural anthropology.

While the status of marginalized faculty produced layers of contradiction, it also enabled full-time faculty to teach their traditionally small loads, get release time and do their research. The flexible workforce, the members of which were considered variously professors-in-training, voluntary part-timers or outright failures by the 'real' faculty, made these benefits possible. At North Urban and other universities, a faculty member with a grant would go on leave, her/his salary paid by the grant, allowing the university to pay an adjunct to teach in his/her absence; saving money on the faculty member's salary. This situation is not uncommon, and has come to be accepted as a business norm. If, as I have argued, this flexible workforce is what maintains the illusion of the older academic way of life for the tenured faculty, it must remain invisible if it is to succeed in maintaining that illusion. To acknowledge this exploited workforce would undermine the notion of a community of scholars, revealing academic power to be as bald and capricious as power in other, less apparently mild-mannered arenas.

Bourdieu's notion of the habitus, social field as structured arenas where position is determinative, is a useful model for the situation and disposition of North

Urban graduates and, increasingly, graduates from more prestigious universities; as they took temporary one-year and other part-time positions in the colleges and universities of the metropolitan area. These individuals' lives did not resemble the professional lives of tenured faculty. For one thing, they had to teach many more courses to make a living. Some semesters some, especially those with families, might teach six to eight courses, an unheard-of load. (Traditionally, three or four courses were seen as a heavy load.) Another irony for these part-time faculty was that disguising how much you taught was as necessary for your survival as a legitimate academic as teaching eight courses was to pay your bills. And disguising how little you were paid became second nature; a way of avoiding social embarrassment after spending six to ten years of advanced graduate training for so little financial reward. The adjunct faculty became very aware in this system of power relations that they were often carrying the department and that teaching was a very important activity. A group of North Urban graduates taught at West Urban Technical University and would jokingly point out you could tell the part-time from the full-time faculty, the part-timers were the ones who taught more courses per term. This was often true. These North Urban graduates were very aware of their status but the fact that they taught a lot and knew many students and were very popular with the students was part of their institutional legitimacy and fit their progressive view of themselves as teachers trying to promote a fairer world. The could not fathom their full-time colleagues' lack of interest in teaching nor their inability to see how unfair the system was. In reality the full-time faculty was very aware of the inequities in the system. Their inability to change things and their fear about their own positions with declining enrollment threatened and budget shortages stopped them from any meaningful political dialogue.

As the part-time market for college teachers expanded all through the 1980s, many PhD candidates were hired to teach a course or two, and everyone expected that getting a permanent job, though a little harder, would be possible. During the next several years universities expanded these part-time roles, sometimes consciously deciding to replace a full-time position with more or less permanent part-time positions. Chairpeople and other tenured faculty, having hired a part-time or temporary person for what they thought in 1983 was a one-time situation, often found that person still working in the department in 1988. Occasionally the part-time person, after being in the department for years, would get a one to three-year replacement position someplace else. Everyone would celebrate their leaving as moving on, as (finally) a step to a more permanent job, only to have the erstwhile part-timer return two years later to go back to part-time teaching.

So, as marginalized faculty members become more popular with students, hustle to their own research and write for publications in the fading hope of making it in an increasingly closed system, averting the eyes from the inequities becomes more difficult. Calling someone a hack for not having a job rings fairly hollow as the numbers grow, and as more and more of the teaching is being done by the aforementioned hacks, two seemingly contradictory trends have resulted. On the one hand adjuncts tend to be treated by administrations and the rest of the faculty as if invisible; not talked about, not invited to faculty meetings, lunches etc.; in

general ignored. On the other hand there is a growing official administra
course that says, 'now that we have a lot of adjuncts teaching here we must .
them how to teach, how to write syllabi, how to interact with students etc'. At many
universities adjunct faculty get publications aimed at 'training' them, are encouraged to come to workshops where marginality and surveillance combine, joining
some older forms of academic discipline that existed on the old route to tenure
and promotion. As a new generation joins the ranks of the underemployed, this one
not having gone through the transformation from the interdisciplinary world of the
seventies to the flexible labor market of the 1980s, the university attempts to manage
the entire flexible workforce as a homogeneous group. Flexible work in the university is no longer a temporary solution to immediate problems, but has become a
structured position. In 1989 William Bowen published *Prospects for Faculty in the
Arts and Sciences: A Study of Factors Affecting Demand and Supply, 1987 to 2012*.
On 13 September 1989, the *New York Times* reported that Bowen's data showed
that in the 1990s there would be faculty shortages in the arts and sciences and the
overproduction of PhDs would be over. Older faculty members left untold numbers
of xeroxes of this article in part-time faculty mailboxes. Bowen's study utterly
failed to take into consideration the flexible workforce. In that same year, David
Harvey wrote that flexible accumulation was a new strategy being used on the part
of corporations to accommodate the developing global economy, what Harvey (1989)
would call the 'conditions of postmodernity' (pp. 141–72). Universities, like the
corporations, had embarked upon a new pattern of labor usage, and it is one that
has produced in the 1990s not a shortage of faculty, but downsizing and retrenchment.

The Entrepreneurial University

In the 1990s the structural pressures that had created the flexible workforce in
higher education continued. More institutions experienced declines in enrollment
despite their best marketing efforts and Federal and State contributions shrank stead-
ily. The regime of capital accumulation brought record profits to the large corporations but less money to the average worker. The political ideology that took hold
in response to these forces is that the small person has too much of a tax burden
and state institutions like education must learn to live with less. The message from
the State capitals was clear — become profitable on your own and stop putting the
squeeze on the poor taxpayer. This has resulted in extreme belt-tightening. At a
state university a few miles from North Urban classes with fewer than thirty students are routinely canceled. Faculty are expected to teach classes of forty or fifty
students. Adjuncts teach fifty-student classes with no graders or other administrative
help for about $2000 a course. Adding faculty is all but out of the question and the
university's budgets for ordinary items like photocopying and paper run out in
the middle of the semester.

As mentioned above many North Urban graduates taught courses at West
Urban Technical University, a private university with large business and engineering
schools. During the Reagan years, West Urban Tech embarked on a large capital

expansion program, taking out many loans. At their middle states evaluation in the 1980s there was some concern over their deficit spending and expansion and the absence of a plan to manage future enrollments. The administration, filled with the confidence of the Reagan years, expected that their enrollments would continue to grow. At the end of the 80s the enrollment crisis hit and West Urban Tech's enrollment fell by a third between 1988 and 1992. One informant discussed the administration and Board of Directors of the university with me, describing how cut-off they were from current realities. Several older members of the board, for instance, believed it was still possible for students to put themselves through school on their own. The administration felt it would be undignified for their members to interact with students, so they were as out of touch with students as economic reality. My informant remembered an incident when the board debated whether or not it would be presidential for the President and his Assistant to go to registration so they could see how the registration system worked and how the students felt about it. The failure of this administration to deal with the problems of the university eventually led to a shake-up and a new President and Provost were hired, but it was too late to avert a crisis.

Even before the new administration arrived the university had spoken of downsizing and most of the flexible workforce was laid off.[9] The permanent faculty then had to take up the slack in teaching schedules, and there was worse to come. Rumors of plans to eliminate departments or lay off permanent faculty began to circulate; finally the administration asked the faculty how they wanted to do this. One bitter faculty member described this as '. . . asking us if we want them to amputate an arm or a foot. It's an unacceptable position to be put in.'

As the plans to eliminate departments proceeded apace it was clear that departments with a lot of majors, especially those with grant money and outside funding, were less likely to suffer cuts. Faculty and departments were openly encouraged to be entrepreneurial as never before. Departments had always tried to have lots of majors and get grant money, to get more of the university's resources allocated. But at West Urban Tech it became a matter of keeping one's job. One of the social science departments at West Tech began to explore a relationship with a computer company to provide software that might allow for a computer and human interface dealing with the growing population of seniors who might need care, with an eye to reengineering, making the delivery of medical services simpler and more reliable. The talks between the company and the department were nearly enough to secure the department's future in the university. The then President had no intention of downsizing this particular department because they had raised the possibility of a large infusion of capital.

As we will see in chapter 4, this increase in cooperative ventures between universities and corporations often bring in big grant money, though sometimes they do not help the financial picture all that much. Operating expenses must come out of the university budget and only capital equipment can come out of the grant. Nevertheless, the talks had the desired effect on West Tech's administration. The departments and colleges in the best position as the discourse of downsizing began were those that had developed relationships with corporations or that had new services and products to be marketed in university/business or university/medical community partnerships. The logic of the market had come to the university. Only if we had something to sell could we justify not being downsized.

Inevitably downsizing came to North Urban as well. The university was reimagined by the administration as primarily an undergraduate institution with only an incidental arrangement of graduate departments. In keeping with this imagination, faculty teaching loads were increased university-wide and graduate programs were cut or eliminated. The interdisciplinary programs developed in the 1970s and 1980s were blamed for North Urban's inefficiency, and each department was forced to look closely at its programs with the intention of reducing or eliminating inefficient programs. North Urban expanded the number of temporary one-year appointments as well. These so-called Dean's appointments, originally devised to keep the part-time faculty from unionizing, are now being used to keep faculty from moving to a tenure-track line. Also, they're flexible and can be renewed if the enrollment is there and eliminated if it is not.

As I will show, full-time tenured faculty are beginning to feel these forces as well. On 26 March 1996 the *New York Times* reported that with budget gaps and declines in state and city funding CUNY plans to eliminate 'more than 1330 full-time faculty and staff positions'. The university Board of Trustees voted for a state of 'fiscal exigency' which will allow them to lay off tenured professors. Governor Pataki is also reducing the size of the SUNY system, and several other states are following suit. In Pennsylvania where the state university has been unionized for many years, the State wants to throw out the old contract and renegotiate from scratch. Many faculty I talked to in these systems know all too well that tenure is no longer a guarantee of a job and that there are real pressures to eliminate university jobs. What was before a shame for a few younger faculty is everybody's problem. University professors have the important and difficult job of overcoming the 'scholastic view', and realizing their situations are very much tied in to larger global changes. For us anthropologists, the circumstances of displaced foragers in the rainforest and workers in new factories set up in the third world are not distant realities but part of a power structure created by transnational flows of capital, goods and information, and decisions made by corporate leaders and governments, particularly our own government. We can no longer afford to deny coevalness with other peoples.

Notes

1   Bourdieu (1984, p. 143) refers to this as a heating up the academic marketplace where ones individual credentials become less valuable and by extension the scarce jobs increase in value.

2   Lois Weis in *Working Class Without Work* points out that in post-industrial economy the struggle is no longer between capital and labor but over symbolic control of information. Citing Touraine and Melucci, she suggests that contemporary social movements will reflect these new structural arrangements and we will see new kinds of struggle (Weis,

1990, pp. 10–11). Certainly these events support her analysis. While many people were still thinking about the conflict between capital and labor, many others saw new forms of struggle with capital, including control of knowledge, nuclear proliferation and the bankrupt semiotics of a consumer society.

3   At North Urban the loss was personal. One of our colleagues in anthropology, a freelance journalist photographing the Nicaraguan revolution, died in El Salvador when his jeep either drove over a land mine or was struck by a rocket. The circumstances were unclear. This loss was for us an important marker of the change from democratic optimism to despair of a global system that could not be fought.

4   The general attitude of the research review board was one of rejecting not supporting grant applications. Interestingly they often did this by imagining all research along a biomedical model. I was talking with a member of the Office of Research at the university and as he struggled to understand my project I pointed out to him that this conversation we were having was part of the data as far as I was concerned. The reflexivity of that comment took him by surprise, for him data was something carefully collected in controlled situations and not something that emanated from the institution itself.

5   A colleague from England told me that the sad situation in his department, where there were no permanent faculty members under 40 and not many in other departments of his university, was not untypical of universities in Great Britain. In his vision a whole generation had been lost in English higher education.

6   We will again talk about this idea more in chapter nine. Cary Nelson (1995) has pointed out that a job applicant who is published is at a disadvantage because they are a known quantity and faculty cannot imagine them in their own way.

7   The recent Yale University Graduate student strike, where graduate assistants refused to turn in their grades until their wage and work condition demands were listened to, is a powerful example of the continuing pressure to organize.

8   The argument I am making here concerns how the social field is constructed and what the symbols of status within that field are. Like Bourdieu I assume that all human interactions take place within a structured social field and different actors take up social positions within that field. My goal here is to articulate the structured positions and the related dispositions of individuals in the social field. I would argue very strongly against Charles J. Sykes, who in his book *ProfScam* (1988) sees the university as a very selfishly and narcissistically motivated group of rogue entrepreneurs who don't care about teaching and are just in it for the research dollars. What Sykes perceives are some of the commodifying pressures on universities to be more entrepreneurial with the decline of state funding and the need for research money to keep things moving. But in my opinion he incorrectly sees these pressures as originating in selfish individuals. The pressures come from the State and the corporations as they push the university to provide education and research for a high-tech economy with less State funding.

9   Actually, a flexible workforce isn't laid off per se; you need only to not rehire them. Budgets for adjunct faculty were simply not approved and department chairs could not rehire people.

Chapter 3

Recent History of Higher Education

Chapter 4 will focus more closely on the last forty years, but first I would like to look at some broad movements in the nineteenth and twentieth centuries, establishing overall trends in higher education and connecting them to the political and economic issues of the time. I will argue that the post-World War II imagination of higher education and the baby boom-driven expansion of higher education in the 1960s worked together to produce an economic boom in higher education. This boom, if it did nothing else, suggested the novel idea that higher education is a business like any other business, an industry supplying a product. This was a new model of education quite unlike previous generations' imaginations.

Of course, after the boom came the bust. 1973 began a slide into economic crisis caused by declining enrollments and the withdrawal of federal money. The crisis mentality developed at this time to deal with fiscal problems became the norm for higher education, and it ushered in an era of enrollment management and marketing; a discourse characterized by the student-as-consumer. Perhaps the most important consequence of this was the rapid expansion of a bureaucratic apparatus created to shape and administer policies, not least of which involved squeezing of the professoriate, the section that produces the educational 'product'.

As already discussed, I have chosen the concept of commodification to explain this process. The value of this trope, it seems to me, is that it allows the placement of higher education into the political-economic framework of the development of capitalism in the United States from its industrial phase in the nineteenth century to the global era of transnational corporations and post-industrial society, while acknowledging cultural developments not directly tied to political economy. The imagination of the university, its contradictory images through history and the various struggles over knowledge and the uses of the university are all clearly caught up in the political economic realities of the United States without being reducible to those realities.

Many historians and other social scientists have talked about education as being caught between the needs of the economy and the needs of a democratic polity, and the fact that these needs are seen as contradictory (Bowles and Gintis, 1987; Cremin, 1989; Katz, 1987; Carnoy and Levin, 1985; Levine, 1986). This is a fruitful approach for thinking about the development of education (higher education in particular) in the United States. It is very clear that as business in America began to bureaucratize and large-scale corporations began to dominate the landscape in the twentieth century, schools, directly and indirectly influenced by business, began to believe that bureaucracy is the most efficient means of educating a workforce and providing the tools needed for new economy, and encouraging the values of group belonging and citizenship that make for a stable polity (Spring, 1972; Veysey, 1965; Barrow, 1990; Katz, 1987).

Keeping in mind some of the current thinking in history, I would like to talk about the imagination of the university (Anderson, 1991), together with the role of nostalgia (Lowenthal, 1985), memory (deCerteau, 1988; LeGoff, 1992), and the invention of traditions (Hobsbawm and Ranger, 1983) in that imagination. Many of our strongest feelings about higher education, not to mention our concerns for its future, are tied to the ways in which we imagine the university. Powerful images like the 'community of scholars' and the 'ivory tower' crucially shape thinking about the strengths and weaknesses of the university, but the images themselves are rarely examined. Any attitude toward the bureaucratization of higher education and the role of business in education is necessarily informed by these root metaphors. Further, ideas having to do with a perceived decline in the quality of education, students and teachers, as well as our fears that 'watering down' higher education will lead to the collapse of our literate culture, are all deeply connected to the ways in which we imagine the university.

Benedict Anderson (1991) in his work on the rise of the nation state, suggests that community, both in its day-to-day functioning and its relationship to the past, is a shared cultural understanding imagined by the inhabitants. He writes, 'all communities larger than the primordial villages of face-to-face contact (and perhaps even these) are imagined' (p. 6). Anderson links the development of capitalism to new forms of consciousness, out of which grow popular nationalistic movements which are then co-opted by various forms of official nationalism. This process involves nothing less than complete transformation of the social notions of space, time, the individual and social identity.

What Anderson ascribes to political community, nations of people; can be extended to theorizing about universities along several lines. First, the development of print, the rise of national languages and the birth of the modern state are all inextricably connected to the rise of the intellectual class (Gouldner, 1979; Bauman, 1992; Habermas, 1987, 1989 and 1992). Universities also play a central role in the canonizing of an standard language and they uphold the political, literary and historical culture of the nation. They are our collective cultural memory. The university is also a site of struggle between conflicting visions of the nation.

Further, and more to the present point, the university can be thought of as an imagined community in its own right. Certainly inherent in its role as holder of culture is the perception of the university as a society apart; the ivory tower. As a community unto itself, it must remain pure, separate from secular society, so that it can uphold all that which is good, true and beautiful. In our culture's imagination, from the outside, it is a sacred space. Within the ivory tower, the university community often terms itself; in its own version of this idea, as a 'community of scholars'.

Following Anderson, I suggest that the 'community of scholars'; this quasi-religious allusion to the medieval university, is in fact a product of the modern imagination. Further the sign is a sword that cuts both ways, representing as it does both the freedom from the constraints of the world to preserve knowledge and innovate new ideas (Tannenbaum, 1965) and a way of describing a community cut off from the 'real' world (p. v). The imagination of the ivory tower or the community of scholars is invoked in times of crisis, not only within the university but during crises in society at large as well. As Lawrence Cremin (1989) has pointed out, we tend to see education, particularly higher education, as the solution to all of our social, political and economic problems (p. 92). A crisis in higher education then, becomes a crisis in the larger society.[1]

Anderson (1991) points out in the process of social imagination, things are forgotten. Memory is a form of forgetting:

> All profound changes in consciousness, by their very nature, bring with them characteristic amnesias. Out of such oblivions, in specific historical circumstances, spring narratives. After experiencing the physiological and emotional changes produced by puberty, it is impossible to 'remember' the consciousness of childhood. (p. 204)

Hobsbawm and Ranger (1983) in their edited volume *The Invention of Tradition* also discuss many traditions, seemingly archaic but really of recent origin, that have been created to serve present-day interests. LeGoff (1992), citing Bourdieu, points out that 'the past serves the interests of the present' (p. 16). Memory of the past involves forgetting the context within which issues in the past developed; often to serve the socially conservative interests of either an elite class fraction in decline (looking back to the good old days when there was order), or the rising masses who cling nostalgically to their 'roots'. In LeGoff's vision of memory the crisis in higher education is understood as the liberal tradition lost. This conservative memory would deny a place to the recording of (among other things) the multicultural traditions in America.

For the rest of this chapter I will examine the ways in which the university is imagined and for whom this imagination functions; what is remembered and what is forgotten. The process will involve a recovery of conflicts that have been forgotten and an analysis of the ways the notion of the university has been used as a symbol of what is wrong in our society or what our society ought to achieve. I want to look at these imaginings as they have been furthered by the language around higher education, the structural changes in universities and their boards of trustees, the changing vision of professionalism and (last but not least) the vision of what education is and what it does for us as a nation.

The Business of Higher Education

As early as the turn of this century, prominent faculty members at the large private universities would occasionally go on record deploring the commodifying process. It seemed to many of them that higher education had turned into a process of students buying degrees. (In a curious way, this may perhaps have been more true of the period from 1900 to 1930 than our own, post-World War II era. At the turn of the century, admission to the private universities depended mainly on whether or not you could afford it (Nasaw, 1981, p. 166).) However there is something else in these comments deploring the decline of education into the buying and selling of degrees.

> It has become an almost traditional part of the rhetoric of the student left in the past decade to declare that the university system is controlled by big businessmen and war profiteers for their private gain and our shared loss. It has become almost traditional to declare that the universities are subservient to the powerful profit interests of the capitalist class; but aside from a few genuinely pathbreaking studies, little proof of this contention has been offered. (Smith, 1974, p. 11)

These are not the words of a conservative administrator trying to undermine the work of student activists in the sixties and seventies. They come from a scholar on the left, (in a book published by *Monthly Review*), trying to substantiate the claims of the radical students. Smith's book does do a good job of contributing to the knowledge of ruling class and corporate control of the universities which was beginning to grow at that time. The quote is interesting for a number of reasons. First, if you compare the attitude of the quote with the overwhelming amount of evidence of the ties between higher education and big business in Ridgeway's (1968) *The Closed Corporation*, or more recently in Clyde W. Barrow's (1990) study *Universities and the Capitalist State,* or even with Smith's (1974) own book *Who Rules the Universities?*, one wonders how a generation of scholars could have been so unclear about the connections.

A possible answer of course is, universities are large complex social institutions within a complex society and the situation was, often willfully, obscured. The scholars of the 1960s and 1970s did some obscuring of their own as they began to awaken from Anderson's social amnesia. Corporate control of the university had in fact been complete for some time but the imagination of the community of scholars still made that very hard to see. David Seymour (1988) in the *College Board Review*, the magazine of the organization which produces and disseminates the SAT exam, in an article dealing with the pros and cons of corporate management procedures being used by universities, tells of a Harvard professor at the turn of the century deploring the selling of Harvard degrees by the businessmen who run the university (p. 38). Seymour's memory of the past is intended to give us the sense that on some level nothing has changed; that commodification has always been with us. Social amnesia can take other forms as well. For example, in the 1980s it was not unusual to hear politically-oriented university intellectuals saying they weren't interested in challenging the policies of their own university: 'It is more strategic to bow to this power so that we can put our energies into a critique of policy in Central America', was the logic. One local college has an active program trying to get students involved in the injustices in Bosnia, but the faculty seem unaware of the ways administrative power coerces them. A department chair there told me that his department had complete control over hiring, despite receiving memos routinely circulated to departments outlining what kind of candidates the university was looking for. This willingness to conform to (or refuse to see) the coercive hold that universities have over their own workers is itself a product of the history of this century.

Clyde Barrow (1990) in his study *Universities and the Capitalist State* documents the development of the relationship between the universities and corporate capitalism. Barrow begins with the transformation of the boards of trustees for American colleges and universities around the turn of the century, and looks at the processes of capitalist penetration, the degree to which the university was transformed by economic forces. His model looks at universities by region because he correctly suggests that capitalism developed at different rates and there are different capitalist blocs for each region of the country. He shows structural similarity but historical particularity. Some universities resisted capitalist penetration because of the period of capitalist development and/or the particular circumstances in which they found themselves. For instance, Barrow (1990) points out that the penetration of universities in the south by capitalism was much slower than in the northeast or the midwest, because in the south political elites maintained a closer control over the university boards (p. 51).

Capitalist groups in the northeast, the so-called eastern establishment, like the Carnegie, Morgan or Rockefeller group, are the earliest, the most successful and today still the largest capitalist groups (*ibid.*, pp. 21–4; Arnove, 1980; Darknell, 1980; Domhoff, 1967). These groups were the ones who spearheaded the appropriation of the university for business interests and are among the ones today pushing the exploitation of the university for capitalist interests. Barrow (1990) shows that the percentage of professionals (clergymen, physicians, educators, lawyers and judges) on the boards of trustees of major private universities and technical institutes in the northeast declined from 60 per cent to 28.7 per cent in the period from 1861–1929 (p. 38). In contrast, over the same period in the same institutions the percentage of businessmen (merchants, manufacturers, railroad magnates, engineers and bankers) increased from 25 per cent to 53.4 per cent. Veysey (1965) discusses this process in some detail (pp. 346–56). He points out that the transformation of the board of trustee to businessmen means that for many they begin to see the university as a business selling a product to a market. Though the boards of trustees of major universities become more interested in what he calls 'the intellectual market' (*ibid.*, p. 351) Veysey is careful to point out that there are some important ways universities do *not* become like businesses. While it becomes popular to think of education as a product being sold the university bureaucracy, with its emphasis on departmental autonomy and decentralized decision-making, is not so instrumental as to taking being profitable into consideration. The process parallels larger developments in public education in the United States in the second half of the nineteenth century. Most historians of education discuss the bureaucratization of education during this period, as well as the new interest corporations take in an educated and properly socialized workforce (Spring, 1972; Katz, 1987; Veblen, 1957; Carnoy and Levin, 1985; Labaree, 1988). While funding is often a crisis in education, the bureaucracy is not seen as a profit making structure. Rather it is seen as an administration of control; a way of controlling the educational process and the socialization of future workers.

It could be argued that universities are so directly influenced by industry and the new corporate trust because they are so directly connected to business interests. The change in university trustees from education professionals to bankers, businessmen and lawyers marks the beginning of the process of commodification in the university. The dominant image for institutions of higher education for most of the nineteenth century drew inspiration from the clergy and promoted the idea of the educated entrepreneurial professional. Beginning around the turn of the century that vision of the university was replaced by a corporate vision. This corporate vision was itself evolving as part of changes happening in the United States in general at the time. As Richard Ohmann (1987) writes in *Politics of Letters*, the turn of the century brought a new complexity to the industrial infrastructure and with it, a new need for technologies of consumption. These technologies of consumption fostered the growth of social sciences, especially as a 'predictive technology for social control', including consumption control (Haraway, 1989, p. 108). As the university began to bureaucratize, it was not only the site for training of workers and the creation of new technology, but also the site of the new industries of consumption, such as marketing. This bureaucratization led to the development of a new middle class and a whole set of changes in values and orientations in American society (Wiebe, 1967, pp. 147–63; Bledstein, 1976, pp. 300–31).

Barrow is careful to point out that by the beginning of the twentieth century corporations were beginning to take over the productive sector of American life as well. The large number of companies producing goods early in the nineteenth century gave way to a small number of large corporations producing most of the goods in the US by the twentieth century. This process of monopolization, which came during a period of economic crisis in capitalism is of course well-known to Marxists, and as Ohmann points out, is another reason why this turn-of-the-century period was an important one for capitalism. In order to survive, companies had invested increasing sums of money in advanced technology and larger factories, becoming less willing to risk their investments in a free market. The monopolizing process was the result, with large corporations actively seeking to control the entire productive process from raw material to finished goods. At the same time and for the same reason, corporate producers began to need to motivate consumption, not merely waiting for a consumer to need their product, but actively inculcating the desire for it. Education, the state and the media were all marshaled to make sure that goods and services were consumed so that these new large organizations and networks of organizations could survive and be profitable.

The university became an important site of science and technology for corporate development (Noble, 1977). Social sciences were newly important for the management of the new mass culture. Workers needed to be managed, buying habits had to be understood and encouraged. Further, the new technologies of the twentieth century required more skilled labor — scientists to invent new products to sell to a consuming public technicians to manage the new factories and processes, managers to understand and manage the new complex corporate structures; as well as lawyers, marketers and others. Universities began a period of growth that would continue for most of the century.

These forces gave corporations a vested interest in the university. Barrow (1990, pp. 61–6) shows that at the beginning of the twentieth century organizations like the Carnegie Foundation for the Advancement of Teaching and the General Education Board began to bridge the gap between the corporation and the university president, by bringing corporate management to the university even when its benefit was not clear. He discusses the role of Henry Pritchett, President of MIT and first President of CFAT who hired Morris L. Cooke, one of time-and-motion-study expert Fredrick Taylor's students, to bring scientific management to the university (*ibid.*, pp. 66–7). It is clear that this group of university presidents joined their interests to corporate America. Barrow (*ibid.*, pp. 66 and 273) cites Pritchett's 1905 article for *Atlantic Monthly* entitled 'Shall the university become a business corporation?' which argued that corporate management brings 'efficiency' to the university. Barrow shows that American universities were in fact not as efficient as European universities which were essentially faculty-run. Pritchett made the opposite case even though the data didn't support his claims. It is important to point out that this trust in corporate management was part of attitudes developing in elite circles during this period of time Veysey (1965, p. 351). Nasaw (1981, pp. 126–58) and Spring (1972, pp. 22–43) also discuss the historical context of the rise of large-scale corporations and the ideology of corporate cooperation that developed in this time. Corporate trusts came increasingly to be seen as the most rational cooperative way to get work done and take care of people in a society.

While corporate interests were merging with the elite class to form the administration of the university, that elite class of university presidents and board members was beginning to create a culture of administrative workers. This culture of the modern university served the interests of corporate capitalism in the name of knowledge, advancement, reason and a better life, while allowing the university to retain some autonomy (that autonomy is what is being whittled later in the twentieth century). Scott Lash (1990, pp. 11–15) in his *Sociology of Post-modernism* has argued that post-modernism is a period of 'de-differentiation'. Following a traditional Weberian line he argues if modernization is a process of the development of autonomous spheres of human social activity, that is separating of the economic from the spiritual, which is also separated from civil society; then, in this view, the post-modern is a period where these autonomous spheres begin to collapse back on each other. In other words, modernization is a process of representing reality where autonomous spheres of social life like the university are given a narrative reality. The post-modern is a world populated by images and signs to be bought and sold. University degrees and certificates are the signs of credentials, available to be bought and sold. In the post-modern world, the sign becomes indistinguishable from the reality.[2]

However, even until late in this century many higher education policy makers and economists have been careful to note that the university is in fact not structured much like a business or a corporation. The needs of academic freedom, the tenure system and the process of education itself have tended to produce a unique institutional structure. Barrow (1990), using Althusser's notion of the Ideological State Apparatus, has argued that higher education is a site of contestation; one where the corporate elite must to some extent concern themselves with education for democracy and social mobility even while attempting to gain as much as they can from university research and technological innovations (pp. 251–9). Carnoy and Levin (1985) also have written about the role of the state and its need to satisfy people's desires for opportunities, while at the same time supporting the powerful groups that back particular politicians and parties. I will discuss this tension in more detail in the next section.

There have been many social forces in the late twentieth century working to wear down the relative autonomy of higher education. These forces, which I call collectively commodification, are similar to Lash's notion of 'dedifferentiation'. Barrow has shown that the infrastructural shifts at the beginning of the century precisely mark the point at which the university in America began to move away from its religious, philosophical and moral orientation toward a science, technology and profit orientation. As already noted, the transformation of the Board of Trustees (Veysey, 1965; Barrow, 1990) was the first step in this process.

The growth of higher education from the end of World War I to the present is inseparable from the rise of the middle class, the creation of consumer society and the success of monopoly capitalism. Noble (1977) suggests that the need for scientific research among developing corporations led to their support for, and involvement in, higher education. Technological innovation was important; new products and ever-increasing profits were crucial to the corporate entities rapidly becoming so large they had to not encourage but *guarantee* consumption. On the productive side this required research and development. The first research labs were set up by AT&T, GE, and Westinghouse during the early twentieth century (*ibid.*, 116); science and engineering labs dedicated to research the production of new products. Later more and more universities developed similar research labs as partnerships were formed between corporation and university. Engineers and scientists began to work in university labs, often doing private consulting on the side. Later, corporations became increasingly interested in founding schools of science and engineering to train a new generation of corporate workers, further binding corporate and university interests together, until the present day when corporations are at the forefront, standardizing scientific research and busily inculcating rational management in the university (*ibid.*, pp. 144–50). Throughout this process the definition of what scientific research should look like and be for has been decided largely by corporate interests. There are other forces, and many struggles as well, but these corporate interests have become dominant during the course of the twentieth century. This is an important route taken by corporate interest into the management of the university.

In order to talk in detail about what has happened to higher education it's necessary to look at the shifts in the American economy in general. Higher education has been directly influenced by the contradictions in American capitalism and transformations of the economy due to those contradictions (Noble, 1977; Barrow,

1990; Slaughter, 1990; Shumar, 1995). I will begin by talking about Fordism, that period of rapid expansion in manufacturing that followed Henry Ford's invention of the assembly line at the turn of the century and the era of consumption that it ushered in.

At the turn of this century America was in a state of rapid transformation. Ohmann (1987) suggests that the amounts of money and numbers of people invested in the new industries of the early twentieth century made it no longer feasible for capitalism to operate in a free market system. Barrow (1990, pp. 14–30) shows the changes in infrastructural arrangements: first, the number of manufacturing firms at the turn of the century was greatly reduced from thirty years earlier, so more and more goods were being produced by fewer companies, and production at individual sites was on a larger scale. Also, corporations had begun seeing the value of research and were actively seeking large numbers of skilled technicians, engineers and inventors, to operate the new high-tech industrial infrastructure (Noble, 1977, pp. 167–70; Levine, 1986, pp. 46–57). Barrow shows that corporate groups formed in this period involved the whole spectrum of the manufacturing process from investment banks to raise money to raw materials to retail; it is clear that the failure of one of these groups would have huge repercussions on whole sections of the economy. Wiebe (1967) writes about the transformation of a formerly rural society becoming urban with a rising managerial middle class and the development of corporate liberalism. Production had become large-scale, expensive and high-risk, and investors needed to guarantee sales if they were going to keep corporate empires afloat. Fortunately for them, there was a new class of urban-dwelling middle class consumers ready to be taught how to consume.

As Ohmann (1987, pp. 144–8) writes, capitalists needed to guarantee markets. It was this need for a guaranteed market that Ohmann believes led to the creation of mass culture and mass media. The need for markets made the psychological manipulation of public desire — marketing and advertising — a high priority for corporations. Advertising did more than guarantee sales, though, as Ohmann points out. The highly effective appeals of advertising created new mass desires and in a new sense, recreated the public. It is the power of advertising that made possible the national magazines which were the beginnings of mass media. Ford, with his ideas of a fair wage and leisure time to consume, did not single-handedly invent consumerism. Government and other public figures recognized the need for consumers to guarantee the future of monopoly capitalism. I will return to the idea of the historical production of the 'public' and the 'consumer' in chapter 7.

Back at the university, all these changes were demanding more university research and more university-trained individuals. While the universities had become important to the corporate world as sites for research in the sciences and engineering, they were also involved in new kinds of research. The new consuming public needed to be managed, and psychology, sociology, and other social sciences were brought to bear on consumer research and public opinion. There was also a growing demand for more skilled workers and experts on both the production and consumption sides of the economy.

After World War II, during a period some call Fordism or Fordism/Keynesianism, there was a tremendous expansion of the corporate/liberal monopoly capitalist model. As Bluestone and Harrison (1982) point out, the call for US goods around the world was at an all-time high. American manufacturers were not only selling goods abroad but rebuilding their own basic industries and receiving royalties on that investment. This period of great sustained economic growth and newly expanded economy (Harvey, 1989; Shumar, 1995; Harrison and Bluestone, 1988) dovetailed nicely, as it turned out, with the new college-educated work force.

Toward the end of World War II, Congress realized there would be a tremendous influx of returning servicemen into the job market and massive unemployment as a result. Remembering the experiences of the thirties, the government was afraid that people would not tolerate the unemployment and there would be riots, and it was this fear that led to the creation of the GI Bill. This Bill provided free tuition for returning veterans, but Congress was less concerned with education than with social control. Congress's idea was that universities could be a holding tank for workers, a place from which there could be slower integration into the work force (Nasaw, 1981, p. 176).

While the universities complained a little, they were receiving massive amounts of Federal aid and so their disapproval was muted. Nasaw (*ibid.*, p. 180) makes several important points about this moment in the development of higher education. First, though GIs were tracked in the sense that members of the elite went to elite schools while non-elite individuals went to state schools, there were no curricula specifically designed for technical or applied skills. Students took the traditional liberal arts track if they so chose. Second, many more students than expected took advantage of the GI Bill, they chose liberal arts tracks and moreover surprised many administrators and educators by doing well. This produced a large population of well-educated individuals which might have been more of a problem at another time; but at that particular moment the expanding economy needed college-educated workers. Everything came together nicely and more people than ever before in history started assuming the American Dream was part of the natural order of things.

It was a time of great structural mobility, with many individuals moving up economically and socially. Bluestone and Harrison (1982, p. 133) observe that management was quite interested in stabilizing relations with labor in this period. There was so much work available that management could afford to give (a very small) piece of the pie to labor to prevent strikes from going on too long and to keep production flowing. There was money in the economy; money for housing, consumer durables, college education and the new infrastructure of highways, (originally designed to transport missiles) which paved the way to the new suburbs. The belief in social mobility that lies at the heart of the American dream seemed to be validated indeed.

Between 1945–1973, Bluestone and Harrison argue that the taxes and tariff structure coupled with the priority to the American dollar created by the Bretton Woods agreement fueled the post-war economic expansion set the stage for the economic crises and changes of the eighties and nineties. American businesses established subsidiaries and leasing to foreign firms. The structure of the multinational corporation took shape and US companies made huge amounts of money leasing American-built factories to foreign firms. Profit opportunities proliferated; for example a US company could make money on the goods produced domestically, get a profit on foreign-produced versions of their goods and receive payment for factories they put up the money to build. The US economy grew at an enormous rate in this period.

> During the 1960s, the productive capacity of the American economy nearly tripled, even after accounting for inflation. This meant uninterrupted, unparalleled, and unprecedented economic expansion from the end of the 1961 (Eisenhower) recession to the 1969–70 (Nixon) crash. It was a period in which economists declared the business cycle obsolete and families saw their real incomes grow by a third. (*ibid.*, p. 114)

While corporations were making fantastic profits the American worker benefited as well. There was more demand for white collar jobs; the university-educated were employed. Blue collar workers saw their struggles pay off to some extent too; their wages rose and thanks to union successes, they had more benefits. Higher education did languish somewhat in the fifties, but the momentum of these events in the economy, coupled with the large number of children born after the GIs return, set the stage for the next big boom in higher education.

The baby-boom generation, beginning to reach adolescence in the early sixties, presented a new set of challenges to business and the state. They were the first generation raised on television, irreverent and born of relative affluence, they expected material well being. But they were not to experience the great economic advancement their parents did. As Bourdieu (1984) says in *Distinction*, this is the generation that expected things to get forever better and in fact experienced decline (pp. 143–4).

Again, as after World War II, there were suddenly a large number of people to integrate into the job market, and higher education was again used by the state as a place to put these people, but this time the move was more carefully planned. As higher education expanded in the sixties to accommodate the baby boomers, its growth was stratified, with community colleges serving as gatekeepers regulating the flow of students to the more prestigious four-year colleges (Jencks and Riesman, 1968; Brint and Karabel, 1989; Shor, 1986).

The relationships between the university and corporations that strengthened and flourished in this period have already been noted. There was an interesting parallel with corporations' development of subsidiaries and multiple offices in the practice of building branch campuses. In general colleges and universities continued to wax ever more corporate in administrative structure, and increasingly to see their problems as management problems. Clark Kerr (1982) accurately catches this shift with his term the multiversity. Universities, like corporations, became by the sixties complex structures with multiple campuses and multiple purposes. Administration was the home office rationalizing this large entity. The managerial section of higher education was growing dramatically, not only in numbers but in power. There had been a long-cherished idea that faculty run the university; rather like a 'medieval guild', but Kerr (1982) is very clear that the modern university is no longer a 'community of scholars' (p. 1).

It could be argued that such a community long ago ceased to be and had been replaced by a model of corporate growth. This fact was only beginning to be felt by the late sixties, because the powerful image 'community of scholars' successfully concealed vast infrastructural changes that only came to light during the social and political ruptures of the 1960s and 1970s. The changes actually began much earlier. Barrow shows that by 1930 corporations had already driven all serious dissenters away from teaching in higher education. And as management power and organization began to be the dominant force in higher education, the culture and the social organization of faculty were relegated to a minority position. The managerial class of higher education experts, often (at the lower levels) themselves at quite a distance from the powerful monopoly corporations, became the majority voice in higher education. Of the two levels of corporate control in the university (the direct wielding of power by the president and board of trustees is the primary one; for instance the recent efforts to downsize universities and bring Total Quality Management to higher education) the second, and more obvious, is in the dominant, ubiquitous imagery of corporate structure. The corporate mentality frames all problems as instrumental issues, effectively silencing non-corporate voices and alienating faculty from the processes of decision-making and problem-solving.

In 1975, the dream of the turn-of-the-century figures like Henry Pritchett had come true. Scientific management had come to the university, the problems of the school were thought of in instrumental terms and each solution conferred greater power on the administrative apparatus. University administrations had grown to out-number faculty, administrators earned more pay and wielded more power in the institution. While faculties still had a guild mentality, a new order had been well-established and developed for years with so little sociological attention being paid to it that in 1975 no one knew who really ran the university.

A 1990 article in *The Chronicle of Higher Education* reported on research on the growth of administrations in universities between 1975 and 1985. Over that period faculty grew nationally by 5.9 per cent while executive, administrative and managerial employees grew by 17.9 per cent. The largest increase by far was to academic support; administrators like financial-aid counselors, auditors and systems analysts; this group grew by 61.1 per cent (Grassmuck 1990). In the evolution of this formal organization it is clear that the faculty are reduced to a factory workforce and the corporate administration and support sectors are expanding and diversifying. This pattern is typical of large corporations.

The expansion of higher education at the beginning of the century, the GI bill and the growth of higher education in the sixties; each produced a crisis for the university. There are a number of possible ways to think about such a crisis but in each case the model adopted by the university was an economic one. Because of the corporate influence put in place early in the twentieth century, when each crisis came along it was thought of in instrumental economic terms, as a crisis of growth.

The adoption of a growth model had other repercussions. Perhaps most importantly, it established precedents for the future interpretation of crises. (When enrollments dropped after the boomer generation graduated, the drop in enrollments was cast as economic decline.) And the business of forecasting had a boom of its own. The Carnegie Foundation established the Carnegie Commission in 1967 to analyze the various problems of the university (particularly student unrest). At the time, it was the only organization of this kind. There are now management consultants and different groups making forecasts for higher education. The university has become an industry, and like industry is dependent on forecasters and planners. Before the drop in enrollments, these planners predicted 'economic boom', in the form of high enrollments, until the year 2000. This assumption of high enrollments was based not so much on the size of the traditional college-age population but on the belief that more and more high school students would go to college, so that the college-educated would be a larger percentage of the general population. This assumption was of course based on the patterns of the past, especially the post-World War II boom. There was little careful analysis of the economic and social conditions of either of the earlier booms but higher education officials were convinced that this trend would continue, and turned their attention to other matters.

Student unrest in general and the free speech movement in particular are some more familiar aspects of the 1960s which I will not analyze here although I do want to look at some of their implications for the university. The students of the sixties questioned the contradictions between the ideal of education in a democratic society and their experience of meritocratic education which they saw was at the base of social stratification. There was (and incidentally still is) much protest over grades, admissions policies, freedom of speech, the denial of college to poor and minorities and many other egalitarian issues. For most of this century the relationship between the state, corporations, and the universities had remained obscure to the general public. But as student activists in campus social issues, and later on the larger canvas of the Vietnam War protest, clashed with what they came to call the military-industrial complex, these struggles served to illuminate the structure of the university and its relationship to capital and the state, and for the first time in the late sixties and early seventies professors and intellectuals begin to write about this relationship. It is at this moment that David Smith (1974) asks *Who Rules the University?* and Jean-Paul Sartre (1974) makes his 'plea for intellectuals' where he questions the role of intellectuals in an advanced capitalist society.

It turned out that hidden beneath the official rhetoric of 'economic boom' was a great struggle over what education was and who should control it. The future prediction of boom and the vision of a more educated and affluent America was a rhetorical tool, wielded by those in power who wished to maintain both the current balance of power and control of the universities. Ira Shor (1986) in his book *Culture Wars* writes that it was a conscious administrative policy in the early 1970s on the part of Sidney P. Marland, Nixon's Secretary of Education, to move higher education to a more career-oriented focus. This was done to diffuse protest and discourage looking into the relationship of the university to the state and capital. 'Marland's success was in focusing the political energy of this bureaucracy around a common program for careerism' (*ibid.*, p. 32). Shor points out it was a successful discourse and vocationalism caught on, especially in community colleges (*ibid.*, p. 38). He cites Marland: ' . . . the future generation of learner in America as coming to maturity at a time when society may not require all their intellectual and developed capacities . . . ' (*ibid.*, p. 39). Marland goes on to say that one day there may be waiters with MAs in French. In the 1990s this no longer seems startling.

The Democratic Vision meets the Legitimation Crisis

The expansion of higher education in the twentieth century was not just the product of expanding corporate needs. As many writers on higher education have pointed out, the expansion also served the needs and fostered the dreams of a growing middle class who, aware that education was the route to greater economic and social opportunity, demanded more access to education (Carnoy and Levin, 1985; Levine, 1986; Cremin, 1989). Nasaw (1981) and Spring (1972) write about the conflict between families and students in secondary school around vocational education. When a group of business leaders and leaders in education, afraid that educational opportunity might create in the public a desire for social mobility that was not satisfiable, began to promote vocational education, Nasaw (1981) shows that many average people rejected this controlling influence and struggled to get the same educational opportunities as other more affluent people. The resultant compromise is still alive today in public high schools with their separate academic and vocational tracks.

In higher education the situation was much the reverse. Most colleges grew out of religious, moral and aesthetic culture, their students primarily the children of elites or individuals training for the ministry (Veysey, 1965; Horowitz, 1987). Beginning around the turn of the century and coupled with the business forces earlier mentioned, colleges began to encourage a more practical, vocational outlook (Veysey, 1965, p. 61; Levine, 1986, p. 45). This orientation served the needs of the new corporations. But unlike the working-class families in the nineteenth century who fought vocational education at the secondary level, middle class families embraced growing vocationalism in higher education in the twentieth century (Levine, 1986, p. 114). Further, colleges began to stratify by the early twentieth century into those that served a lower middle-class, (where career anxiety was high and a vocational orientation was supported) and colleges dominated by a more secure elite and upper middle-class more interested in a liberal arts back ground. Levine (*ibid.*, p. 128) writes that by the 1920s and 1930s the upper middle-class is 'over-represented' at prestigious liberal arts colleges. This stratification suggests there has been a correspondence of interests at various moments between a lower middle-class interested in securing their positions and government and corporate leaders wanting to direct them there.

Magali Sarfatti Larson (1977, pp. 150–8 and 200–7) documents the role of the university and the rise of professionalism and the professional middle classes in American society. With the economic demand for new kinds of experts as well as workers, the university has evolved into the modern-day system of meritocratic sorting that we have come to accept as the function of higher education, with the middle class seeking to scale the hierarchy of schools and professions, competing for credentials to be converted into capital in the form of occupational success and position in society. But the expansion of higher education began to create its own dilemmas as well. With expanding opportunities there was expanding demand and an increasing politicization of higher education. As higher education in the post World War II period sought to meet the needs of a growing middle class and provide equal opportunity, while the working class was demanding the opportunity to move into the middle class, the economic and political conflicts came to a head.

In the 1960s these issues were often confronted directly around notions of open access to education and questioned around the status and functional uses of knowledge. The 1960s raised serious legitimacy questions not only for higher education but the government as well. Cremin (1989) citing an article by Hannah Arendt suggests that the crisis coming to a head is our tendency (as a nation of immigrants trying to get ahead in life) to believe all our social problems can be solved with education (p. 93). In the sixties and since, that belief hit the wall repeatedly. Education is both the sign of, and the solution to, crisis. I also suggest, along with Carnoy and Levin (1985), that the crisis of a nation of immigrants is only part of the contradiction education has tried to manage. Education and higher education have also had to satisfy both the demands of a people in a democracy for greater opportunities and a say in things and serve the needs and interests of the large corporations as well.

The current round of crises in higher education are both heir to, and symptomatic of, the conflicts mentioned above. On the one hand there is a continuing concern for who controls the status of knowledge. Should our official history be the story of ruling elites or the history of common people (Zinn, 1980). The conflicts around multiculturalism and fears of cultural decline are a symptom of the democratization of higher education. With a greater number of people attending college from different backgrounds the issues of whose interests are being served becomes heightened. Further this crisis of what is legitimate knowledge is exacerbated by the inflation of credentials that necessarily happens with university democratization. With more working class students attending college the college degree becomes devalued and only prestige degrees are distinctive. Ideas about the decline of education are often about a college degree losing its cachet in the marketplace (Bourdieu, 1984, pp. 143–4).

When conservative commentators talk about the decline of education they often point to an imaginary past innocent of the contradictory forces that have developed higher education. The 'community of scholars' image is also often invoked by conservative voices, projecting an idyllic past where quality was controlled. Russell Jacoby (1994) points out that while the culture wars have been raging in higher education they have made us miss the real issue of colleges becoming more stratified, with the most prestigious schools dominated by elite students. Many less privileged students attend universities but that education has been robbed of any meaning other than the job you can get in exchange for the degree. And with more and more high paying jobs being replaced by lower paying jobs, students who attend less prominent universities and colleges are increasingly — and realistically concerned that their education may not get them the economic opportunities they desire. Lasch (1995, p. 180) points out that while the right discusses the problems of higher education in terms of cultural decline and the left discusses them in terms of issues of diversity, both groups fail to see that history of corporate control has gutted the meaning of liberal education and replaced it with instrumental techno-cratic concern for nothing but the 'bottom line'.

The history of the developing relationship between business and higher edu-cation, together with growing cultures of professionalism and class aspiration have led to a crisis of legitimacy. Higher education is increasingly stratified into elite colleges and universities where discussion and debate over the liberal culture and a critical literacy is the inheritance of a privileged class and the very few students who find their way into this culture through merit scholarship. The irony of this situation is that there is a small group of elite students attending elite institutions that provide a liberal arts education and many other students have been moved to technical training (*ibid.*, p. 193). The vast majority of higher education is the ground of an increasingly disenfranchised lower middle class and a more affluent working class who see higher education as an empty sign, only a necessary creden-tial to a middle class job, one that is moreover increasingly difficult to trade on. The idea of liberal education is superfluous at best, seen as irrelevant to one's mobility needs; the alienation from schooling in secondary schools discussed by Carnoy and Levin (1985) is widespread in higher education as well. In an article from a large urban daily newspaper a government professor teaching a course on the sixties had a group of students who didn't want to take a traditional exam on the material he had been teaching because they said it would be hypocritical. The students indicated that they had learned all about the sixties and how people had questioned and challenged the status of knowledge; to then have to take a traditional exam on the material would be too absurd. When the professor asked the class in a discussion over the examination how many of them had ever had the opportunity to 'actively participate in their educations' he said no hands were raised (Vigoda, 1995). The story illustrates in capsule form what has happened to much of higher education. Students, far from actively seeking information, passively receive knowledge they secretly question the value of but never confront openly, and they have little sense that it should be otherwise. But it's like the Emperor's new clothes. Nobody is willing to point out the obvious because most students believe that they need to keep their mouths shut, get a degree and get a ticket to a good job. As the job opportunities decline, or students fear declining incomes, the disaffection with what they are being taught and its irrelevance increases. More colleges, especially at the lower end of the socioeconomic ladder, experience serious problems with student resistance in the classroom, not unlike what has happened in many high schools. Should that dissent be opened up and given expression, or managed?

The next chapter looks at how that silencing of college students came about historically, its political context and its consequences for the future. I will also look at the economic context of a decline in higher education that began as a demo-graphic phenomenon, but lives on as fiscal crisis of the state as capitalism globalizes and government is increasingly dominated by the interests of transnational corporations. That fiscal crisis, and the government's role in bending the workforce to the interests of transnationals, has led to new crises as universities have been forced to retrench and downsize in the face of less funding and financial aid for higher education.

Notes

1   Further, a crisis of education is related to a crisis of youth. Writing about youth culture Dick Hebdige (1988) has suggested that we use youth as a sign of crisis. Youth is often seen as to blame for the ills of the society even when it is clearly the case that youths are a product of the society, not the cause of social problems. We look to education, as the institution that is supposed to solve the problems of youth, to deal with all of our social problems. Higher education makes the bridge between the adult word and the troubled world of youth. It is also supposed to preserve our culture and traditions, advance our knowledge and socialize the next generation.

2   Along a slightly different line Gosta Esping-Andersen (1990) has argued that the role of the state in a social democracy is to limit the role of the economy or engage in what he calls decommodification of the spheres of social life. In Esping-Andersen's view there is a dynamic tension in capitalism. The economy depends on arenas of the social being separate from the economy and yet capitalism has a tendency to commodify all aspects of the social (Haraway, 1989, p. 108).

Chapter 4

Political Economy of Higher Education

Introduction

The last chapter discussed the development of higher education in the United States
and its expansion over the course of the twentieth century, particularly as it expanded after World War II; that expansion was spoken of as an economic boom
while real infrastructural shifts in higher education were disguised by an imagination of the 'community of scholars'. It wasn't until the social crises of the late
sixties that people began to awaken to the growing ties between corporate America
and higher education.

This chapter will explore developments in higher education over the last thirty-
five years beginning with the aftermath of the political crisis of legitimacy of the
1960s. In a larger sense in America, the political challenges to the state posed by
campus unrest and war protest declined significantly after Kent State. Many analysts, still engrossed in writing about campus unrest and the significance of the
cultural upheavals of the sixties, were caught by surprise by the recessions of the
1970s and the drop in enrollment — a new fiscal crisis. Nationally, the new problems were inflation, declining jobs and rising taxes; economic concerns that have
dominated the national stage ever since.

The chapter will explore changes in the economic structure of the country as
it moved from a prosperous post-war period of economic plenty to a society where
the relationships between the transnational forces and economic flows have begun
to eclipse the power of the nation state (Rouse, 1995, p. 358). It will also discuss
the impact of globalization on personal identity and the growing crisis of the state
as it is pressured to reduce the tax burden on American workers whose earning
power is decreasing as unemployment problems deepen. The twin crises of finance
and legitimacy have had a profound effect on institutions of higher education, both
in the form of decreased federal and state support and also in the new notions of
rationalized work process, which have brought concepts like the flexible workforce
and Total Quality Management to teaching and research.

Finally the chapter will look at faculty consciousness. The economy-driven
rapid changes in higher education have engendered new forms of labor discipline
and new ways to define teaching and knowledge, forcing faculty and students to
realign themselves with the university. Reflecting on the future of higher education,
I will argue for a return to questioning the purpose of higher education and the
status of knowledge. What role will universities play in the nation as our national

interests are increasingly dominated by global corporations with incomes that rival the GNP of most nations (Bodley, 1996, p. 21)?

1971–1972: Pivotal Years

The early 1970s brought new crises to the economic system. David Harvey (1989) places the breakdown of the economic system of capital accumulation he calls Fordism at around 1973. According to Harvey, capitalism developed specific 'regimes of accumulation' (Agglietta, 1979) that not only allowed for accumulation of profit, but also worked to socialize the workforce, encourage consumption and regulate the flows of finance such that the accumulation process could go on relatively free of crisis. Fordism, was the system of large-scale production, mass production of standardized goods and minimal competition (Harvey, 1989; Machado and Shumar, 1996). The 'regime of accumulation' began after the second World War when the Bretton Woods agreement began to falter in the 1960s (Harvey, 1989, p. 141; Strange, 1986, pp. 5–7), threatening crisis for large corporations. Harvey sees this crisis as resulting from saturation of domestic markets, causing the industrial structures of the post-war nations to seek more exports at the moment technological innovation was fueling greater productivity. This problem of market saturation also coincided with an embargo by the OPEC oil nations, further exacerbating the problem by increasing energy costs and flooding the financial markets with petrodollars (Harvey, 1989, pp. 142–5). As both Harvey and Strange argue, the problem was the Fordist system was too rigid. Corporations needed more fluidity in financial markets, which they sought by moving away from regulation, the gold standard and fixed rates of interest. That led to greater volatility in inancial markets (Strange, 1986, p. 8) which in turn led to an emphasis of finance over production (*ibid.*, p. 11) and a shifting of the risk in currency exchange from the State to the consumer. This is what Strange calls 'Casino Capitalism', and others have referred to as flexible accumulation (Harvey, 1989) or 'disorganized capitalism' (Lash and Urry, 1987).

Bluestone and Harrison (1982) look at the forces that changed the global structure of capitalism and their impact on the domestic economy of the United States as the productive sector of the society — including of course the American worker — was sold off in the Casino-like atmosphere of the financial markets. According to Bluestone and Harrison, American industry's problems stemmed from decisions made directly after World War II. We have already seen that the post-war boom made it easy to move the large group of GI Bill college students into the work force, creating upwardly mobile careers for them (Nasaw, 1981), possible only because corporations were making phenomenal profits at the time. Bluestone and Harrison (1982, pp. 111–41) suggest that these huge profits were the result of American industry's role in the rebuilding of the economies of Europe and Japan. For a time, US industry had more work and money than it knew what to do with, as American corporations built factories overseas and collected profits on the products produced in those factories. Orders from foreign companies for US equipment was high, US firms sold goods manufactured in the United States and the dominance of the US dollar and favorable tax policies made global expansion and huge margins of profit possible.

There were several important repercussions. First, US labor got more at the bargaining table, because while there were still major struggles between labor and capital, businesses could easily afford concessions to labor in order to keep production moving. This was no time for a strike. That meant that costs for American labor went up. While this was good for the economy in that it produced savings and consumers; it also made US-produced goods more expensive. This is what Harvey calls Fordism — the world economy demanding US goods after the Second World War, large-scale mass production to rebuild the economies of the world, an organized industrial labor force and fixed rates of interest.

Another result was that American corporations begin to internationalize, opening offices in Europe and the Far East. The multinational corporation began to develop. In the immediate post-World War II context, these foreign subsidiaries were a just way to get American goods around the world. Later, when large-scale mass production began to go into crisis in the 1960s, by which time communications technologies had become more advanced, institutions were in place for the more global, decentered system of production.

Bluestone and Harrison point out that US companies created their own competition. The new foreign factories, built with the help of fiscal policy brought on by the post-war, were newer and more efficient than US factories, able to produce more product more efficiently and their labor costs were much lower. This meant that as these new factories saturated their own domestic markets they started to give US firms competition in the international markets. As a result, US-based firms started to move away from the production of consumer goods, where foreign competition was too great, and into production of goods for military contract or into the production of services. Some began to look for new sites of production.

What Bluestone and Harrison saw as the coming of flexible accumulation, characterized by US plant closings and the beginnings of a globalized system of production, began in the 1970s to have profound implications for the American economy. Table 1 shows the decline in net rate of profit for several industries during the early 1970s. This period began a decade of wild inflation with decreases in demand for US goods. At the end of the Vietnam War, military production was cut back as well. The oil embargo and the creation of petro-dollars created cash gluts and furthered the inflationary cycle. Businesses closed or moved to other areas (such as the sunbelt) to reduce labor costs. The stage for deindustrialization was set; jobs down, costs up.

As the larger societal economic boom began to collapse at the end of the sixties, there was a decided conservative turn to the mood in America. The coalitions of the left had broken up in the sixties, with students, feminists and the civil rights movements all going their separate ways. Campus radicalism had all but died and student protest focused on the single issue of ending the Vietnam War. By 1972 when the US realized the war was lost and began pulling out, campuses across America became very quiet.

Table 1: Net pre-tax profit rates in selected manufacturing industries (1963–75)
(in per cent)

Industry	1963–68	1969–75	Percentage Change
Rubber products	9.1	6.1	−36.2
Glass products	12.0	7.9	−34.2
Steel industry	7.3	4.4	−39.4
Fabricated metal products	8.0	6.4	−20.4
Radio, television equipment	12.2	3.8	−69.2
Machine products	13.9	9.3	−33.4
Farm machinery	8.4	4.1	−51.4
Machine tools	12.9	6.1	−53.1
Electrical equipment (heavy)	13.2	7.7	−49.1
Motor vehicles and parts	16.3	6.7	−64.8
Shipbuilding	5.8	3.1	−47.0
Railroad equipment	7.8	3.4	−56.9
Average for the twelve industries			−46.3

Note: Net profit rate = net pre-tax corporate income (less deficit) divided by total assets.
Source: US Department of the Treasury, US Internal Revenue Service, *Sourcebook of Statistics of Income*, Publication 647, (Washington, DC, US Government Printing Office), 1963–75. Reprinted from Barry Bluestone and Bennett Harrison, *The Deindustrialization of América*, New York, Basic Books, p. 148.

It was at that moment that higher education administrators, researchers, and planners noticed a very disconcerting thing. Enrollment was dropping off. If something was not done quickly the colleges and universities in America were going to experience 'economic crisis'. The perception of this crisis was odd because it was so abrupt. In 1971, all forecasters were still forecasting great success — continued high enrollments — until 2000. The very next year predictions turned ominous. Suddenly, it seemed, the college-age population was shrinking, fewer people were enrolling; universities and colleges had grown too quickly during the 'boom' years, etc.[1] I would like to suggest that the crisis in higher education in the 1970s is a product of imagination. It was an invented crisis following the thinking of Benedict Anderson (1991) in *Imagined Communities*. I am not suggesting that the crisis wasn't real, but rather that the ways in which it was imagined, structured and dealt with were a product of the coming of corporate management to the campus, part and parcel with the ways in which the larger economic crises of the 1970s were imagined and dealt with.

There were larger political-economic issues helping to produce the effect of lower enrollment and influencing the perception to that effect on the part of higher education planners as well. In 1972 higher education began to experience degree inflation. The expansion of the system of higher education had served to produce many new college graduates entering the workforce in the early 1970s, but in the economic stagnation of the early 1970s the pay-off for a college degree seemed to be receding rapidly. More advanced, more prestigious degrees were needed to get the same jobs that a college degree once guaranteed. There was federal policy in place advocating career-oriented education as a way of reducing the tide of dissent, but at the same time the economic depression produced by the post-war globalization discouraged students from going on to college. Even before the college-age population dropped significantly colleges were already beginning to experience a downturn. The hardest hit, as Aronowitz and Giroux (1985) point out, were the independent liberal arts colleges which had thrived on the sixties goal of education for an informed and democratic public but which were not particularly career-oriented (p. 171). Higher education officials, experiencing the economic decline of the 1970s and declining enrollments for the first time in twelve years (and later the slowing down of federal money as the federal government experienced cash shortages and rampant inflation), began to manage their perceived crisis with the instrumental techniques of the marketplace.

One of the interesting features of the crisis of Fordism in the general economy is that the responses of flexible accumulation had the effect of bringing more aspects of the society under the influence of the economic. The traditional conservative view, that government should not interfere with the free market, was not, in fact, policy under Fordism. Regulation under Fordism not only guaranteed the smooth working of the market, but also made sure other aspects of the culture lined up in support of the market; laborers were trained and consumers were encouraged to consume (Agglietta, 1979). As financial markets (and later other aspects of the economy) began to seek new arenas of profitability, selling a company for scrap (destructive of culture and community, but profitable) could be preferable to producing product. Flexible accumulation had pressured business to prioritize financial speculation over production (Strange, 1986). Not only that, but while the reproduction of capital accumulation under Fordism involved other institutions, the shift to flexible accumulation demanded that these arenas; schools, healthcare, government, find ways to be profitable themselves, that is, to act like businesses. One of the roles of the state under Fordism was clearly to limit the movement of capital and the market (in other words to restrict the range of commodification) but under flexible accumulation the metaphor of the market became more than a metaphor and extended the range of the market.

Higher education under Fordism was in an interesting and ironic situation (Shumar, 1995). On the one hand, the boards of trustees and the power figures in higher education were controlled by business and economic interests (see chapter 3) and it was very clear that the institutions of higher education served the needs of industry by providing research and trained workers for the advanced industrial workplace. But higher education served an ideological function as well. Liberal scholarship managed to survive under Fordism and while it may not have been as free as it imagined itself from business interests, there was a dynamic and vital tension as well as pressure from the state to keep education a public institution[2] instead of in the complete control of business. Often seen as the source of genius for the great capitalist expansion, education was also still seen as valuable in and of itself.

The ironic position of Fordism in the university quickly gave way to a new commodifying of the university. The economic crisis of the 1970s and the deregulation of the financial markets tended, as already noted, to bring market logic to other aspects of the culture, and this new logic coincided with the deep crisis of confidence in the culture brought to us by the cultural revolution of the 1960s. And another revolution — the information revolution ushered in by the explosion of computer technology — facilitated commodification of culture by making possible rapid transmission of images and information. The effects on the university were profound; moreover it can be shown that the practices of flexible accumulation, strategies of inventing markets and products; the pushing of the economic into previously non-economic arenas which has characterized the 'post-modern' appeared on campuses even earlier than in other institutions.[3]

Many signs of change in the universities were already clear by the early 1970s when the enrollment crisis was announced. One way of understanding the invention of this crisis is as a particular way of responding to these signs. University administrators and researchers had just finished a decade of concern with crisis (the crisis of cultural revolution centered on American college campuses). People were used to thinking in terms of needing to manage the crisis. The cultural crisis had been perceived as a threat to the State; an example of its reaction was the killings at Kent State. The new crisis was a different kind of threat, one perhaps even more profound; certainly one with serious long-term implications for our culture. Higher education had seen the early increase in enrollments in the post-World War II period and the early 1960s as 'economic boom'; and they now began to predict and prepare for an 'economic crash' *well before the crash actually came*. The legions of new higher education professionals produced by the booms of the post-war, organized by the Carnegie Commission and other professional organizations, began to plan a number of responses targeting the expected crisis.

First, education began consciously to be seen as a product or service; something to be sold to a public. If it could be sold, a demand could be created for it. Consumers could be found, or invented. This increased the image-producing — public relations, advertising, market research etc. — functions of the university dramatically. College degrees, subject to market forces, started to be managed in new ways. If degree inflation depressed enrollments, then we needed to seek new markets, like non-traditional students, or produce new specialized degrees and certificates in order to make buyers desire the product.

Second, since education had become a product or service, then the faculty had become laborers. If they were laborers, then they could be treated as such and be made to produce more product, more efficiently and for less cost; they could be degraded. The number of faculties seeking to unionize went up dramatically in the seventies. Faculty were forced to respond to the increased pressures to proletarianize them.

Management's drive to proletarianize faculty benefited from degree inflation. When the number of BAs and BSs increased dramatically in the sixties and seventies, so did the PhDs. This dramatic increase in PhDs was strategically imagined by university administrations as a surplus labor pool, working alongside the permanent labor pool as a flexible, temporary and inexpensive group of workers. Even before most universities experienced enrollment decline in the late seventies and early eighties, the numbers of unemployed PhDs was large enough to provide a permanent surplus labor pool. This enabled colleges to teach about half of their classes with part-time labor. Some institutions, especially community colleges, might have been happy to go to an entirely part-time faculty, though most universities and colleges used their permanent faculty to create the image of prestige and value and used part-time faculty to deal with the ups and downs of enrollment; especially those ups and downs occasioned by new programs and degrees.

Finally, administration bureaucracies continued to grow in order to manage the new education industry. While the business of universities is nominally teaching and research, judging from employee growth and salary levels it is clearly the 'business' sector of higher education which has become the business of education. Management of the new functions of the school required scientific rationality and a new name, 'strategic planning' (Uhl, 1983; Clark, 1987; Hardy, 1987; Newman, 1985). The creation of image, coordination of the faculty and students in this new environment of educational products, along with new corporate alliances like bookstore chains and other promotional ventures, together with the traditional relationship with corporate research; all these functions required a growing capitalist professional class to manage the university.

Planning for crisis allowed institutions to avoid the so-called enrollment crisis. Advertising works! After a brief dip, many schools found their enrollments recovering. However, the price of this success was continuing crisis, crisis as norm. Institutions found themselves in a new era where the effort to recruit new students, put out new images and make new products could never end. This required permanent flexibility. The faculty had to be proletarianized for the new model to work and further, they needed to be stratified into temporary part-time workers, permanent teachers, and permanent researchers. The product (education) was mass-produced and, like all goods produced in capitalist society, was being tailored and targeted to special consumer groups. Not large-scale mass production of goods under Fordism, this was production of specialized educational commodities for selected groups. Under these new conditions of seeking new students and providing them with new certificates, degrees or programs; image became more important than product. More money, time and care was put into the creation of the image of the college and its education than in the education itself. An article in the 28 March 1990 edition of the *Chronicle of Higher Education* reports on the related growth in academic support staff and new categories of administration that provide counseling and other services to students. The data presented in table 2 from the National Center for Educational Statistics in 1989 also show that for two-year institutions administration increased by 21 per cent from 1977–1986 while instruction increased only 6 per cent; and for private universities instruction increased by 21 per cent over the same period while administration increased 39 per cent. The *Philadelphia Inquirer* on 31 March 1996, citing US Department of Education statistics, claims university administrations have grown by 83 per cent nationally from 1975 to 1993 while faculties have grown 22 per cent and enrollment has grown by 28 per cent during the same period.

The new success of colleges and universities was modeled on the images of scarcity (of students) and surplus (of labor). The way these images were used was the particular reinvention of higher education in the late seventies and early eighties. An institution needed to constantly produce images of its prestige and desirability

Table 2: Index of expenditures in constant dollars per full-time-equivalent student at public institutions of higher education, by type of institution: Academic years ending 1977–1986

(1977=100)

Year	Total	Instruction	Administration[2]	Educational and general expenditures[1]			Operation and plant maintenance	Scholarships and fellowships
				Research	Libraries	Public service		
				2-year institutions				
1977	100	100	100	(3)	100	(3)	100	100
1978	101	100	105	(3)	101	(3)	102	76
1979	102	100	108	(3)	98	(3)	103	78
1980	97	96	102	(3)	89	(3)	102	78
1981	93	92	97	(3)	83	(3)	99	71
1982	93	93	98	(3)	90	(3)	102	66
1983	90	90	97	(3)	77	(3)	98	65
1984	92	92	100	(3)	78	(3)	100	64
1985	103	101	113	(3)	85	(3)	111	76
1986	108	106	121	(3)	89	(3)	115	81

[1] Data are in constant dollars, adjusted by the Consumer Price Index for the academic year (July 1–June 30). Mandatory transfers are included in the total but are not shown separately.

[2] Administration expenditures include institutional support, student services, and academic support minus library costs.

[3] Not calculated; expenditure category constituted 2 percent or less of total expenditures in most years.

Source: US Department of Education, National Center for Education Statistics, 'Recent trends in higher education finance, 1976–77 to 1985–86', *Higher Education Administrative Costs: Continuing the study*, (based on the HEGIS survey Financial Statistics of Institutions of Higher Education, Institutional Characteristics of Colleges and Universities, and Fall Enrollment in Colleges and Universities), January 1988. Reprinted from National Center for Educational Statistics, *The Conditions of Education*, 1989.

to draw students, so the need for a large and ever-expanding imaging-making apparatus became the norm. If public awareness of the university's prestige (images of product) were to decline, the scarce student might go elsewhere. And since colleges could never be sure how well their advertising would work in any given year, they needed a group of teachers — laborers — they could hire and fire at will in order to deal with the unpredictable ups and downs of consumption.

The next chapter to this story is a crisis in the larger economy of Reaganonomics due to globalization and corporate downsizing. Harvey (1989) argues that Fordism began to break down around 1973, and accumulation based on the large factory model began to go into crisis; what with big government spending, mass consumption, and inflation; and corporations had to seek new arrangements to try and preserve profit (p. 189). Harvey calls these various strategies flexible accumulation. Further, corporations began to put pressure on the government to promote policies to smooth the way for these new transitions.[4]

On the consumer side beginning in the 1970s there was a phenomenon called market segmentation. Companies began to produce specialized products for smaller target audiences in the hope of selling more goods. For instance, instead of one shampoo, a manufacturer offered shampoos for dry, normal and oily hair, and/or separate products for babies, men, teenagers. These specialized products were often made of the same raw materials but constructed or packaged in a different way. In a sense, the auto industry pioneered this a long time ago when they took what was basically the one car body and engine, added an array of different details and called it an Oldsmobile, Pontiac, Chevrolet, etc.

The production side saw the break-up of the assembly-line model, and advanced communications technology accelerated this process in the 1980s. Not only were foreign factories able to produce goods more cheaply than US factories, as Bluestone and Harrison have shown, but all companies began to use a global system of production to make goods cheaper. This could include some combinations of assembly-line methods with other older methods of production. For instance, GM closed plants in Michigan, (one of them the subject of Michael Moore's film *Roger and Me*) and opened assembly plants in Mexico, to benefit from the cheaper labor, fewer safety regulations, less benefits to be paid. Parts for these cars come from all over the world. The engines may come from high-tech plants in Asia, parts may be produced in small villages using labor-intensive techniques. Farmers' wives in the midwest US may assemble taillights by the piece in their homes and mail them to GM. Computer technology has made it possible to monitor this process from Detroit. This is 'flexible accumulation' in action (Harvey, 1989, pp. 189–97).

With flexible accumulation there is only a small 'core' group of employees who get the traditional good salary and benefits that Americans got used to in the post-war era. Supplementing this core globally is a much larger group of part-time workers, (temporary or independent contractors), who get little or no benefits and lower wages. This group is flexible; which is another way of saying they work cheaply and have no job security. The similarity between this group and part-time teachers is an issue I want to explore but first I want to look at another aspect of flexible accumulation that affected the universities greatly in the 1980s.

In the early 1980s the federal government changed its policy on research produced under federal grants (Cowan, 1990; Noble, 1989). Corporations, as Barrow and Noble have shown, had been using universities for research since the turn of the century, and corporate priorities had greatly influenced the structure and orientation of university research. Formerly, the federal government held patents that were the result of such research. New government policy gave ownership of the patents to the university, and this produced a deluge of changes in the university and made it possible for corporations to close their own R&D facilities and get what amounted to publicly-funded research[5]. Corporations in this period gave universities large grants targeted to buy research equipment (money that could moreover be used to obtain federal matching funds). Of course there were corporate guidelines: typically, grant money could not be used toward maintenance of equipment; maintenance had to come from the university's operating budget. And any inventions coming from this research would be patented by the university and leased exclusively to the corporation. This gave corporations the best of both worlds. Research took place in an environment with little constraint on creativity, was publicly sponsored, corporate costs were kept to a minimum and there was a guaranteed return.

The breakdown of Fordism and the new image of flexible accumulation led directly to a new arrangement, and its impact on universities was dramatic. The solution to the corporate cost problem was to create a new level of crisis for American universities. Many schools found themselves forced to raise tuition even higher than it already was. Even very wealthy and prestigious universities now needed to use temporary and/or part-time faculty. Students got channeled into two groups: those who received a basic education for their tuition dollar, having bought a prestigious diploma at a high price; and the very exceptional few who would be part of prestigious research teams and experience the benefits of capitalism.

In September 1990 *Academe*, the publication of the American Association of University Professors (AAUP), devoted an issue to the 'entrepreneurial university', a response to the above-mentioned changes in the university. Research universities, forced to cope with new costs in the late 1980s, were not able to cover them out of operating budget alone, no matter how high tuition went. Tuition increases eventually reached the level of diminishing returns; that point at which, costs too high, students go elsewhere. Further, as I'll discuss below, the State found itself under pressure to decrease its commitment to higher education, passing the burden of payment for higher education to the consumers.

Ivy League universities these days often lament the loss of diversity. 'Where have all the working-class and minority students gone?', they ask. The answer is (of course) the same place middle class students are going — less expensive universities. As costs cannot be covered by tuition a number of universities, hoping to go into the business of business (money-making), seek to profit-share with corporations on the fruits of their research. This is a new level of commodification. From the turn of the century when American universities were 'rationalized', through the imagined 'booms' of 1945 and 1960, to the enrollment crises of the seventies and the transformation of the university into a system that operated 'as if' they were selling a service to the student; in a sense, up to this point, the commodification of the university has been a metaphor. We can say that its stucture is 'modeled on' corporate America. But metaphor changes into literal reality at the point at which universities begin to produce research for profit.

Globalization and Downsizing in the 1990s

In the 1980s social scientists attempted to quantify changes in global competition and the new information technologies. The process that in the 1980s was called 'post-modern', or 'disorganization' (Lash and Urry, 1987), or 'flexible accumulation' (Harvey, 1989); in the 1990s was referred to as 'globalization' or 'transnationalism.' (Waters, 1995; Sklair, 1991; Featherstone, 1990; Rouse, 1995). In this new market-place goods and services are more individualized; instead of simple mass production of standardized items there are items customized for and marketed to individual users. Image and information has a new role with computers, video and other electronic media driving the new economy. Virtually instant transmission of data makes possible an increasingly globalized system of production, with different aspects of the manu-facturing process in different countries targeting products in a global marketplace.

All this represents not so much of a change in the regime of accumulation as its spread to a global system and the concomitant dramatic growth of transnational corporations. In the new globalized economy, there is increased market competi-tion, a refiguring of boundaries of space and time and a new global consumerism. Underlying the development of transnational corporations is what Sklair (1991) and Rouse (1995) call transnational practices. For Rouse, that entails the movement of people, goods, money, information, images and ideas across national boundaries. As more people participate in the global economy, their practices are shaped by that economy and it becomes increasingly more complex and problematic to talk about the economy of the United States. This global movement has enabled corporations with new information technologies to reduce and rationalize workforces and pro-duce more product. Often these products are information and images capable of moving rapidly around the globe in search of a market.[6] One way to see the new global practices is, as a further result of the contradictions of Fordism that Harvey, Bluestone and Harrison and Strange, among others, have discussed. The development of multinationals led to the instability of Fordism, which encouraged the seeking of greater flexibility which coupled with the new communications technologies worked together to create a world of giant corporate organizations existing without borders and capable of rivaling the economic power of nation-states. In this new borderless economy, the State takes on fiscal responsibility without the affluence of a growing economy and finds itself in crisis as a result.

The transnational global economy has had a number of interesting effects on the national economy. At first, there was an inverse relationship between the worker doing well and the financial markets doing well — if the information was good about employment the Dow was likely to dip; if unemployment was up the Dow did well. Labor Secretary Robert Reich has said publicly that it used to be if a company was doing well workers could expect to be rewarded with job security

Table 3: *Phase of productivity growth (GDP per Man-Hour) 1870–1987 (annual average compound growth rate)*

	1870–1913	**1913–50**	**1950–73**	**1973–87**	**1870–1987**
Australia	1.1	1.5	2.7	1.8	1.6
Austria	1.8	0.9	5.9	2.7	2.4
Belgium	1.2	1.4	4.4	3.0	2.1
Canada	2.3	2.4	2.9	1.8	2.4
Denmark	1.9	1.6	4.1	1.6	2.2
Finland	1.8	2.3	5.2	2.2	2.7
France	1.6	1.9	5.0	3.2	2.6
Germany	1.9	1.0	5.9	2.6	2.5
Italy	1.7	2.0	5.8	2.6	2.7
Japan	1.9	1.8	7.6	3.5	3.2
Netherlands	1.3	1.3	4.8	2.4	2.1
Norway	1.6	2.5	4.2	3.5	2.6
Sweden	1.7	2.8	4.4	1.6	2.6
Switzerland	1.5	2.7	3.3	1.2	2.2
UK	1.2	1.6	3.2	2.3	1.9
USA	1.9	2.4	2.5	1.0	2.1
Arithmetic average	1.7	1.9	4.5	2.3	2.4

Source: Angus Maddison, *Dynamic Forces in Capitalist Development,* (New York and Oxford, Oxford University Press) 1991 p. 51. Reproduced by permission of Oxford University Press.

and raises, but under Fordism and large-scale industrial production competition has been minimized, the old social contract is gone. Even if the company does well, it may still downsize to become leaner, meaner and more able to swallow up other global competitors; laying off workers in the process.

As indicated earlier, the pressures of deregulated global capitalism tend to put the concerns of financial markets above those of productivity and this fact creates some interesting problems. A current problem for the standard of living of average Americans, who are certainly affected by these forces, is the need for continual economic growth. Table 3 shows that while economic growth increased dramatically from 1950 to 1973 for most industrialized countries, it declined as dramatically from 1973 to 1987.

The decline in economic growth, (an indication of the market saturation in the 1960s talked about by Harvey), has forced business to seek even greater flexibility in the drive to keep profit levels high. The new communications technologies of the 1980s made possible the new forms of production and capital accumulation that Lester Thurow (1996) called a real revolution in capitalism, which he said may require a redefinition of economics to understand. The first phase of this process is one we are quite familiar with; the 'globalization of production' and the 'deindustrialization' of American cities and industrial areas Bluestone and Harrison (1982). This process is better be thought of as not deindustrailization but the development of new global spatial relationships. Many de-industrialized areas in the US are reindustrializing new workforces that have become used to much lower wage rates. Further, many foreign companies are building plants in the US to seek those markets. The new communications technologies make even more new flexible regimes of production possible. GM can build a new plant in Thailand to seek the growing Thai market, Mercedes Benz can build a factory in the US. Steel, motors and parts can be made anywhere in the world to bring together with 'just in time' inventory at the plant and the product can be monitored by information technologies from a home office anywhere. With the declining power of unions in the globalized production system, corporations are increasingly freer to seek the most advantageous facilities from a market location perspective.

More recently the middle classes have begun to feel several effects of global flexible accumulation. First, many corporations are seeking to reduce the size of their relatively high-paid, university-trained white-collar workforce, and have employed a number of strategies. The first strategy is outsourcing. Outsourcing — farming jobs out — has been part of the strategy of the productive sector since the 1970s (Head, 1996, p. 48) and has recently become part of the strategy of corporate headquarters as well. Jobs that used to be done internally are now done by contractors who are encouraged to compete for the job. This increases the efficiency of the organization because they only pay for a particular job and do not have to pay for the worker (or his/her benefits) during slower periods of the year. In practical terms, outsourcing is a way to get the same employee for less money. A man in middle-management for a large corporation, who earned about $60,000 dollars a year, was fired one day and rehired the next as a consultant on the same job he had been doing. This man, who had no other options, was forced to take the job and find other clients to start his own consulting business. (This kind of situation is incidentally good for the electronics market. He now needed his own computer, fax, photocopier, business phone and so forth, to run his own office.)

Another change in employment brought about by new communications technologies is reengineering (*ibid.*, p. 49). Reengineering is the designing of software to do the job that service workers used to do; a way to bring to the service sector the kind of efficiency of production that has been brought to the manufacturing sector. We are familiar with this strategy at the lower end of service work (for example the new automated phone trees one gets when calling companies on the phone), and it clearly has far-reaching potential. Many of us in higher education are concerned with the development of certain models of distance learning, for instance, because the use of image and information technology could make it possible to automate college courses. Simon Head in a discussion of what he calls the 'new, ruthless economy' points out the potential of reengineering to create a kind of technological aristocracy in the corporation which could control most of the power in the organization (*ibid.*, p. 50).

The 1980s helped to produce a growing inequality between the professional middle-class, many of whom benefited from 'casino society', and the working-class who were forced out of well-paid manufacturing jobs to low-paid service sector jobs. The 1990s promise to increase that income inequality as many more of the middle class are downsized and the technological aristocracy benefits from their positions. Also in the 1990s it is becoming clearer that the movements of flexible accumulation in the 1980s, the priority of the financial markets and the new ways to guarantee profit levels are not good for American workers. No matter how hard corporations and politicians try to put a positive spin on downsizing, free markets and global competition, workers are losing wages. Unions, once very powerful, are unable to stop these programs and people are increasingly worried about the future although they may not understand all the complex forces that have gone into the production of their personal situation.

Slow to respond to American concern for these new economic circumstances, George Bush was defeated in 1992 by Bill Clinton, who told Americans that he was aware that the main problem in the country was the economy. But when economic indicators improved during the first two years of his administration, Americans were not relieved and rewarded Clinton with a no confidence vote in the 1994 election, turning the Congress over to the Republicans. Clinton's Secretary of Labor, Robert Reich, sees the current economic problems as a problem of education. Returning to the comfortable metaphor 'to get a good job, get a good education', Reich suggests that to draw high-paying jobs, all American workers need is to have computer litearcy and training for the communications industries. Reich has a point but his vision is limited. The number of high-tech jobs is unlikely to be as large as the loss of manufacturing jobs experienced by the US in recent years. Further, with reengineering, it is questionable how much job growth there can be in this new high-paid service sector. Government finds itself in a crisis.

Throughout the twentieth century, the US has been in a position to mediate the aspirations of a democratic public with the interests of large corporations in the United States (Carnoy and Levin, 1985, p. 44). One of the ways this has been done is by advocating educational opportunity for Americans. Because education is often seen as the way to encourage upward mobility, there has been a tendency for the interests of business to be the interests of government officials and educators (Barrow, 1990, p. 252; Carnoy and Levin, 1985, p. 41). In the earlier years of the twentieth century this relationship between the interests of business and the interests of citizens and educators was fraught with conflict. Business has always been in the complicated and contradictory position of wanting a skilled workforce and needing creativity for new inventions, new products and new strategies to encourage Americans to consume these products and services. But the current crisis is a new one. For the first time in the history of American capitalism the state has to deal with not national companies but global transnational corporations who want a deregulated economy. Deregulation comes with its own contradictions, and in any case at this moment in history 'what's good for business is good for America' rings hollow. This always ideological pronouncement, justification for class inequality and unequal access to resources, now doesn't even make ideological sense to American workers. If employment is up the Dow dips? It feels very much to the average American that what is good for business is *not* good for them.

In the new global economy government is in a very difficult position. Pressured to do the bidding of the capitalist class, it sees less and less domestic benefit. This is particularly the case in the United States and Britain where there has been a strong cultural tradition of 'free market' and absence of government intervention (Hoover and Plant, 1989; Gamble, 1988). Further, throughout the twentieth century, the State has been mediating the conflict between labor and capital by providing more jobs and benefits directly to the workers through State funding. Carnoy and Levin (1985) point out that the State has increased its share of employment from 9 per cent of the labor force in 1920 to 16 per cent in 1980 (p. 60). If one takes into consideration forms of indirect subsidy to private business and education, the State role in supporting the public has grown considerably. The crisis of Fordism in the 1970s was not just a crisis for the economy but the beginning of a crisis for the State as well. Many workers were concerned with high taxes and a declining economic position. The revolution of Reaganomics, a critique of big government, was supposed to fuel economic growth, defense and military spending, creating a small economic miracle while giving new tax breaks to corporations and affluent individuals. The result was that the Federal deficit soared (Harrison and Bluestone, 1988, p. 147).

The culmination of this situation is that the contradictions of the State in American capitalism are coming to the surface. The State can no longer effectively mediate between the interests of average Americans and the demands of business, since many large corporations are now transnational and under less pressure to respond to the domestic concerns of the United States. Further, the Federal deficit is so great that a large portion of the tax base must go to refinancing debt, making it difficult for the government to spend money on citizens in an effort to reduce their financial problems. Finally, Americans want government to reduce their taxes and get rid of what they see as wasteful spending, while at the same time to better manage an increasing number of social problems exacerbated by poverty, crime, drug addiction, illiteracy. The State at every level is caught in a crisis of legitimacy, unable to stem the tide of moral and social decay, at the same time in fiscal crisis, without the funds to mediate the contradictions of capitalism and under pressure to reduce deficits and taxes but still provide Medicare, social security, and education; to name just the most important services Americans don't want to lose.

Universities in a Global Economy

It is in the context of the above-discussed crisis of the State that the position of universities must be assessed. The first major problem of universities in the 1980s and 1990s is finance. As already pointed out, the universities have many new strategies to reach new educational consumers; these strategies are particularly important to private colleges and universities. But both public and private education has continued to experience decreases in direct state and federal support and decreases in the availability of student loans. Families have in recent years had to pick up a greater percentage of the college costs at a time when many family incomes are stagnating or declining. Table 4 shows the decline in financial aid to college students and table 5 the contraction of the middle class over twenty years from 1969–1989. Families are aware that college is even more necessary now, but they are also aware that a college education is not going to guarantee their son's or daughter's future. The effects of these forces and concerns can be seen in the popular periodicals, many of which have run special issues on the best colleges, the best buys in higher education, the best graduate schools.

The effects of these decreases in public support are different for public

Table 4: The shrinking federal student aid grant, school years beginning in 1977–19
(1991 Dollars)

Year	Maximum grant ($)	Student cost (tuition, room, and board) ($)	Maximum grant as percentage of student cost
1977	3,017	5,196	58.1
1979	3,313	5,170	64.1
1981	2,524	5,274	47.9
1983	2,461	5,698	43.2
1985	2,658	6,183	43.0
1987	2,518	6,606	38.1
1988	2,533	6,757	37.5
1989	2,526	6,886	36.7

Source: Lawrence Mishel and Jared Bernstein, *The State of Working America* (New York, Economic Policy Institute Series, M.E. Sharpe, Inc.) 1993 p. 367.

Table 5: Percent of families* with low, middle, and high relative income, by region, 1969–1989

Region/Income Group**	1969	1979	1989	Point Change 1969–1979	Point Change 1979–1989
Northeast					
Low	27.6	31.8	29.5	4.2	−2.3
Middle	60.0	55.8	50.9	−4.2	−4.9
High	12.4	12.4	19.6	0.0	7.2
Total	100.0	100.0	100.0	0.0	0.0
Midwest					
Low	28.7	30.7	34.4	2.0	3.7
Middle	60.3	57.0	52.6	−3.3	−4.4
High	11.0	12.3	13.0	1.3	0.7
Total	100.0	100.0	100.0	0.0	0.0
South					
Low	42.7	40.4	41.7	−2.3	1.3
Middle	49.0	49.7	46.2	0.7	−3.5
High	8.3	9.9	12.1	1.6	2.2
Total	100.0	100.0	100.0	0.0	0.0
West					
Low	29.5	32.6	35.5	3.1	2.9
Middle	57.1	53.0	48.7	−4.1	−4.3
High	13.4	14.4	15.8	1.0	1.4
Total	100.0	100.0	100.0	0.0	0.0

* Income adjusted for family size. Individuals are considered one-person families.
** Low-income group refers to 0–0.75 of the median; middle-income group refers to 0.75–2.00 of the median; high-income group refers to 2.00 and above times the median.
Source: Lawrence Mishel and Jared Bernstein, *The State of Working America* (New York, Economic Policy Institute Series, M.E. Sharpe, Inc.) 1993 p. 320.

universities and private universities. Many public institutions have begun to deal with the realities of retrenchment and downsizing. When these tendencies began in the late 1980s, many state university systems in the 1990s saw large portions of their state subsidy withdrawn and were forced to reduce staffs and programs dramatically. Many private institutions have had to consider downsizing as well, but in the private institutions heightened marketing and fund-raising efforts have been the main effects of the decrease in State support. With the above-mentioned changes in federal patent law, more private and state universities can seek advantageous corporate partnerships. Prestigious universities and colleges engage in massive giving campaigns; one prestigious private university in North Urban's area held a billion-dollar fund-raising campaign. Finally, private institutions can market to different segments of the population. There has been a dramatic growth in categories of non-traditional students as people in the workforce trying to get a leg up getting new skills and universities seeking to sell them those skills.

One of the dangers in all of these changes is that the universities are increasingly servants of the marketplace, and in ways different from the past. The logic of the market is rapidly becoming the only logic on the university campus. There is less and less dynamic tension between the pull of liberal culture and economic rationality. State universities to survive must both seek corporate research partnerships and prove that they are vital to an economy of the area, and they must also rationalize their faculties, departments and curriculums. Private universities have to sell a product and it must be a product that people desire, if not high prestige than a program or skill that serves a special niche market. Many traditional comprehensive liberal arts colleges that survived the eighties did so because they developed a hotel management school, a physical therapy program or some other form of practical education that could be sold to the public. The problem with such planning of course is that shifts in demand for labor mean that a program hot today may be over-saturated tomorrow. And last but not least, lost in all of this are the goals of a liberal education. The loss of our liberal cultural traditions, I would argue, is due less to multiculturalists and feminists than the rhetoric of the right would have us believe and more to the instrumental logic of the marketplace which has our colleges and universities in a stranglehold.

All of these problems produce a crisis of legitimacy for the university which parallels to the legitimacy crisis of the State itself. Higher education is very costly and there are pressures on schools to control tuition, get less State funding and provide more service. At the same time, universities are encouraged to be more rational and provide skills that people need. Many professors at state and comprehensive private schools talk about the decline of quality in their students, but it's not so much that the students have less ability than that they seem to have less interest in what they are taught. For the students, education is not an empowering process in which to gain a voice in public affairs and acquire knowledge and wisdom to be a fruitful contributor to one's society, but just a necessary hoop, a product dispensed, one that may help in the future or not. They know they need the credential but they are alienated from the process, a phenomenon sometimes referred to as overeducation (Carnoy and Levin, 1985, p. 170). The frustration of expecting of the material benefits of a college education coupled with the realities of downsizing and fears of underemployment have left many undergraduates wondering about the purpose of their college education and their future.

Faculties and university administrations have had to respond to these political and economic forces. The issues are very different for the few hundred highly selective schools in the country (because their market draw is their prestige, a commodity sign in and of itself) from the vast majority of institutions that do not have the draw of prestige, and it is on these I will base most of my observations. Some of these issues have been explored ethnographically in chapter 2 and I will return to them later in chapter 9. At the moment I will discuss some general implications for faculty and administrations. First, university faculties, beginning to feel some of the economic forces in the late 1960s, and coupled with the political awareness at that time, began to unionize. There was a flurry of union activity to be discussed in more detail in chapter 6. Ironically at the moment that trade-unions began to see a decline in their power, unions in higher education began to expand. I have argued elsewhere that this is part of the metaphor of Fordism coming to the university (Shumar, 1995). But if universities began in the 1960s to see themselves as factories of knowledge that produced workers and research for the Federal government and corporations, the so-called 'military-industrial complex; they just as quickly moved through Fordism and became one of the early professional bodies to experience the new pressures of flexible accumulation.

The centerpiece of these changes is the dramatic increase in PhDs and the increased use of part-time faculty, temporary full-time contracts and other non-tenured faculty. Bowen and Schuster (1986) point out there is nothing new about the use of part-time faculty in higher education. They argue that while the use of part-time faculty has increased in the last twenty years it may be leveling off and if part-time faculty do not become too prominent then they should not be a threat to the quality of university programs. What is missing from this analysis of part-time faculty use is the growth of what Barrow (1995) calls 'flexible specialization', which gives the university greater flexibility in staffing courses by using temporary full-time positions or part-time faculty. It allows the institution to staff its liberal arts courses with a flexible workforce while concentrating on developing programs that attract students because they promise skills for a particular occupation. The flaw in looking at the numbers of part-time faculty versus the numbers of full-time faculty is that this does not illuminate the changes going on in many universities and undermining morale. Many younger faculty members spend years as part-time temporary faculty — a person may go from a series of regular part-time jobs, to several one-year contracts; maybe even a three-year contract, and then back to part-time work. Humanities and social science programs especially have to staff their courses with part-time or temporary people. While the university's overall statistics may look good, liberal arts programs are suffering. The absolute numbers of part-time and temporary faculty may have leveled off in the 1980s, but structurally they are still central to the maintenance of the new university, allowing, as they do, the university to maintain its illusion of having a core based in the liberal arts tradition. Table 6 shows the percentages of PhD recipients with academic employment

Table 6: Percentage of new doctoral recipients with definite employment plans in the United States who had job commitments in higher education, by field of study: Years of doctorate 1970–93

Field of Study	1970	1971	1972	1973	1974	1975	1976	1977
All fields[1]	**68.1**	**69.3**	**67.7**	**65.0**	**62.6**	**60.4**	**60.5**	**58.8**
Humanities and social/behavioral sciences	86.4	85.3	83.3	80.7	78.3	75.5	73.8	71.6
Humanities	96.1	94.4	94.0	93.3	91.0	89.3	90.0	87.4
Social and behavioral sciences	80.3	79.7	76.6	73.2	71.2	68.7	66.0	63.9
Natural and computer sciences and engineering	46.6	50.5	48.4	45.5	41.4	39.2	42.8	40.5
Natural Sciences	56.4	61.1	60.9	57.2	53.2	47.7	51.9	48.7
Life sciences	70.9	73.2	68.8	68.4	66.0	61.7	61.7	63.3
Physical sciences	38.2	41.9	45.5	38.0	32.3	25.8	31.6	29.8
Mathematics	80.3	85.7	78.7	77.6	77.1	74.3	77.8	72.6
Computer sciences and engineering	28.6	31.3	27.0	25.3	21.1	24.9	27.0	27.0
Computer sciences	—	—	—	—	—	—	—	50.0
Engineering	28.6	31.3	27.0	25.3	21.1	24.9	27.0	26.7
Technical/professional	71.6	69.0	66.4	63.3	62.2	60.3	59.0	58.7
Education	70.9	67.6	63.5	60.2	58.5	56.4	54.7	54.5
Other technical/professional[2]	73.9	73.3	75.8	71.8	72.0	70.3	70.8	69.7

Field of Study	1978	1979	1980	1981	1982	1983	1984	1985
All fields[1]	**56.9**	**55.1**	**52.6**	**51.4**	**50.3**	**51.7**	**50.7**	**50.6**
Humanities and social/behavioral sciences	69.1	65.7	62.7	61.8	61.8	62.5	60.2	61.0
Humanities	85.3	82.3	80.7	82.3	82.7	84.4	81.9	81.9
Social and behavioral sciences	61.3	58.2	54.6	52.8	52.5	52.5	50.2	51.1
Natural and computer sciences and engineering	38.6	36.8	35.2	34.2	33.3	38.0	36.9	36.9
Natural sciences	45.1	41.7	39.4	36.4	36.1	38.9	38.8	39.6
Life sciences	61.4	59.3	53.8	55.0	50.3	49.9	45.1	50.3
Physical sciences	24.9	22.2	20.1	16.8	19.2	23.1	22.5	23.4
Mathematics	71.4	70.8	72.1	70.3	74.6	77.2	79.4	76.4
Computer sciences and engineering	27.5	29.1	28.4	30.6	28.6	36.7	34.1	33.2

Table 6: Cont'd

	1986	1987	1988	1989	1990	1991	1992	1993
Computer sciences	60.6	53.2	47.4	52.7	50.4	53.6	50.3	54.2
Engineering	25.6	26.6	26.5	28.0	26.2	34.4	31.7	30.6
Technical/professional	57.4	57.8	55.2	53.4	52.1	51.7	51.9	51.4
Education	52.5	52.6	50.0	48.2	45.9	45.0	43.9	42.8
Other technical/professional²	68.6	69.8	68.2	65.8	65.6	66.3	68.6	68.3

Field of Study	1986	1987	1988	1989	1990	1991	1992	1993
All fields¹	**50.3**	**51.9**	**51.9**	**52.7**	**51.9**	**52.2**	**51.8**	**51.9**
Humanities and social/behavioral sciences	58.4	61.1	61.2	63.2	63.9	64.6	64.6	65.3
Humanities	80.4	84.8	82.7	83.1	84.9	84.9	85.3	86.0
Social and behavioral sciences	48.9	49.2	50.9	53.2	52.8	53.8	52.6	53.4
Natural and computer sciences and engineering	35.9	37.6	38.4	37.9	34.1	34.4	32.8	33.5
Natural sciences	36.6	37.7	40.0	39.6	37.5	39.3	39.5	39.6
Life sciences	45.8	44.7	49.8	49.2	47.1	48.2	45.2	45.4
Physical sciences	20.6	24.4	23.3	21.6	20.8	20.8	22.0	22.3
Mathematics	76.5	75.4	81.5	82.5	81.1	79.1	77.4	73.6
Computer sciences and engineering	35.0	37.5	36.9	36.3	31.0	29.8	26.7	27.8
Computer sciences	51.3	68.5	58.9	64.9	57.1	49.6	42.1	47.2
Engineering	32.6	32.1	32.8	30.6	26.0	25.8	23.5	23.5
Technical/professional	52.8	53.6	53.4	55.0	54.5	54.7	54.1	53.1
Education	45.0	45.0	44.4	46.0	46.8	46.7	46.9	44.8
Other technical/professional²	68.5	69.6	69.4	70.2	68.9	68.5	67.0	68.1

—Data not collected as a separate field of study.
¹ Includes those for whom field of study was unknown.
² Primarily composed of agricultural sciences, business and management, communications, health sciences, and other occupationally oriented fields.

Note: Only new doctoral recipients with definite employment commitments in the United States are reported here. A 'definite commitment' is defined as a signed contract, acceptance of a formal offer, etc. Employment in higher education includes positions in 4-year colleges or universities, medical schools, and junior or community colleges with the exception of postdoctoral fellowships.

Source: National Research Council, Survey of Earned Doctorates, Doctorate Records File, various years. Reprinted from National Center for Education Statistics, *The Condition of Education*, US Department of Education 1995 p. 310.

committments. Dramatically in 1970 96.1 per cent of all humanities graduates and 80.3 per cent of all social science graduates had jobs in higher education. By 1993 those percentages have dropped to 86 per cent and 53.4 per cent respectively. While not all of the current 1993 graduates are looking for academic employment anymore, the statistics give a good feel for the contraction of academic employment.

Junior faculty members are particularly demoralized as the laborious, demoralizing route to a tenure-track job becomes longer and less certain of reward. Far from being poor teachers or scholars, many of these junior faculty have multiple publications, grants and teaching awards but find themselves still unable to secure full-time positions. A flexible workforce not only allows the university to develop new programs and courses, increasing and decreasing offerings rapidly, but at the same time it allows the university to maintain traditional benefits of leaves and reduced course loads to the senior faculty. The use of part-time and temporary faculty has resulted in many efforts to unionize the part-time faculty as well. One of the ways research universities have attempted to side-step the part-time faculty issue is to use graduate students as their flexible workforce, and increasingly graduate students too see themselves as an exploited workforce in the university. The recent increase in graduate student strikes and orgainizing efforts on the part of graduate students is an indication of the incorporation of graduate students into the flexible workforce.

Flexible specialization has brought a new culture of assessment (Tierney and Rhodes, 1995) to the university. Coming under different names (total quality management, responsibility center management) this culture of assessment is the logic of the marketplace directly brought to bear on the university department or college. Work must be rationalized in order to make the university more efficient and less wasteful, and this often involves specialized administrators trained to bring these new disciplinary logics to the university. It is the university's version of reengineering. Ironically, Noble (1977) pointed out that many corporations discovered in the early twentieth century that the rationality of the business environment had a stifling effect on creativity, and that is therefore was in their own best interest to move their research parks away from the corporate headquarters. Increasingly business uses universities as the site of creativity for research into new products. By the end of the century, the present fiscal crisis of the state will bring a new financial discipline to the university demanding once again an instrumental view toward productivity. In chapter 9 I will look at the impact of this logic on North Urban University as it encouraged departments to be more financially viable. The effect of this has been to create a university where the knowledge and courses that sell are the only ones the university will support — knowledge that does not draw students and/or research money must be either eliminated or reduced to general curriculum where it can be taught by the flexible workforce.

The culture of assessment or quality management is part of the way faculty are used in the university. With ever-larger numbers of temporary faculty (both full and part-time) the administrative apparatus perceives a need to control the quality and efficiency of the product being sold to the students. In the absence of an illusory community of scholars to create a moral tie to bind faculty together and give them a sense of fulfilling the university's mission, administrators attempt to exert bureaucratic control to get departments to police themselves. The question of whether part-time faculty are good enough is not so much a question of how well-trained or how good they are; after all in the boom periods many people were hired into tenure track jobs sight unseen; the question is more one of social control. Do these temporary workers have the institution's goals in mind and at heart? They may be very good teachers and researchers, but if they are not good team players, they may be seen by the administration as detrimental to the university and dismissed. The official justification of a person's being a poor teacher can be used by the administration, but it rarely has to come to that because most temporary workers are aware of their precarious positions and effectively controlled by that weakness. For them there is no academic freedom. Whole departments can be effectively controlled by administrations along these lines; for example in one sociology department we will discuss later there are four full-time faculty (one emeritus, one retiring and two temporary), and four or five part-time faculty. This department is composed entirely of marginal people and as a result it has no standing at all with its college, but is simply labor.

Finally, quality management dictates that what the consumer wants is the final arbiter of what education should be. If a department has a lot of majors and is efficient in delivering its product to the students (lean production), then that department is in good working shape and is doing well. If there are few majors and too much overhead then administration will prune that department back. This model pressures faculty to sell their courses to students and to market effectively with little or no concern with the quality of teaching or ideas. Many social science programs look for practical application disciplines like gerontology to draw students. In this climate student evaluation of a course is very significant and there are pressures, especially in private institutions, to avoid giving low grades.

Between the images of the 'community of scholars' and the strong ideological belief in meritocracy, university faculty are often at a loss for assessing these forces. Many senior faculty feel very bad about the lot of junior faculty; yet see themselves powerless to do anything about their situations. The mandates from state universities to downsize and the drive among private universities to keep paying students coming in have produced between them a survival mentality. Many faculty are concerned with the quality of students and their level of interest in the work but know that above all that student's presence in their class or majoring in their department is central to their survival.

As administrative power gets exercised in more direct ways and the bureaucratic structures of many schools becomes more 'top down', faculty are increasingly pressured to turn against deviant members of their department, to cooperate with quality control, and to ignore the many violations of academic freedom to which temporary faculty are subjected. The next chapter looks at the powerful impact of the Supreme Court's Yeshiva decision in which faculty were denied collective bargaining on the ground they were managerial employees because of the control they exercised over their own work process. Ironically that control was minimal even then and in the fifteen years since Yeshiva has been considerably eroded.

The younger generation in higher education has gone from youth to middle age working and hoping for tenure-track jobs. It is clear that most wait in vain. All along they have been told that the meritocracy still works; if you are good you will be rewarded and if you're not rewarded you must not be good. Reduced to statistics, they are written off, told there is only a small percentage of part-timers unsuccessfully seeking full-time employment, encouraged to 'see the big picture'. Ironically, a significant portion of the non-academic middle-class is also joining — or being pushed out into — the flexible workforce under lean production. So more and more of our neighbors are joining the part-time faculty and temporary faculty on the highways, commuting to their clients as they move from full-time management to consultants.

Lost over this century has been a democratic and participatory model of education, one not modeled on corporate bureaucratic efficiency and the profit motive. Worse still, the profit model is now being extended to high schools. Soon they too will be modeled on corporations. Commodification is the hegemony of economic structure being imposed on institutions which once had an autonomous place in social life. This is a situation difficult to struggle against because many people working in these situations often fail to see what is happening. Higher education is at an important juncture where educational priorities must be redefined and the downsizing imperatives of the state and the transnational vision of a world of lean production, high profit and slower economic growth must be met with a new vision for the future; hopefully one where higher education plays an important role in revitalizing a citizenship for a democratic culture and works toward an environmentally sound sustainable future.

Notes

1 For instance the Carnegie Foundation for the Advancement of Teaching (CFAT) published as late as 1975 a volume titled *More than Survival: Prospects for Higher Education in a Period of Uncertainty*, where they identify these problems in higher education. They see a growth of new students, faculty positions or federal spending looming in the 1980s. The proposed response to these potential problems is flexibility and the exploration of new markets.

2 From this perspective I would argue all universities and colleges are public institutions and this is the case whether we are talking about private universities or public ones. The government had a vested interest in free scholarship, scholarship that was not directly influenced by the market. This is clearly seen by the levels of Federal funds that have been given to private universities and financial aid given to private university students. We will see later in this chapter a decline in that support, the erosion of funding support could be seen as a sign of the state abandoning its role in keeping the colleges from being commodified.

3 Similar things were going on in healthcare a little bit later in the early 1980s with the arrival of the new HMOs. The majority of the first HMOs were non or not-for-profit organizations, but were later turned to profit making industries and were bought up by insurance companies.

4 Andrew Gamble (1988) suggests that the rise of the new right in Britain and the United States was part of the creation of a 'strong state' that could discipline a workforce for the new needs of capital accumulation. This would include ideologies around the inefficiency of unions and large government and the support of a 'free-market'.

5 Here we see the universities were drawn into the strategies of flexible accumulation as they developed throughout the 1980s. It might be important to say here that these were new strategies and they began to take shape in the 1980s. By the 1990s (next section in the chapter) transnational corporations were much stronger and the state was be in a new state of crisis.

6 You can get a taste of the new global economy by putting a small personal ad in a newsgroup on the Internet. Many people do this to sell used items, notably out-of-date computer hard- and software. You can reach thousands, perhaps millions, of people worldwide. A handful of years ago, the same ad in the local newspaper could have reached a few *hundred* people.

Chapter 5

Imagination and the University

Yeshiva: The Landmark of 1980

Almost everyone in higher education is familiar with the Yeshiva decision. The Supreme Court of the United States decided in a five-four decision that faculty at Yeshiva University did not have the right to collective bargaining because they were managerial employees (US Reports, 1980). The test of whether one is a managerial employee or not comes down to whether or not there is autonomy and primary control over the work process such as being able to make decisions about the direction of work. Further, management is defined as individuals whose interest do not significantly differ from the company's interests. When the Yeshiva case came before the National Labor Relations Board the NLRB's opinion was that the faculty at Yeshiva, while having a great deal of autonomy nevertheless acted in their own interest as professionals but did not exercise the managerial control that would have precluded their right to organize a union (Sussman, 1981). The NRLB argued that the Yeshiva faculty should be able to organize a union. The university administration disagreed, saying that faculty were managerial employees in that most of their recommendations in hiring, raises and firing were carried out and also that they had autonomy over their own work such as the creation of curriculum, syllabuses, exams and courses. The Court found for the administration, although it is significant that there was a large dissent.

While the decision was appropriately described by Justice Powell as a 'starting point'[1] intended to apply only to that particular set of circumstances — the court left other university situations open to other interpretation — it has in fact been used as precedent in other cases. In 1988 the First Circuit Court of Appeals in Boston decided, based upon the Yeshiva opinion, that Boston University faculty were managerial employees and therefore did not have the right to collective bargaining. In the BU instance it was clear that the faculty had very little autonomy within the university, but the court still held that the precedent set by Yeshiva applied.

The Yeshiva decision is important to collective bargaining in higher education and not just because of its effect as a legal precedent. The decision also nicely illustrates a set of contradictions having to do with the nature of the university and the roles of its faculty members, within both the university and society at large. Arthur Sussman (1981) begins his analysis of the Yeshiva decision with an interesting anecdote:

Dwight Eisenhower early in his brief presidency of Columbia University greeted a group of faculty members expressing his delight a meeting some of the 'employees' of Columbia. The resulting silence, as the story continues, was broken by a senior professor who rose and said, 'With all due respect, sir, we are not the *employees* of Columbia university. We *are* Columbia University.' (p. 27)

It is this model of the faculty *being* the university that underlies the Supreme Court decision on Yeshiva, despite the fact that the history of higher education and the real-life experiences of university faculties since World War II call it severely into question. Within the quote itself it's not hard to see symbolic struggle. Even if the Columbia faculty unanimously did believe they were nothing less than Columbia University itself, the President's gaffe made it clear that at the very least there was some question about it. Personally, I see in the story not only admission of weakness (The professor stood up to make his point because he was aware his standing within the university was on shifting ground) but also evidence of denial; an unwillingness on the part of faculty at that time to confront unmistakeable changes in their status.[2] Perhaps this speaks to the question of why thirty years later faculty still have no clear idea who's running the university, in whose interest. The confusion between faculty *being* the university or being *employed by* the university reverberates throughout the institutional structure of higher education, from the level of individual consciousness of faculty members, to support staff, to university administration, to federal policies affecting higher education, including of course the Supreme Court.

Forces of commodification in recent decades have moved both faculties and administrations toward seeing teachers as workers. For instance, since the late 1960s the number of faculty unions has increased dramatically. Forces identified in earlier chapters have pushed university administration to act more like business management and their response to the enrollment crises of the seventies and eighties has had the effect of proletarianizing the faculty. As education becomes a commodity it necessarily turns teachers and researchers into commodity producers or laborers. And torn between their traditional standing as autonomous, high-status professionals and the need to protect themselves from exploitation within the newly profit-motivated university adminsitration, teachers have responded, however reluctantly, by forming labor unions.

Reluctantly because this process is resisted by many faculty. Ideological concerns aside, university teachers and instructors are not a homogeneous group. They run the prestige gamut from prominent superstars and darlings of prestigious universities through the more ordinary tenured professor, the tenure-track instructor, visiting faculty post-doctorate teaching assistants and part-time faculty and adjuncts. Not surprisingly, these groups have different takes on their changing position(s) within the university; and there has been much tension and friction between types of faculty. But in general, as faculty members have been treated more like laborers they have increasingly sought the protection of labor organizations. This is what the Yeshiva faculty tried to do.

The Taft-Hartley Act, which provides for the right to organize labor unions, states that when a person acts in the interests of the company (and hence as management) s/he is not covered by the act. Only those who act in their own interests and (who are) subject to management abuses are protected by the Act. Sussman (1981) observes that Congress rewrote these guidelines to the Management Labor Relations Act (MLRA) in 1947 to make it clear that any employee acting in the interest of the company was not covered by the Act (p. 36).

For Mr. Justice Powell and the majority of the court the faculty of Yeshiva '. . . exercise authority which in any other context unquestionably would be managerial . . . it is difficult to imagine decisions more managerial than these'(US Reports, 1980, p. 686). The court agreed with the administration that since decisions made by the faculty were for the most part carried out by the university, faculty therefore had a great deal of control over the work process, and as such were managers and therefore not entitled to the protection of MLRA. Not only were they not entitled to it, said the Court; giving it to them might actually endanger academic freedom by creating a conflict between professional concerns and the demands of a union. Writing for the majority, Mr. Justice Powell evokes the medieval university: 'This system of shared authority evolved from the medieval model of collegial decision-making in which guilds of scholars were responsible only to themselves.' (*ibid.*, p. 680) and his conclusion was '. . . the university has both the need and the right to expect the "undivided loyalty" of its faculty' (Sussman, 1981, p. 43) Mr. Justice Brennan in a dissenting opinion felt that academic freedom was in danger from the institution *without* the protection of the right to organize into a labor union: '. . . the Court denies the faculty the protecction of the MLRA and in so doing, removes whatever deterrent value the Act's availability may offer against unreasonable administrative conduct'(US Reports, 1980, p. 705).

Unclear about how to imagine the faculty, the NLRB had attempted an amalgam of factory work with entrepreneurship. They (and dissenting Mr. Justice Brennan, in the subsequent Supreme Court decision) envisioned the university as an odd sort of factory, where entrepreneurs (the faculty) come to produce in their own interests but (also) produce a product that the university can sell. Increasingly being exploited for their knowledge which was being sold to students, faculty in this view had little control over financial issues and the direction of the university. Under this logic the NLRB argued Yeshiva faculty should be able to organize. Yeshiva's faculty had autonomy in their work — like managers — but they were seen by the NRLB as exercising it in their own professional interests — unlike managers — *not* that of the institution.

Most of the court disagreed, but there was clearly no consensus in the opinions as to what role faculty does play at a university, and there are several conflicting models of what the university in fact is. Mr. Justice Powell, for instance, used the community of scholars image to argue that 'the university needs protection from the Act more than the faculty need the Act for protection from the administration' (Sussman, 1981, p. 43), greatly romanticizing the relationships within the modern American university. It is clear from Barrow's (1990) history that the American university has never been very like its medieval ancestor and what similarity there

once was has been eroded by industry and the profit motive over the course of this
century.

In *The Taft-Hartley Act: One Year After,* a pamphlet put out by the government, several interesting points emerge. The first question dealt with is the inclusion or not of foremen's groups. In the factory model, foremen are the dividing line
between workers on the shop floor and management in the front office; go-betweens,
in fact. In writing the Act the NLRB left the question of whether foremen were
labor or management ambiguous.

The second interesting point is that all the industries cited are primarily large-
scale producers in the retail, automotive and construction industries. There are other
industries but only treated as special cases. Congress understood how to deal with
industrial production and that is the model under which the Act was written. Other
industries had to be forced into this model and decisions were then made based on
how closely they fit the factory model. The problem of foremen was dealt with
similarly — in each case it had to be decided if that foreman group looked more
like workers or more like management, and decisions came down accordingly.

Blame It on Fordism

The Management Labor Relations Act was based on the large-scale factory model
of Fordist production, and at the heart of the factory model is the icon of Fordist
production. The Wagner Act was passed in 1935 after decades of violent and
radical labor unrest; for some time before and certainly in the decades that followed, Congress was looking for ways to deal with the radical segment of the trade
union movement. As we saw in chapter 3, the development of the trade union
movement in the United States cannot be separated from the historical changes
brought about by the end of the Second World War. With the end of the war and
the Bretton Woods agreement, the United States was in the very privileged global
position of being an economic producer to the world, which led to both a need for
large-scale industrial production and also the need to minimize competition, secure
the cooperation of labor and stablize financial markets. It is not surprising that the
Taft-Hartley Act reflects the dominant system of production. The structure of the
system of accumulation under capitalism, and the conflicts and contradictions associated with it, are part of the consciousness of all of us, including lawmakers writing law. The Wagner Act and the Taft-Hartley Act took their form in this period
of large-scale industrial production and have Fordist-Keynesian images of production embedded in their structure.

Those images of production have suffered major sea-changes since the end
of World War II. As Scott Lash (1990) puts it, the autonomy of different social
spheres has begun to collapse under post-modernism (p. 11). Arenas of social life
that used to have their own autonomy, such as family life, health care and education, to name three, have become bound up in economic concerns. Harvey's (1989)
notion of flexible accumulation makes a similar point. Under Fordism, production
was done in the factory, leaving the family, the university and the medical community

to pursue different autonomous goals. These other spheres of life were separate from the economic and played their own role in smoothly reproducing society and socializing the workforce (Agglietta, 1979). With the collapse of Fordism discussed in chapter 4 and the subsequent advent of flexible accumulation, there were not only significant changes in financial markets, corporate structure and the ways labor is employed to produce, but as Harvey (1989) points out there was a significant time-space compression caused by the new patterns of capital accumulation and the advent of new communications technologies (p. 306). The space-time compression, central to the redefinition of the productive sector, involves all sorts of new redefinitions. Factory work combined with piecework in the global economy as products began to be tailored to niche markets and new computer technology allows the combination of work done by horticulturalists in the rainforest with work of factories in major cities and the compression of space and time also resulted in loss of autonomy for different spheres of life. Education, government and healthcare; institutions that had previously been seen as support industries maintaining the industrial economy had become industries in themselves along the lines of commodity production.

For instance, the medical community formed HMOs originally as non-profit attempts to cut patient cost by streamlining and centralizing medical services. The HMOs were then purchased by insurance companies and changed from non-profit to for-profit, and became subsidiaries of insurance groups whose primary goal was not the health of its clients but the accumulation of capital. Within the family, as a result of flexible accumulation, one or both parents may spend evenings perhaps assembling taillights for GM on a per-piece basis, since rising labor costs have encouraged manufacturers to return to piece-work. The family home, no longer an autonomous arena, has become a site of production. Under flexible accumulation, university professors' teaching and research can be used by corporate-sponsored research and development groups. This resource has the advantage of being subsidized by tuition and federal funds.

None of these new configurations of labor can be addressed under the current Management Labor Relations Act, because they simply do not fit the images of production generated in a prior era. To further complicate matters, corporations in their unceasing attempts to increase or guarantee profits have consciously moved away from the Taft-Hartley image of production, because it is simply more profitable for them to exploit labor groups that aren't protected by the law.

At the same time the dictates of 'flexible accumulation' are dismantling Fordist industrial production at the manufacturing sites where it arose; the factory model is being used to understand work in the university. In many ways, the university of the nineties has come to look like a factory. Administrators think of themselves as management and faculty as workers, and students are spoken of, and encouraged to think of themselves as, consumers. A careful look at the forces that have commoditized the university reveals that, as corporations have shut down traditionally-run, no longer profitable American factories, the work has been shifted to unprotected and more easily exploitable groups at universities, in the home, and among third-world women. This forces us to see the world in new ways and it's hard to make sense of these new ways with old ways of talking and thinking about them. This is what happened to the NLRB and the court in the Yeshiva decision. Justice Powell said in his opinion that if the NLRB came up with new categories of laborers such as 'non-tenured' or 'part-time' perhaps these groups could be seen 'as if' they were industrial workers and a case could then be made for them needing protection of the Act. But a majority of the court could not see tenured faculty as employees entitled to the same protection as labor. That inability on the part of the Court was the result of not only by sweeping changes in the economy and the difficulty of representing them but also by the power structure of the modern university. The problem for the court, and for all of us, is that the university as 'factory of knowledge' is itself ironic because the university has already moved to 'flexible specialization' (Barrow, 1995). While I would argue that education is being commodified in that students and corporations are being imagined as consumers of a product produced by faculty and controlled by administrations, the result is not factory production, but flexible accumulation. There are highly tailored products for various markets: the traditional student market, the adult market and others; all packaged and distributed by various kinds of faculty laborer, not just tenured professors.

Academic Power and Corporate Power

New regimes of power rarely materialize out of thin air. With the exception of major revolutions there is usually a more or less gradual transformation of an older order of power relations. This led Michel Foucault (1973) to observe in the case of the transformation of the fourteenth-century leprosariums of Europe into the later asylum system, that the structure of exclusion at the heart of each remained the same (p. 7). Only who was excluded changed. Although there are obviously many differences between the American university and European asylums, Foucault's observation serves as a point of departure. Power relations in the modern university have changed dramatically during this century. Those changes accelerated after the Second World War, by around the time that the faculty at Columbia were telling Ike that they were the university, administrators and university presidents were busily working to bring scientific management, Taylorism, to the university. At the time, the old academic hierarchy was still in place. Deans, provosts and presidents were academics; it was still accurate to call the university a community of scholars. But even during the Eisenhower administration, this was beginning to change. University administrations were coming to be dominated by trustees whose careers originated not in the ivory tower but on Wall Street and Madison Avenue. Further, new programs in business administration brought oganizational dynamics and strategic planning to the university in all of its many new layers of administration. It was difficult even for those of us who work in universities to quantify the effect of some of the changes at the time and it is certainly something the court would have a hard time addressing.

In retrospect it is easier to see that faculty and administration, no longer similar groups with a confluence of interests, have become two distinctly different groups, with different and not infrequently opposing agendas for the university. Deans and provosts have become the foremen of the university; they are liaison between administration and faculty. While university administrations these days may be headed by an academic President, the President's advisors and staff are almost invariably managers of a very corporate managerial type who often have the ear of significant members of the Board of Trustees; and it is typically they who generate the rules and legislation that the President approves. It is also the case that a university President who understands the way power operates in the university may grab this new role directly and run the university like a CEO. Whether the President retains the mantle of scholarship or takes on the corporate role, the situation results in a series of duplicities. A university President will be expected to speak in the interests of humanistic scholarship and cultural diversity but many of the policies carried out will in fact contradict these public expressions. The role of the President is to speak publically for the virtues of academic values while legitimating the administrative apparatus behind the scenes doing the trustees' bidding. This often gives public rituals in universities ironic overtones, such as when faculty and staff go to the convocations or holiday parties and listen to the President speaking of the 'university community' or the 'university family' knowing that a large sum of money has just been denied to an academic program in favor of a new building project or renovation of the administration offices. For example, one state university expanded so rapidly they had to put the political science, history and other social science faculty into a temporary building. The faculty were told that the situation was temporary and new headquarters would be found for them. But after more than ten years and a renovation of the main adminstration building, the temporary building was still housing the faculty. Faculty joked that carpets had been replaced twice in the administration building while they were waiting for a permanent department and that even the old carpet administration threw away would be an improvement in their quarters.

Deans, who are members of the faculty who traditionally represented the faculty to university administration, have become instead a funnel of communication for top management's interests. They tend to outline the parameters of what is acceptable. Deans in the modern university take, like foremen, a position on the line between the power structures. In the university this role serves also to obscure the position of the rest of the faculty members in the university. For instance, there is a tendency for the deans to outline criteria to the faculty for candidates to be presented. If candidates do not fit the administration's criteria they are rejected, so faculties learn quickly not to send unacceptable candidates to be hired. Deans in some schools are begining to take on the role of arbiter of curriculum standards; what students should be taught and how they should be evaluated in certain core courses is being managed by the dean. This is often the case where the student population, after being recruited, is seen as sub-standard or non-traditional and thus in need of remedial teaching or inculcation into university culture. Consent for this pedagogical intervention is sometimes secured by the administration's having the dean convince the faculty that certain academic standards require behind-the-scenes coercion. Clearly, here the dean is not the faculty's representative to top management but the reverse. Of course, as far as the official record is concerned, a dean can usually say that all the faculty's recommendations for hire are carried out by the administration, as Justice Powell said in the Yeshiva case. The reality is that the faculty are exercising less and less managerial control in the choice process and are instructed to make the 'correct' recommendation. This is just the kind of corporate bullying that the Taft-Hartley Act is supposed to protect workers from. Clearly, looking realistically at faculty power within the university, faculty should be entitled to collective bargaining.

The stratification of the faculty spoken of at the beginning of this chapter makes the lines of administrative control even more difficult to assess. Some faculty members are rewarded with senior positions for 'voluntary' cooperation with the administration, which unsurprisingly includes union-busting efforts. Managerial control of faculty is effectively total. The older power structure, a status hierarchy based on academic prestige, is harnessed to the management interests of a capitalist board of trustees with the reins firmly in the hands of the expanded administrative class. But the picture is even more complex. In a university divided into management, administrative and academic sectors, administrators often have bigger salaries and more actual power in the running of the university because they are doing management's bidding. Faculty, however, have greater symbolic prestige, so administrators pay a kind of ritualistic deference to faculty. This is a kind of social group distinction along the lines of Bourdieu's analysis. Administrators have greater capital and managerial control, faculty have a greater symbolic and academic prestige. Everyone knows this, but we have no way of talking and thinking about this. The failure of American intellectuals to theorize their own social and professional space (as Bourdieu does for French culture) has left them weaponless in the struggle against universities who are ironically throwing the Columbia prof's claim in their faces: If you *are* the University a union is not appropriate.

Yeshiva's Impact

We have seen that embedded in the Yeshiva decision are images of production and their contradictions as they have worked themselves out in US history since the end of World War II to the present. At a deeper level in this landmark decision there is a philosophical assumption that people and their labor are commodities sold in the marketplace. There is also an implicit assumption of a need to keep the buyers of labor power separate from the sellers of labor power. Finally, and very central to the Taft-Hartley law, is the principle of trading small tokens of control to the sellers of labor in exchange for the legal right to insist on depoliticization of the marketplace and the right of the state to the absolute final word on the subject. It is just this Fordist contract that capitalists, because of the current crises of capitalism, cannot abide by. There are several ways out of this apparent cul-de-sac for higher education. We might entertain the notion that higher education, despite the commoditizing tendencies since the end of World War II, is *not* an industry and professors are *not* employees. Or we might acknowledge that the Taft-Hartley understanding of labor, and its resultant contract, is inadequate to the situation we find ourselves in and that we need to move beyond it.

During the 1980s Yeshiva had a big impact on other institutions, the most famous being the case of Boston University. The faculty at Boston University attempted to make the case that they did not have the managerial control that faculty at Yeshiva had and that therefore they ought to be entitled to collective bargaining. But when they sought to organize a union, the First Circuit Court of Appeals argued that Boston University's faculty was essentially no different from Yeshiva's faculty and based on the Supreme Court decision in that case they were management and not eligible for collective bargaining. Though the Supreme Court suggested that each university situation could be different and should be looked at separately, the First Circuit Court did not find the differences. Further the NLRB has made decisions (at Farleigh Dickenson University and others) since Yeshiva, ruling that private universities may not form collective bargaining units. When the University of Pittsburgh began the collective bargaining process, the university's administration, though a State university, argued before the Pennsylvania Labor Relations Board that faculty were managerial employees citing Yeshiva. The PLRB did not agree with the university and ruled in favor of the faculty. Interestingly, in one ethnographic interview I was told by a department chair at a private university that his dean loved to bring up Yeshiva in meetings. Yeshiva was actually used by this dean as a 'friendly' threat to control his faculty, 'if you try to unionize it won't work because of Yeshiva'. The Supreme Court's decision, in this instance at least, was used as an informal coercion to accomplish exactly what the court said in its reasoning for denying collective bargaining rights to the Yeshiva faculty was not done in universities, exert management control over faculty.

Even in small colleges where faculty have no tenure and no decision-making responsibilities, Yeshiva is being used to keep faculty from organizing. The NLRB has been forced by Yeshiva to revisit its criteria for deciding if collective bargaining can be allowed in a particular university. Chastised by the Supreme Court for not coming up with acceptable criteria to determine if faculties should be able to collectively bargain, they have been forced backward into a position of non-approval. They can less afford to risk a challenge and so refuse to allow many private university faculties to create bargaining units.

Finally, the Yeshiva decision further separated the public university and the private universtiy. A split into a public and a private tier was already widening due to economic forces; tuition demands making many private schools out of reach for many students. But Yeshiva went further in that it legitimated some structural differences between public and private universities. The professoriate will not be the same for all universities; but managerial employees at the private schools and (potentially) unionized employees at public schools.

Ideological State Apparatus

Yeshiva's importance is in the way it shows up the relationship between the State, the corporate sector and the universities. The original opinions of the court indicate a deep rift in the court itself. One way to read this is to say the majority of the court felt it had to maintain the status quo and uphold traditional ideological categories of intellectuals, scholarship, management and labor. But the dissenters — nearly half the court — recognized the transformation in American society and that the contradictions of capitalism have changed the game. They acknowledged there need to be new rules and new definitions, that faculty are becoming intellectual laborers and need protection. The pressures of flexible accumulation and the shrinking Federal and State budgets for higher education mean that lean production has come to campuses throughout the nation. New forms of power within the university are needed to discipline labor and produce more work for the same cost. Total quality management, forms of stategic planning, and using debt to retrench or scare faculty into submission are all part of the ways universities are being reworked. These are the discplinary tools of administrations and governing boards to attempt to realign the roles of universities in the changing climate of a less stable economic order. The 'community of scholars', with the faculty in control of the university, exists on very few campuses. Most colleges and universities are under the new discipline of the global order. Many faculty cling to the old vision, and some are fighting back, but the courts' response to Yeshiva is symptomatic of the early days of this crisis. What the future will bring is an interesting question. University faculty are well poised to be the leading edge of a new wave of unionization in the service sector economy.

This is what Gramsci (1971) meant by hegemony. The lower courts and the NLRB do not philosophize, they simply apply. The forces moving in the economy and in the university encourage them to apply decisions which are good for IBM and Martin Marietta while still paying lip service to a mythical medieval bastion of independent scholars. Of course capital does not win without struggle. There is and has been a deep philosophical struggle; after all many people are concerned, but in the end capital often wins by default. On the other hand, power is plural in the United States and often there are avenues of struggle even when it looks as if things are hopeless, The Pennsylvania Labor Relations Board (PLRB), aware of the NLRB's problems in Yeshiva, came up with new criteria to argue that the faculty at the University of Pittsburgh should be able to form a union. Their argument in the Pitt case was that only a very small percentage of faculty has any input on budgetary matters and that it is budget and financial decisions which define management, not academic issues. Therefore the PLRB found that the faculty at Pitt were not managerial employees by the Yeshiva criteria and should be allowed to form a collective bargaining unit. This was a strong response to the Supreme Court President set in Yeshiva.

Subjectification and Yeshiva

The dean I mentioned earlier, who used Yeshiva to discourage union talk among his faculty, talked about Yeshiva a lot. In his role as go-between, the Yeshiva decision reassured him, allowing him to see the university differently than it really is. It also justified his bringing the decisions of management to the faculty, insisting upon their cooperation and then calling it a group decision by a community of scholars. This dean would very undoubtedly tell the NLRB that 100 per cent of his faculty's decisions were approved by the President of the university.

But not just deans engage in this kind of double-think. What is interesting about the ideological lack of consensus on the court in the Yeshiva decision is that it is reflected in ideological struggles among the faculty themselves. Yeshiva symbolizes our confusion over what has happened to us in the commoditizing of the American university; there are parallels between the court and the consciousness of faculty at America's universities and this is another reason Yeshiva is pivotal. Faculty have the same rift in their understanding of the social and academic worlds the court revealed in the Yeshiva case. In the case of faculty members their symbolic identity as professors is also at stake. They may resist collective bargaining because they see it as giving up their superior symbolic status in their struggle with management. But that superior symbolic status has not protected them from domination by administrations becoming more and more aligned with corporate interests.

As indicated before, very few faculty members really like the idea of unionizing. When North Urban University was in the midst of a long and difficult strike, I heard many disparaging things about the striking faculty from teachers at other institutions. Even unionized faculty members who theoretically support the idea of a union often have trouble with the idea of being labor. One inevitable effect of the commodification of higher education is that each new crisis puts more pressure on faculty members to see themselves for what they are, workers.

The split in the consciousness of faculty members also falls along the lines of the older system of academic prestige. Faculty at larger, more prestigious private institutions tend to cling to the identification of scholar as an independent activity. They tend not to see themselves as employees. On the other hand, faculty at community colleges and part-time faculty at most institutions have to deal with the exploitation and managerial control directly and on a day-to-day basis, so it is very clear to them that they are employees and need protection from management. Faculty also split according to whether they see themselves as teachers or as researchers. Teaching, in old academic terms, is a lower-prestige pursuit than research, so teachers have less trouble seeing themselves as labor while faculty who engage in — or aspire to — research tend to see labor activity as an aberration imposed on them by outside circumstances.

The growth of part-time and visiting faculty unions has furthered awareness that universities exploit workers like the business sector does, but it has also created a another kind of rift between the faculty groups. Part-time faculty needs are often very different from full-time faculty needs. This can lead to a three-way conflicts between management and the different faculty unions. It can also lead to worker solidarity. Part-time groups can often lend support to the full-time faculty and help raise the consciousness of those faculty members who buy into the ideological construct of independent scholar, failing to see their position as workers. Part-time faculty harbor no illusions that they are independent scholars and are usually very clear about their positions as workers.

Faculty members cannot afford to fail to see what the court failed to see. They know that their recommendations on hiring, promotion, tenure and curriculum must all fall within the guidelines set by management, so they know they do not exercise professional control in these arenas. They can also hardly fail to see that their symbolic prestige as scholars affords them less and less in the way of personal rewards or even control over individual professional concerns. But their commitment to an identity shaped by a mythological past, a past that never existed in America but that is nonetheless important to their symbolic prestige, continues to make the idea of collective bargaining unattractive to many faculty members.

In spite of this symbolic difficulty the huge increase in university and college faculties organizing since the late sixties indicates the extreme and systematic exploitation that faculty members everywhere in the US experience as commodification proceeds apace. In the next chapter we will look at the problems of seeing faculty as either factory workers or managerial employees. With the expansion of bureaucratic apparatuses and the crisis of falling rates of profit, all institutions are part of a global structural rearrangement. These rearrangements are bringing new forms of corporate or government discipline to many arenas formerly not part of the economic. The pressures of commodification are both produced by the crisis of capital and the expansion of the economic into different arenas. Old metaphors do not nicely fit the contemporary sitation and may serve to obscure it. Collective bargaining is one of the tools faculty have to fight the decline of the economic positions and the new forms of technocratic control on the production of knowledge. But it is not a panacea. Formed during the Fordist era, present models of collective bargaining fail to come to grips with the way faculty are being controlled by an administrative apparatus that uses new mechanism of social control and surveillance to both manage the system and serve the interests of powerful individuals and corporations. Further, unions provide a limited model for how faculty can respond to these new situations. They are an important step in creating collective response to protect faculty interests, but faculty will need to find new ways to imagine themselves as well.

Notes

1 Sussman (1981), quoting from the SC record.
2 Interestingly, it should be pointed out that shortly after Eisenhower's speech at Columbia, the 'community of scholars' became a movement incorporating a set of ideas that were developed into a series of seminars to — one might imagine — keep the 'community of scholars' imagination alive.

Chapter 6

Collective Bargaining in Higher Education

North Urban's Faculty Union

The process of unionization at North Urban was typical. University faculty, faced with falling wages and benefits, voted in 1972 to establish a union through the American Association of University Professionals (AAUP). The resulting organization, while formally a union, functioned simply as a professional organization at first. Then in 1980 the university administration pushed through changes in contract language to make the retrenchment of about 150 faculty and staff positions in the university possible. The retrenchment plan was not based on fiscal exigency and was ultimately unsuccessful, but the university's attempt served as a wake-up call to the faculty, alerting them to the weakness of their position in dealing with the administration and to the fact they could not take job security for granted. As a direct result the faculty union turned serious, got the university censured by AAUP in 1984 and got the contract language changed to protect tenure.

The Board of Trustees at North Urban took from the beginning a strongly antagonistic stance toward the faculty and the union. In 1982 a new President came to North Urban and, with the cooperation of central members of the Board of Trustees, embarked on a ten-year battle with the faculty, the purpose of which, many faculty thought, was to 'bust the union' and gain total administrative control over the university. The new President was much disliked by faculty and tensions rose.

In the mid-1980s salary was the big issue for North Urban's union. Their salaries were low by comparison with other state research universities and the union wanted to bring them into line with national averages. In 1986 contract negotiations broke down and the faculty of North Urban began the fall semester without a contract. Tensions continued to rise and the vast majority of faculty voted to go out on strike in October 1986. The faculty wanted not only to increase salaries but by now they also wanted to get rid of the President. (They had demonstrated their lack of support for the President by holding a referendum in the faculty senate; a large majority voted no confidence in the university President but failed to remove him.)

The strike ended badly for the union. The university went to the Common Pleas Court and when it was clear that the judge would issue a back-to-work order, the faculty returned to work, accepting a two-year contract on essentially the university's terms. Animosity between faculty and administration ran high; ten years later there is still a strong sense of resentment and distrust of the administration among North Urban faculty. University administration was seen by most as remarkably ruthless in its anti-union tactics, cynically spreading untrue rumors about the faculty and student lack of support for the strike.

The strike revealed weakness in the faculty's position. When the university played hardball, faculty were forced to either back down or behave like a much more militant trade union, and it quickly became clear that the necessary level of militancy was something most faculty could not achieve. Joining a professional union was one thing; behaving like a trade union member was another for the North Urban faculty. Some faculty did feel the strike should continue until the court actually issued the back-to-work injunction, increasing the pressure on the administration to settle (because class time was being lost). Others thought the union ought to defy the back-to-work order and put even more pressure on the administration. But in the end most North Urban faculty suffered from role conflicts. Their professorial image of themselves militated against any in-the-trenches trade-union behaviors like defying a court order.

The strike had other effects as well. One of the difficult things about school strikes is that they are hard on the students. Some students lost work-study or other payments and were forced to make other financial arrangements. But the students, — both undergraduate and graduate — university rhetoric notwithstanding, were very supportive of the teachers' strike and even more so of the drive to remove the university President. The graduate students, some of them teaching assistants, graduate assistants and part-time faculty, were put in a very difficult position by the university administration. The university tried to carry on business as usual, using the faculty who were not part of the union: the part-time faculty and the teaching assistants. Unlike the full-time faculty, part-timers and teaching assistants had no strike fund, no support mechanisms and moreover they could be fired if they refused to hold their classes. In spite of this, the graduate assistants and part-time faculty were very supportive of the strike, many of them standing on the picket lines with faculty. (The faculty's situation made part-time faculty realize they needed to protect their interests as well and after the strike they began to look into a union of their own. More on this later.)

Another aspect of the faculty brought out during the strike was the way in which the field of professors was structured. As Bourdieu argues, university faculty is not just a collection of people with similar backgrounds and training. The academic world functions as a structured field and within that field different dispositions tend to be associated with position with the field. The strike had a bigger impact on the Colleges of Arts and Science and Education than it did on the Law School and Medical School, because those schools' faculty had a greater tendency to see themselves as managerial and therefore did not participate in the strike. In the Business School there was a split, with some faculty participating in the strike while others did not. In Arts and Science almost all of the faculty supported the strike.

But the political field at North Urban was divided another way common in many state universities. There are two ways to reach prominence (i.e., promotions, higher salary, more leave time) in the university. One way is to become an important scholar in your field; bringing in money in the form of grants, getting major publications that lend luster to the university. A different route is to collaborate with the administration and get appointments to posts and activities within the university; positions often having less to do with scholarship and more willingness to do the administration's bidding. Faculty members in administration's camp not only benefit personally, they actually become part of a system of control, and as we saw in chapter 5 this allows the university administration to say there is faculty autonomy because the faculty can seem to be participating in administrative decision-making. In reality only a small percentage of faculty participate in these ways.[1] There has always been tension around the fact that some faculty have relatively powerful positions like Assistant Dean or International Campus Director; at North Urban that tension came to a head during the strike. Some faculty were unhappy that they now had to report on colleagues and act as a surveillance team. Others in high administrative positions, found themselves caught between a tradition of left politics and wanting nothing to do with the union in the strike.

In several ways North Urban's strike forced a confrontation with identity. Proletarianized worker struggling for better benefits and wages against an oppressive employer? Or member of a professional association trying to negotiate differences with a university administration? Perhaps in other universities faculty were not forced to confront these issues of identity in quite this way, but at North Urban, because the administration took such a hard anti-union stance, the faculty had no choice. North Urban faculty were not only forced to confront these issues in the strike but to also to acknowledge that their lack of clarity meant they failed to achieve either goal. They lost money in the strike and failed to remove the President from office.

Following the strike the faculty sought new union affiliation, striking up an agreement with the American Federation of Teachers, creating a joint AAUP-AFT union. The union felt that the AAUP hadn't helped them much and they were looking for a union offering a little more support. (Eventually they dropped the affiliation with the AAUP.) In 1988, when their contract came up again, the faculty were not ready for another strike. They complained loudly but settled without pushing their demands.

The next time the contract came up in 1990 the union was ready to take the administration on again, and this time they went out in September, making it possible for students to make other plans for their semesters. This strike was again at least ostensibly about wages, but the big issue was really benefits. The university wanted faculty to begin co-paying on health insurance and they did not want to allow any faculty input on how healthcare was arrived at. Faculty felt the university could offer a managed care package, which would provide good healthcare benefits and save the university money. Once again, for the university at least, the issue was clearly not money but control. The university, determined to establish the precedent of co-payment, did not consider managed care or faculty input.

There was less faculty support for the 1990 strike than there had been in 1986, but the faculty got more in the long run. The strike showed the administration unequivocally that strikes are bad for enrollments, because students began to transfer (or not even consider North Urban because of the fear of a strike). The administration realized that cooperating with the faculty was not only more effective but a better message to send to the outside world. Even so, the university did not back down right away. The 1990 strike ended with a back-to-work order from the court and a big debate over how to handle makeup pay due to faculty for the time made up during midwinter break. The university, to finish classes, had carried the semester over into January 1991 and there was much debate over how to compensate faculty for their research and administrative time during this period. Each faculty member had to present a case to the PLRB with administration and union people present at the hearing, a slow and expensive process.

As the university and the faculty settled these issues the faculty ended up in a much better position. The university agreed to settle the outstanding pay issues after a protracted fight and subsequent contracts were negotiated with salary increases for faculty at North Urban. The university finally agreed to explore managed-care options, resulting eventually in good faculty healthcare benefits that saved the university money. North Urban faculty are now very well-paid by national standards. With a new Provost, the relationship between the faculty union and the university administration seems to have improved though there are still visible scars. In a second referendum vote against the President, the faculty Senate again voted no confidence in the President. Many faculty continue to deeply mistrust university administration.

It does seem the administration has realized it needs to work with faculty instead of taking an oppositional position. But the 1990s has brought new problems. The twin dilemmas of declining student enrollments and declining appropriations may well lead to new conflicts of governance as the university moves forward with its vision of responsibility centered management. In theory, this vision of management decentralizes decision-making in the university and in practice it would force each school or department to be profitable in terms of dollar input and output. This kind of reengineering in the university raises many questions about what constitutes important knowledge and how that importance is measured. These issues reach beneath the basic issues of salary and benefits to the broader issues of control of the institution. I will return to the issues of control at the end of this chapter.

Other Unions, Other Issues

After the 1986 strike the part-time faculty realized they were not in a good position at North Urban and needed to organize themselves. At the time some estimates put the percentage of North Urban classes taught by part-timers and graduate assistants at 50 per cent, a not unusual number. The part-time faculty had no benefits, were paid abysmally and during the strike were pressured to do the university's bidding or not be rehired. (One of the many dilemmas for part-time teaching, because contracts are semester by semester, is that it is difficult to show you have been fired. The university can simply say there is no course.)

The part-timer situation was complicated. Some people teaching courses had teaching assistantships which at North Urban carried a fairly typical package of stipend and tuition remission. Teaching assistants taught their own courses and functioned very much like part-time faculty but were often at earlier stages of their graduate career. It was typical for a department to award a two-or three-year TA to an incoming graduate student. They were later encouraged to find other funding so their assistantship could be freed up for incoming graduate students. Older graduate students (and even recent PhDs) were often hired on a course-by-course basis to teach part-time. These people were at varying stages of PhD work and were sometimes teaching elsewhere as well, or living on grants or doing other work. They were often less connected to the university culture. Finally there was a group of part-time teachers who saw their work as a more permanent status. In the English department, for instance there were remedial writing and reading teachers with master's degrees who saw the part-time work as a more or less permanent job, not as a step to a future career. It was this last group that spearheaded the movement to create a part-time union. Perhaps the most exploited, they were not duped by propaganda of the temporary nature of their work. PhDs and ABDs were strongly supportive of this group, as they were beginning to realize that part-time work might be a long term reality for them as well.

As the part-time faculty got closer to voting on collective bargaining the university took the unprecedented action of eliminating most part-time positions. It replaced them with a series of training positions built on the teaching assistantship, also creating some new pre- and post-doctoral fellowships. These latter involved teaching two semesters, two courses per semester. The annual stipend for the fellowships was a significant increase over the average part-time rate but there were still no benefits. The university called these 'training fellowships' and (although some part-time positions did remain) argued that now there were no part-time faculty, only graduate fellows engaged in training. Despite efforts to keep the movement for a part-time union going, the effort ran out of steam.

An interesting repercussion of this ploy was that departments who didn't need the whole fellowship pushed the university for the right to break up the fellowship (rather than add cost to the department budget). The university paternalistically agreed and departments began offering half and even quarter fellowships. A one quarter post-doctoral deans' fellowship meant teaching one course for one semester for what was admittedly a better rate than what had been offered before. The rate change brought North Urban's part-time pay a little more in line with what was available in the marketplace, so it might be argued that this was a partial success of the full-time faculty union. The administration clearly did not want another union and was willing to make some concessions to buy off the part-time faculty. The move was also a success for administration in that it resulted in departments doing the dirty work of disarming the part-timers by breaking up the fellowships.

There have been other efforts to organize part-time faculty in North Urban's metropolitan area. One state university has fought for years to establish a part-time union through AAUP. The part-time faculty, which had good organization and a lot of support, voted for a union and negotiated for a contract with the administration.

For many years the administration simply ignored them. Job actions by part-time faculty are necessarily much more difficult but the part-time union did successfully pressure the university into giving them a contract in the early 1990s. It was a significant achievement, setting minimums for part-time pay and establishing a scale of seniority and increases. This contract has recently expired and the university is again simply ignoring the part-time union. This university has also ignored their full-time faculty's efforts to renegotiate a contract; so both groups are currently working without contracts.

The most successful part-time union in the region is at Metro College, a community college in the city that has been unionized since the 1970s. Metro College has been very successful in not only unionizing the part-time faculty but in coordinating efforts between part- and full-time faculty. The full- and part-time unions have been at odds at various points and there have been times when the interests of the two groups diverged significantly, resulting in tension not just between faculty and administration but between the two unions as well. But as the union leadership sought to resolve these issues and foster a sense of mutual respect, the bargaining position of each group strengthened. Early on some full-timers took the position that part-timers were merely not good enough to get full-time work, but as time has gone on it has become increasingly clear that part-timers are not inferior scholars and teachers but people caught by the changes in the labor market in higher education. Both unions now have an agreement in principle not to sign a contract with the college administration until the other group has a contract to sign. This presentation of a united front has made the faculty much stronger because the college cannot operate until they have contracts with both groups. Metro College has managed to avoid the situation at North Urban where the administration put part-time and temporary workers into the difficult position of being strike breakers.

The National Context

Richard Freeland (1992) ties the rise of collective bargaining among university faculties to the overproduction of PhDs in the 1960s and 1970s (pp. 381–2). As shown in chapter 3, the boom in higher education post-war and in the 1960s left many universities scrambling for faculty. That severe shortage of faculty stimulated the expansion of many universities' graduate programs, resulted in a large number of PhDs produced with fewer positions for them. The overabundance of labor created a situation that gave administrations the upper hand. With an abundance of potential new faculty, existing faculty could be pressured into accepting lower pay and going along with administration programs. Freeland points out that it is no accident that faculties begin to seek collective bargaining arrangements at this point, the first being at City University of New York in 1969. Freeland also points out the rise of regulatory controls by state and Federal agencies in this period as well (*ibid.*, p. 381). Faculty compensation, which had risen in the 1960s, began to decline significantly in the 1970s as indicated in Table 7.

The number of faculty unions grew dramatically beginning in 1969, tripling

Table 7: *Percentage changes in faculty compensation by rank in public and private institutions of higher education, by AAUP category, 1971–72 to 1978–79*
(in current and constant [1967] dollars)

Control and rank	Current dollars (%)					Constant dollars (%)				
	I[a]	IIA[b]	IIB[c]	III[d]	IV[e]	I	IIA	IIB	III	IV
Public										
Professor	47.1	48.3	44.3	31.9		−11.4	10.9	−13.3	−20.8	
Associate professor	47.6	50.2	46.6	41.6		−11.3	−9.8	−11.9	−14.9	
Assistant professor	46.4	46.6	45.8	38.0		−12.1	−11.9	−12.4	−17.1	
Instructor	49.8	46.2	41.6	48.1		−10.0	−12.2	−14.9	−11.0	
No rank					52.9					−8.2
Private (independent)										
Professor	46.4	39.2	43.1	30.0		−12.1	−16.4	−14.0	−21.9	
Associate professor	45.2	41.0	41.5	41.4		−12.8	−15.3	−15.0	−15.1	
Assistant professor	43.3	39.6	39.7	30.7		−13.9	−16.2	−16.1	−21.5	
Instructor	47.8	34.8	33.1	34.4		−11.2	−19.0	−20.1	−19.3	
No rank					27.8					−23.2

[a] Category I: includes institutions which offer the doctorate degree and which conferred an annual average of 15 or more earned doctorates in the most recent three years in at least three nonrelated disciplines (essentially universities)
[b] Category IIA: includes institutions awarding degrees above the baccalaureate but not included in Category I (similar to Carnegie classification of comprehensive universities and colleges).
[c] Category IIB: includes institutions awarding only the baccalaureate or equivalent degree (similar to Carnegie classification of liberal arts colleges).
[d] Category III: two-year institutions with academic ranks.
[e] Category IV: institutions without academic ranks (mostly two-year).
Sources: 'Coping with Adversity' (1972, table 5); and 'An Era of Continuing Decline' (1979, table 13). Reprinted from The Carnegie Council on Policy Studies in Higher Education. *Three Thousand Futures: The Next Twenty Years for Higher Education*, Table H-2, p. 300. Copyright 1980 by The Carnegie Foundation for the Advancement of Teaching, San Francisco, and Jossey-Bass, Inc. Publishers, reproduced with permission).

by 1978 (Stadtman, 1980, p. 69). Growth of faculty unions has continued significantly into the 1980s. Table 8 shows the number of collective bargaining agreements by bargaining agent from 1975 to 1987. While collective bargaining agreements have grown for all the unions they have increased very dramatically for the AFT and the NEA, the stronger and more established teachers' unions. This statistical evidence supports experiences at North Urban where the faculty moved to the AFT because the bargaining strength of the AAUP was not sufficient.

AAUP's own history around unionization is a paradigm of the difficulty university professors have with seeing themselves as unionized employees. The AAUP was founded in 1915 amidst important changes going on in the university. Its concerns were supporting scholarly work and finding a collective voice for a growing profession (Metzger 1987, p. 156). The collective expression of the modernizing of a community of scholars, the AAUP is situated in the rising professionalism of the early twentieth century; scholars who saw themselves as being largely independent and motivated by a set of concerns that had more to do with reason and knowledge than with workplace conditions. It was a modern version of the transformation of a traditional guild to a modern independent body.

Table 8: Number of faculty collective bargaining agreements by bargaining agent (1975–87)

Year	Total	AAUP	AFT	NEA	Other	Combination of Any Two Agents
1975	211	24	53	87	28	19
1976	218	26	75	88	27	2
1977	234	29	83	92	27	3
1978	266	35	92	100	33	6
1979	301	39	96	137	24	5
1980	337	41	105	162	24	5
1981	359	43	112	173	26	5
1982	382	48	110	188	30	6
1983	377	44	108	188	31	6
1984	393	43	110	191	36	13
1985	395	40	118	191	38	8
1986	412	43	119	198	45	7
1987	427	43	125	200	50	9

Source: The National Center for the study of Collective Bargaining in Higher Education and the Professions. Reprinted from Dennis McGrath and Martin B. Spear, 'A professoriate in trouble: And hardly anyone recognizes it' in *Change*, (1988) p. 30. Reprinted with permission of the Helen Dwight Reid Educational Foundation. Published by Heldref Publications, 1319 Eighteenth St., NW, Washington, DC, 20036-1802, Copyright © 1988.

One way of looking at the rise of the AAUP as a professional body is as a function of the opposition between faculty and boards of trustees. Tension between the Board of Trustees and the faculty is illustrated by a story from Harvard where President of the University Lawrence Lowell threatened to quit if the Board went ahead with the firing of a faculty member who had supported the Boston police strike of 1919 (Kauffman, 1993, p. 223). (Lowell, unlike his latter day counterpart at North Urban, clearly identified with the faculty.) Events like this started to draw the political lines in the sand between governing boards and university faculty. The AAUP, as a professional organization, was always interested in trying to work jointly with boards of trustees in developing models of governance (*ibid.*, pp. 224–5).

The original vision of the AAUP fit the early twentieth century well. Business had not yet completely dominated the university; universities were still largely elite institutions serving an elite class. But with the historical changes in higher education documented in chapter 3; the expansion of higher education and the growth of government and business control over boards of trustees, the image of a professional body was not a strong enough protection against pressures being put on faculty.

The problem is illustrated by the AAUP's flip-flop on collective bargaining. In the mid 1960s the association debated the possibility of forming a union but there was strong vocal opposition to this. *Academe* (May/June 1989) published a special article on collective bargaining, collecting quotes from the history of the association. One passage (from the Special Committee on the Representation of Economic Interests, published in the summer 1966 AAUP Bulletin) reads:

The Association prefers that all faculty members participate in making decisions and protecting their economic interests through the structures of

> self-government within the institution, with the faculty participating either directly or through faculty-elected councils or senates . . . It is fundamental, however, that whatever means are developed for representation, *the faculty must have a truly effective voice in decisions of the institution and . . . the economic interests of the faculty must be adequately protected and promoted.* (my emphasis)

In this statement is the glimmering of a recognition of the decline in faculty power. The statement uses the word 'must' twice, which it clearly would not need to if the faculty could take 'an effective voice' and the 'promotion of their interests' for granted. The musts underscore the reality that these things are changing.

With the expansion of universities and growth of federal and state funding, with awareness of big deals being made in the sixties between the military and universities and business, faculty became aware that a majority of them did not have a whole lot to say about their positions. By 1972 the AAUP had reversed itself and begun to act as a collective bargaining agent. While the AAUP reluctantly agreed to the need to begin collectively bargaining, its original vision of faculty as a professional body remained central to the identity of the AAUP. Collective bargaining for faculty should be a meeting between rational managers who negotiate an agreement about their respective positions; it did not, in the AAUP's view, involve militant union tactics. But as the North Urban case shows, not only was the rational meeting simply side-stepped by the university, the faculty were weakened by the consciousness promoted by the AAUP. Only when they began to act like a militant union did they make progress.

As shown in the last chapter, the vision of 'professional' versus 'worker' is widening the split between state and private universities. Collective bargaining agreements have grown more in public universities than in private universities since the Supreme Court's Yeshiva ruling. The NLRB has ruled in a number of cases since Yeshiva that the faculty *at private universities* cannot form collective bargaining agreements because they are managerial employees. Certainly at many of the elite colleges that represent in our national consciousness the image of college, faculty are managerial employees. The President and Provost are often chosen from the ranks of the faculty and are very collegial. Faculty senates and governing bodies have a great deal of power. At an elite school, these are all people who carry a great deal of weight nationally and have a lot of 'cultural capital' and if they have an argument with administration it may end up on the pages of the *New York Times*.

But many less prominent private institutions suffer under the Yeshiva decision. Part of the image a private school sells is the image of a scholarly community, but the reality at non-elite institutions is otherwise. Threatened with the loss of enrollment and the risk of position, and with little hope of being able to form a collective bargaining agreement, many private university faculty must endure the administrations top down control. At West Urban Technical University, the faculty are virtually powerless. They view the university administration as corporate top management. The most recent new President was hired from the outside, came in and replaced the top management team with his own people, all newcomers to the university. This new President sees the university as a service industry to be run efficiently in a corporate fashion. Little mention is made here of the 'community of scholars'.

There has been, since Yeshiva, a continued increase in collective bargaining among public university employees. There is a tendency to see Yeshiva as putting a damper on the development of faculty unions in general but as the table above shows this is not the case. As those public sector employees develop collective bargaining they face a new threat, the use of the 'fiscal exigency' club to downsize the entire university. In New York, Pennsylvania and other states, the state governing boards have already moved to reduce funding severely, rewriting their entire relationship with the state university. This is nothing less then a wholesale attempt on the part of political conservatives to change state systems of higher education from universities that employ professional scholars to universities with flexible workforces. States seek to eliminate or restrict tenure, do away with sabbaticals and to redefine how academic worktime is measured. All of these efforts involve mechanisms of surveillance and control that would deal a death blow to university scholarship and independent thinking.

Many of the employees of these state universities are unionized but the unions are either very weak or have structural limitations. (In New York the SUNY faculty are not allowed to strike.) Many state employees' unions have not to deal with a serious challenge in a very long time and so are not geared up for a fight with the state. These are, of course issues that other state employees will have to face as well; faculty will need to support, and depend on the support of, other state employees. These fiscal crises and efforts to downsize are linked to the global arrangements discussed in chapter 4. Faculty need to understand the context of the situations they find themselves in, think about creative responses to debt being used as a weapon to beat workers into submission.

Technocratic Control and the Future

The last two chapters have shown how the history of the university and the history of labor in the United States have shaped two images of university faculty. These are the image of the 'community of scholars'; a professional group that in the modern word may be much larger than traditionally and likely to be producing more highly specialized research, but they are neither management or labor in the corporate sense. They are a new class (Gouldner, 1979). The other image is factory worker, the person who comes to work, stamps out a product, has little control over the labor process and is managed by an elite who shape the production process and determine the use of the product.

Neither of these visions fit what has happened in the United States in higher education. The expansion of the institution of higher education and its twin systems of public and private universities represents the complex development of an institution — the American university — that deals in its many forms with the most basic contradictions in our society. It can provide real opportunities for personal upward mobility — college graduates earn more than high school graduates. It has opened up the world of thought and scholarship to a broad public, making the United States a highly educated democracy. It has provided research for the development of new products and new markets, commercial as well as military. It has also been used to track different students into different career paths, leading the upper middle-classes to the more prestigious liberal arts degrees and the lower middle and working classes to technical and vocational training. Universities have created an institutional setting where intellectuals can flourish, but it's also one where their ideas can be contained and limited, where their impact on the larger society can be mitigated.

What has evolved in universities are various technologies of social control. Issues of social control have become more and more about managing a bureaucratic system and less about its relationship to a larger society with values we might question. Some have referred to this as a technocracy (Postman, 1993). Technocracy as a system tends to neglect ideological concerns and political decisions in favor of working to preserve the system (Burris and Heyderbrand, 1984, p. 205). The North Urban situation is instructive. North Urban seems to be heading in a direction of greater cooperation between faculty union and administration, the years of militant unionism having receded somewhat leaving a structure where each group cooperates and helps the other out. What the groups share is a vision of the university as a corporation that produces research and degrees and that must cope with problems of funding and enrollment and public image. The old ideological issues of the status of knowledge, the role of public intellectuals, the purpose of an education, are all avoided. This fact is the core of a potential crisis of institutional legitimacy and must be confronted by both groups, administration and faculty. In the technocracy, the system is what matters; the system is that which gives professional identity and so individuals are hooked into maintaining the system. But that system may increasingly be running into contradiction as it serves to promote the professional image of management, faculty and student alike.

Dennis Carlson (1992), in his study of urban school reform, is very critical of the union in the school district where his fieldwork is set. For Carlson, because the teachers' union limited themselves to wage and benefit issues, they were incapable of presenting a plan to deal with curriculum reforms brought about by the administration. When the administration imposed a system of basic skills and programmed curriculum the faculty had not developed mechanisms for dealing with these issues. In a sort of metacommentary Carlson argues that because the union accepted the 'rules of the game', as they were dictated by the administration, they were left with little position but to play the game.

I would argue that teachers' unions tend to do this because of the structure of US labor law. As we saw in the last chapter, labor law was written to accommodate the structure of the industrial factory at a time when unions were making political trade-offs in economic power; a reality nothing like that of the modern university teacher. As a result labor law does not speak to the realities of teachers today. The teachers' union needs a different model. The school is not a factory, curriculum is not management's prerogative but is a crucial part of the craft of teaching. Teachers cannot simply leave content and curriculum to administrations and school boards concerning themselves like the factory worker only with wages and benefits. When they do the classroom becomes alienated as the shop floor, further delegitimating the process of education that is everybody's reason for being there in the first place.

As university faculty unions grow they face a similar problem. Colleges are already beginning to be large impersonal bureaucratic systems where students and faculty alike are alienated, simply go through the motions for a credential that has less value than it did in generations past. Faculty unions need to address themselves to the meta-issues which include how to deal with being part of a vast technocratic system where rational system regulation takes precedence over all other human ideological issues. This won't be easy, but if higher education as a system is to survive the alienation and apathy that already runs rampant in the high schools it will be necessary.

Note

1   Interestingly when the faculty at the University of Pittsburgh appealed their case to the PLRB, they made this argument. They argued that Pitt faculty were in fact not managerial employees because only a small group of faculty influenced by the administration participated in decision making.

Chapter 7

Planning, Advertising and Consumption

Introduction

Modern higher education is inextricably bound up in images of the marketplace. The purchase of goods and services, once a metaphor for tuition and learning, is now the central reality of college life, with learning itself imagined as a purchasable service commodity. A generation ago this was not true. This model of higher education evolved during a period of perceived crisis when the applicant pool was declining dramatically. The ways in which that crisis was handled are related to an increasing preoccupation with signs in the larger culture and with a tendency to use those signs to understand and manage social life.

This chapter will look at evidence of this semiotic shift in the brochures and bookstores in America's colleges and universities and will relate these changes to political and economic changes discussed in previous chapters. These semiotic shifts can be shown to be both ways to manage consumption and ways to commodify the university. The chapter will also examine the relationship of commodification to democratization. Democratization often brings with it, or is carried out through, commodification (Capra, 1989, p. 3), resulting in an uneasy association in our society between these forces. The recent history of higher education in the USA can be seen as an object lesson in moving from a democratic movement into the commodification of a social arena. Advertising and the other technologies of consumption are the mechanisms of this commodification.

The Semiotics of College Life

The forerunners to the linguistic revolution — a long history of developments in sociometrics and cybernetics, systems of information and control used in the military, business and industry-were all created to be a 'predictive technology for social control' (Haraway, 1989, p. 108). When structural linguistic revolution hit American academia around 1963 it had already had a huge impact on the other humanities and social science disciplines, creating an increased interest in semiotics and the birth of a new theoretical discipline in the social sciences called structuralism. Structuralism asserted that social life was constructed from various systems of signs and that those systems were relational systems of meaning. These ideas generated, at the beginning of the mid-sixties, much discussion in American academia, as they were already doing in Europe. Journals proliferated with articles and seminars on language, language structure and language's relationship to other aspects of social reality. The development of semiotics and structuralism in France, Britain and the United States was, significantly, paralleled by a dramatic increase in the number of commodity signs in use in the culture during the same period. The understanding of language and signs developed and changed simultaneously with accelerated change in social sign use; scholars were developing the vocabulary to talk about this in the midst of an enormous proliferation of signs both in the larger culture and on the smaller academic stage. Certainly I would not say that the linguistic revolution *caused* the change in sign use (or vice versa) but there clearly was a dynamic interaction between sign use in American society capitalism, and the language to discuss these phenomena.

As often happens, the first models were idealist. Scholars imagined a semiotic realm independent of economic, political and social forces. Structuralism in all its varieties had persistent flaws in that it saw the sign system as having an autonomous nature rather than existing in relationship with the forces of capitalism in a particular historical setting. Richard Ohmann (1987) talks about an early semiotic transformation in national magazines around the turn of the century (see chapter 3). He shows that transformations in the print ad are central to the development of advertising in the twentieth century. Print ads at that time moved from intellectual argument techniques to affective appeals, which was achieved partly by relying more heavily on the visual. Instead of intellectual persuasion, the modern ad strives for an image that appeals to the emotions. The exact nature of the appeal varies; it can draw on popular fantasies (often but not necessarily sexual), reinforce deeply felt attitudes around racial, gender, or national stereotypes, evoke childhood pleasures — the possibilities are endless. The image is then associated with a brand name or a slogan evoking the product, grafting the affect onto perception of the product.

This new form of advertising developed at a time when, as already noted, businesses needed a guarantee of consumption. The enormous investments in large-scale production around the turn of the century demanded a predictive way to guarantee consumers. The new kind of advertising images were very effective. They not only guaranteed consumption but they generated enough revenue to take over the magazine publishing business. Magazines became an image-oriented public format.

Academic journals and college catalogs before 1960 looked more like bibles than magazines.[1] There was no attempt to make college catalogs look like advertising circulars because the laws of the marketplace were considered to have nothing to do with the university. In 1964 the look of the *Harvard Educational Review* changed from a journal with double-column print and no graphics (a format reminiscent of a bible) to single-column print, larger, more modern typeface and advertising in the back of the book; a familiar format resembling a mass-market magazine. The *Harvard Educational Review* was certainly not unique; many other journals made similar shifts to a new 'look' at this time.

People impose the image they have of a social world onto that world. The college used to look like a monastery and the publications of it like bibles because this was the model imposed on it in people's collective imagination. New universities look like corporate R&D parks or military bases because often these are the images the new leadership has in mind. Modern university publications all look like magazines, annual reports or mail-order catalogs (whether the university itself still looks like a gothic cathedral, a modern research park or some hybrid of the two). The catalogs and other publications use the commercial idiom of the marketplace because, first of all, this is the lingua franca of the class of businessmen, bankers and lawyers who now dominate higher education. But it is also the way the rest of us in our culture have come to imagine all institutions. Institutions today find themselves in the marketplace needing to deal with market forces and they have few other ways to imagine their situation.

Semiotic changes in American culture, coupled with pressure on the university to seek students, have made marketing the overriding concern. The admissions office in the sixties typically was in a small, matter-of-fact, low profile corner of the administration building. Now it is likely to be the biggest, highest profile office in the university. Even Zemsky and Oedel (1983) have warned that marketing higher education like a business will have potentially disastrous results, but they admit the need for, and Zemsky has himself been central in, developing ways to use marketing data to solve college admission needs and keep tuition money coming in as the government's contribution shrinks (p. 5). I would like to look at the semiotics of the college brochure and then at the other ways marketing functions on and around the campus of the nineties.

This year's brochure for a small, local, non-competive four-year college is about twelve inches square and twenty-six pages long, in look and layout (four-color gloss, staple-folded) it resembles an upscale clothing catalog. On the cover, to the left hand side of the page, is the picture of a young man skiing down a hillside, the brand of his goggles and boots prominently displayed. The skis, snowsuit, poles and gloves are clearly detailed although we cannot see any specific brand. Wrapped from the right around his image is copy that begins, 'my mom and dad and lots of aunts and uncles went to (college X), but I just wasn't sure . . .'. The copy continues as the boy obsesses about the college's 'pretty campus and friendly atmosphere' and then decides 'it's been a part of his family for a long time'. When he tells someone he's decided to go to X, they say 'who?' and at the bottom of the page, in answer, is a dictionary definition of the college including a quote from Edward Fiske saying college X is one of the best buys in college education. Below that is the name of the college in large bold red print, like a magazine name. The whole picture is bordered by the black edge of a Kodak negative, complete with arrows and frame number. This whole fantasy scene is (fresh from the documentary cameraman's darkroom) a pleasing image of fun, affluence, excitement, activity, and has no reference to college anywhere. (Even inside the brochure only the last five pages devote any space at all to information about programs, financial aid packages or requirements.) The definition at the bottom referring to Fiske vaguely suggests college evaluators to legitimate college X but the bulk of the brochure is devoted to images of affluence and fun and the copy is about feelings.

It's no accident the catalog looks like a *Gap* ad; this is a typical product of mass advertising, complete with demographics on the projected college audience and assessments — read conscious manipulation — of that audiences' concerns. The demographic segment this ad appeals to — the student population college X is seeking — doesn't have parents and relatives who attended college. In fact, a decade ago this four-year college was itself a junior college. But the working-class people being appealed to enjoy the fantasy of affluence and have no way of knowing what college is really like. The brochure gives them a pleasant image that tells them college is structured reassuringly like institutions they are familiar with; notably the department store.

The next six pages continue with this motif. It looks like a six-page ad front-of-the-book fashion ad; fantasy images of students stereotyped by role: the bookworm, the chemist, the businessman, the actress, the jock. Each image, complete with testimonial, invents a little fantasy. The brochure then moves into the meat of describing college life and beyond. The application is a blow-in card exactly like the ones that advertise exercise machines in *TV Guide*, only bigger. The back cover features another testimonial, this one a cheerleader fantasy.

This catalog is typical, although, of course, different marketing strategies are used for different social groups. When advertising to the working class, people likely to be the first in their families to attend college, images like the ones described above are most common, tying college to the purchase of goods. A catalog advertising to a more middle-class audience might use a different testimonial format — images of graduates from the school telling their stories of great jobs they got after graduating. There would be more copy and a certain assumption that the reader knows more about college. The most prestigious universities, appealing to the scions of well-to-do and well-educated elites, adorn their brochures with the images of status and culture; ivy-covered buildings, important sculptures; libraries filled with books; showcasing the tradition and cultural capital to be obtained by going to this institution. Still a kind of purchase, but at Sotheby's instead the mall.

David Riesman (1980) concerned about the development of the marketing approach in college catalogs, has suggested that an outside auditor should validate claims made by catalogs (pp. 241–7). The results of another study, looking at the marketing of competitive liberal arts colleges, suggest that while college catalogs may color the way a college is perceived they usually contain a concise statement of the institution's goals and make reasonable claims (Ragan and McMillan, 1989). But while competitive liberal arts colleges might be forthright in their advertising, many less competitive schools rely on less than ethical means to acquire students. The larger point is we have entered into a new era of college admissions, one that is rapidly changing and not well defined.

At one time there was just one bulletin for a university or college. That bulletin looked like a bible and it told you everything — how to apply, about financial aid and programs of study, requirements, lists of faculty and their research-everything. Now there is typically a whole array of glossy advertising flyers. The publications have different purposes — one to hook the audience, or in the case of larger institutions, a separate hook for each college or area of study. There are separate brochures for evening and special programs. There is a brochure for before you apply and one for after you apply and one for after you're admitted. And like the advertising images at the turn of the century described by Ohmann, these catalogs don't tell you anything substantive. The catalog I just described could be a TV promo for college life in America, very televisual, no specific information, lots of fantasy and lots of effect.

Another campus arena transformed by the advertising semiotic is the college bookstore. Many of the bookstores on campuses where I work have been taken over by Barnes and Noble, one of the largest book retailers in the United States. Colleges sell their bookstore franchises to commercial retailers because of their inability to run the bookstore in the black. There are several reasons for this, the most important of them stemming from a corporate decision by print capitalists. About a decade ago, in order to keep profits at their outrageously high levels, publishers said they would accept only a small percentage of returns on books, instead of allowing booksellers to return virtually any book that did not sell. This put colleges and universities in a impossible situation. There was no way to accurately guess the number of students in a class and books had to be ordered early. Bookstores can try to pressure faculty into using the same books over and over but this is only partially successful at larger institutions, so it has been harder and harder for college bookstores to break even. The university could subsidize the bookstores but the pressures on college budgets and the movement toward a businesslike 'cost accounting' approach in higher education has required bookstores to be profitable.

There have been two main approaches to being profitable; selling things besides books, (the gift shop approach); and selling the franchise to a larger retailer (monopolization). A large bookseller, like Barnes and Noble, can deal with the problems because of the size of their retail organization network. This is one of the reasons college bookstores have moved to commercial retailers. Even before the move to commercial retailers, bookstores at some universities had begun to look like small specialty shops. At an Ivy League university where books used to occupy 80 per cent of the selling space, they have been reduced about 30 per cent, with the remainder devoted to CDs, tapes, cameras, walkmans, calendars, specialty foods, magazines, clothing; what was once a place to buy textbooks and school supplies has become a small up-scale specialty shop that happens to also have books.[2] There have been a variety of transformations. As is common in the retail industry, bookstores market to the appropriate class faction. At an elite highly competitive university, for instance, the bookstore may resemble an upscale cappuccino bar, which does carry books, though many fewer than a decade ago. It has become an up-scale retail shop with good books catering to its upper-middle class constituency. At a more comprehensive university, or the typical state university, the Barnes and Noble bookstore has become a trinket shop and resembles *K-mart*. Often the books are kept behind the counter and you must present your class list to get them; there is no browsing through the books. Books are still available at the university bookstore. But the bookstore, that place unique to the university, with books stacked from floor to ceiling and students actively experiencing the value and prestige of reading; that bookstore no longer exists on many university campuses.

University life itself has become an important sign in the consumer sign culture.

Major daily newspapers run regular Sunday supplements on college life; the *New York Times* runs no less than two annual Sunday pull-outs, indistinguishable in style from the advertising circulars also included with the paper. The college-life supplements are glorified ads, with articles about how to choose college and what to do when you get there tucked in between pages and pages of ads for schools. Universities and colleges constantly bombard all of the media TV, radio and print, with ads for their schools. College fairs have become opportunities to hand out brochures and look more like trade shows than the traditional college recruiting. *US News and World Report* runs three special magazines a year on the best colleges. It's easy to see how this form of journalism can become thinly-disguised PR, any opportunity to advertise is used. A recent article (Wright, 1991) in *The College Board Review* discussed increased pressure on families and the confusion they experience as a result of the college rating game played by the media.

Families are confused because although the magazine rating articles are ostensibly intended to clarify, there is something other than the need for information driving the rating mania. While everyone in higher education is at least theoretically cautious about marketing, many private, less competitive institutions find it increasingly necessary to advertise and market extensively, given the decline of the so-called traditional college-age students and ever-less government funding. A major daily newspaper headline in March 1996 announced 'With competition fierce, colleges turn to hard sell'. The article reports on a number of colleges which, through aggressive advertising campaigns and computer-designed individualized direct marketing campaigns, have not only increased their applicant pools but increased their enrollments and succeeded in offsetting the fiscal problems that began with declining enrollment. The pressures on these institutions are such that they will do what is necessary to survive even if concerns can be raised about the methods.

And as already observed, with the increased competition in the global economy and the resultant growing competition for scarcer middle class jobs, there has been inflation in the academic credentials market. The job that used to require a college degree may now take a degree from a *good* college. McDonough (1994) has discussed this pressure in the economy and also documents the fact that high schools' funding cutbacks on counselors have spurred the development of a new industry — the private admissions counselor to advise affluent low-achievers about their college options. Colleges are desperate for students and students are increasingly interested in colleges with good names, so the image of the university has become doubly important.

Amidst the slick brochures and college catalogs, and the expensive logo-ed clothing and paraphernalia where books used to be, and the PR stunts and the ubiquitous commercial advertising, the signs of college life have changed greatly. Imagination is fetishized in a new, more image-rich and rapid semiotic, which is keeping pace with movements in the mass culture as it too is reduced to images of the commodity and exchange. It appears that the intense and seamless flow of images has a life of its own, but these images did not begin proliferating magically. There are infrastructural forces in the economy and higher education behind this

semiotic, forces that have generated new ideas and new institutions which participate in image production.

Technologies of Control

In 1967 the Carnegie Foundation for the Advancement of Teaching (CFAT) established the Carnegie Commission on Higher Education (CCHE). Its goal was an
organization empowered to undertake a series of research problems dealing with
contemporary campus issues. It is clear that the initial impetus for the CCHE was
student unrest and the civil rights movement of the 1960s. They were very turbulent
times, affecting universities and colleges across America. Only a few years after the
establishment of the CCHE the student movement began to die down but almost
immediately another problem took its place, the caving enrollment picture. It was
the CCHE's report in 1972 that began to reverse optimism about college enrollments
and predict an enormous decline in college enrollment. Seemingly overnight the
sixties were forgotten and the seventies were upon us with economic depressions
and the newly-limited horizons. As previously noted, the university's response
was 'economically reasonable' and it's certainly possible to see why that form of
reasoning was applied to the situation. The sudden shock of this crisis changed
forever the way colleges and universities planned. One factor that insured this was
that demographic research, thanks to new disciplines and technological advances as
well as the colleges' need for information, improved by quantum leaps. Marketing
came to campus and it found not only new ways to lure students but new and better
ways to accurately predict trends. Empowered by success, the scientific study of
college enrollment was here to stay.

The College Board, the organization which administers the SAT test, traditionally saw itself as an organization primarily concerned with the standards and quality of education. It also has a history as a gatekeeper. Barrow said at the turn of
the century if you could pay you could get into Harvard (and perhaps with current
college tuition costs we may return to that system), but changes after World War
II called for a way to regulate who got into the more prestigious universities and
colleges. The College Board became an important part of that process by admin-
istering a standardized exam supposed to measure basic academic ability. In the
boom era of the sixties the SAT was an important ticket, used by admissions
officers and sanctioned by a Federal system of educational support that saw access
to higher education in stratified terms. With so many students knocking at the doors
of higher education, the SAT was a way of determining who was capable of university work and who needed to start in a community college. The SAT legitimated
notions of intelligence, quality; the great man myth.

It also gave students a way to internalize exclusion, seeing it as personal
failure. They didn't get into the good school because of personal failure, they
lacked the intellectual ability, not because they were excluded by forces beyond
their control. That these methods of exclusion followed racial, class and gender
lines suited the purposes of the system — it was a means of restricting access and

maintaining existing boundaries — and did not (in this early era) occasion much protest. The College Board is also a barometer of the times, responding to the concerns in the educational community. In recent years, it has struggled with these issues of quality and sought to identify what defines education. It has certainly tried to make its examination less biased along gender, racial and class lines over its history.

As more and more people began to take the SAT the average score went down. Students from working-class backgrounds who took it, because of their less advantaged culture and education, got lower scores. The partial democratization of higher education in the sixties pushed scores on standardized tests down because more people with less educational and cultural 'capital', to use Bourdieu's term, began taking them. This produced an interesting phenomenon in the seventies. Average SAT scores fell every year, because more students from less advantaged backgrounds were taking the test and they were a growing percentage of the whole because the total pool of college students was shrinking. College officials decried the decrease in SAT scores, pronouncing it evidence for the decline of a culture. At the same time they were growing desperate for warm bodies with which to fill their classrooms (Shor, 1986, p. 74).

Not until the 1980s did the College Board shift its understanding of what they were. Gatekeeping, by measuring the potential performance ability of students, used to be a way the College Board could be part of a school strategy of increasing institutional prestige. (If you are taking high-scoring students you have a better school.) While this is still a strategy used by colleges today, the gatekeeping function began in the era of shortage to assume secondary importance. And as the need for gatekeeping receded, the College Board (finding itself in a culture suddenly awash in market metaphor) began to see itself as a marketing firm. More and more businesses were looking for solid demographic information and the College Board was sitting on a mountain of suddenly interesting demographic data.

In the days when school choice was a simple matter of students searching for the right institution, the College Board used to fund its operations by charging students to take the SAT and then charging them for each school the scores were sent to. Robert Zemsky and some colleagues at the University of Pennsylvania wondered if it was possible to use the wealth of information the College Board had to model the kinds of patterns that went into college choice among students (Zemsky and Oedel, 1983). For Zemsky, this project was a matter of rationalizing the college admissions process such that market segments could be identified and efficiently targeted. In his view this would help the right students get to the right universities and would also help the university to efficiently find students that fit the university and incidentally plan for the future because the university would also be able to accurately predict future enrollment.

Zemsky's vision certainly had many advantages. However, in the competitive climate for non-prestige schools, the goals of Zemsky's project are often put aside in favor of increasingly aggressive advertising coupled with the more refined marketing techniques made possible by the College Board's fund of demographic data. The College Board was capable of generating lists broken into categories, cross-referencing demographic information like family income, region and ethnic background with SAT scores. The College Board was willing to sell those lists to schools. This enabled an institution to send promotional literature to pre-selected audiences, of people likely to want to attend their school. The College Board still officially sees its role as facilitating the movement of students to college and measuring their potential for college performance, but the fact that their activities are in service to marketing imperatives — it just too easy to use College Board lists in a target marketing strategy, tailoring the imagination of the university for each consumer group — is often lamented in their own magazine (Johnson, 1988).

The College Board has now moved into a new era of management, beyond their original gatekeeping function to become a part of a technology with several purposes. They are in the business of desire production. This mechanism includes the older gatekeeping function because we want appropriate desires for the right institutions. But, moving beyond the old system, it is now necessary to nurture desires in all potential consumers, and this can be done with the right demographic information. If you know what peoples' backgrounds and interests are, you can encourage them in the right fantasy. It is also important to be able to forecast trends, which has become very complicated because attempts to produce desire will also change trends.

There are many contradictions here. Colleges in the United States have become much more democratic in the sense that there are more high school graduates going to college. The College Board can be part of the attempt to get many kids to college, still monitoring the quality of students, but it's a tricky issue. Increased opportunity and democratization is often, in our society, in an uneasy relationship with forces of commodification. There are other difficulties as well. It is unequivocally difficult to measure a person's college potential in unbiased ways; all knowledge is culturally based. Whose knowledge is being tested? Issues of curriculum and cultural elitism are only a small part of this whole difficult discussion.

Marketing and advertising of colleges threaten to produce a system of highly prestigious sought-after institutions in high demand, a second layer of less illustrious institutions doing their best to imagine themselves illustrious and a huge number of institutions using all the market techniques they can get their hands on to sell their product to a consuming public. The rapid growth of adult student populations, which is the result of the survival strategies of many universities, shows that the buying public can, and will, be wooed successfully with images of prestige and credentials promising to get you out of your humdrum life and into an exciting new career.

The crisis of higher education is a crisis of capitalism, which tends by its nature toward overproduction. The 'boom' in higher education necessitated the bust. The bust in college enrollments, of course, was tied to not only declines in student-age population but declines in demand due to economic weakness. Bourdieu (1984) speaks feelingly of the generation of the 1970s (p. 143). He calls it the generation promised great hope, only to see economic opportunity decline. The truth of this causes more and more high school students to turn away from college because the pay-off was uncertain at best.

Economic declines of the seventies wrought changes in capitalism as well. I've talked about the slow transformation of the productive sector toward globalization and the development of lean production strategies on the part of corporations. Meanwhile, the consumer sector changed as well. New marketing technologies had made the sale of goods and services possible in tight times, by tailoring products to specialty markets. These new technologies were part of the shift away from a civil society and toward one permeated by the economic on every level. In a culture where college professors use the J Peterman[3] catalog in writing courses, it is increasingly difficult to tell the difference between art and advertisement, film and commercial, literature and mail order catalog.

Baudrillard (1981) discusses this idea with his notion of the 'commodity sign', however he essentializes the notion rather than making it historical: the Baudrillard model developed in opposition to Marxism. In contrast to Marx, who assumed the realism of production and the idea of real needs, Baudrillard argues that capitalism has always invented need, that there are no real needs. Therefore the commodity is merely a sign, something important to the actor who wants to enter the semiotic of commodity-based culture. A person consumes because of the value or meaning of the sign, not because of any 'real' need. Capitalism — and consumption — has always been about produced desires.

Sidney Mintz's (1986) work on sugar production in the Caribbean supports this line of thinking. In the early days of sugar production, sugar had three functions in society: as spice (not food), medicine and preservative. When more sugar started being produced in the colonies it was marketed as a sign of affluence and cultural superiority to the ruling class, the gentry of Europe. It became tied in to the symbolism of world domination, the symbolism of white as pure and superior and the symbolism of wealth and power, and the ruling class began to use sugar more and more as a food. As the rich ate more sugar, the sugar producers became richer and produced more. As they produced more the price dropped and then the middle class bought sugar to emulate the rich. More profits, more production, even lower prices; eventually sugar reached all the way down to the working class. No longer distinctive, sugar was no longer something for the rich to revel in. It became a mass-produced and widely-consumed good and then a basic necessity of life. Indubitably something that satisfied biological needs, though never a real need, sugar was used because of its sign function. Its history is an object lesson in the commodity sign and its transformation of a capitalist society.

Demand for sugar was produced before the modern technologies of demand production developed and is unique in that it did not require force. Earlier attempts to ensure consumption often did. For instance, capitalists in the nineteenth century forced farmers off their land and into the factories so that they would make factory-made textiles. Demand for sugar was produced nonetheless. Demand has always been produced.

The Hidden-hand and the Death of the Real

As the media became more complex and each time the market's attention declined, businesses and marketing firms moved to new and better means of getting our attention. One popular way has been to link a series of products into a campaign. A fast -food store gives away free toys with food purchases, toys which are themselves advertising a movie or TV show. The toy advertises the TV show and the TV show advertises the fast food and the toy manufacturer. This kind of semiotic chain encourages a participant in the consumer culture to move around the chain, i.e., buy lots of things. Many products have small ads for other products, for instance a soda can might advertise a radio contest, and be (certainly not merely a drink!) both an ad for the radio station and the car company giving cars as prizes in the contest. In return the radio advertises the soda and car dealers advertise the radio station and the soda. Recent trends in film demonstrate the Lacanian term 'suture'. In film and television it is increasingly common for sponsors to pay to have their products shown within the narrative. And there is the Internet with a series of advertisements on every Web page. The boundaries between advertising, the world of commerce and other social arenas, begin to collapse in this semiotic chain where all aspects of the culture are on sale. MTV is the ultimate conclusion; the ad for the band (the music video) is the product itself, producing an odd and ironic effect when the programming cuts to a 'real' commercial, and the 'real' commercial seems somehow more substantial than the program, the music video. Colleges, in marketing themselves, have no choice but enter this arena as well. It would be difficult to present images *not* part of this commercial semiotic.

Before going further I want to look more carefully at French post-structuralism. Certain insights appeared in the 1970s among social scientists who were, I believe, unconsciously reflecting on the new technologies of demand production and the resulting implications for the ways we look at society and people. Lacan, Baudrillard and others brought our attention to the semiotic realm, to what they called the death of the real and the signified. Baudrillard in particular abandons traditional infrastructural analysis in his assumption that all demand is a sign and commodities are signs. While these contributions are important, it is the historical unfolding of the technologies and infrastructure of desire production which needs to be addressed. Production is arbitrary, as Baudrillard maintains, but in capitalism there must be production so that people can be encouraged to consume. It is a materialist process that has only in more recent times been possible to see in all its complexity.

At the same historical moment Baudrillard is saying all commodities are signs, and Lacan is saying there is no signified but only chains of signifiers; marketers, advertisers and business people are developing new technologies to deal with the market slump in the seventies. These new technologies are of two orders. There is first of all a movement toward more 'soft,' image-based products and services (for example, videotape, software, TV programming, Disneyland), products that are not primarily signs but are in fact nothing but signs. The social arena is reconceived as a field of possible arrangements where an individual occupies any number of places, in place of the old model of a single joint public space, with a market and a set of consumers to buy goods in it. In Baudrillard's terms, a movement beyond the real.

Mintz's history of the sugar industry shows that desire under capitalism has always been produced. However until very recent times Western culture saw the world in 'real' terms. There were real needs and even after the technologies of consumption learned to produce needs, consumers were still thought of as rational individuals. This vision of the real holds through the Fordist era where large-scale production and mass consumption reinforced the idea of a society of individuated rational producers and consumers. It was still possible to see supply and demand as an equation, even if demand was goosed a little from time to time. However in the 1970s, as a response to crises in capitalism at this stage, new technologies like market segmentation radically changed the Smithian view of capitalism.

Market segmentation saw the social field populated not with individuals but with demographic centers, social groups from a particular set of socioeconomic backgrounds. These demographic centers reverberate with other groups. Marketers speak of primary, secondary and tertiary markets. Markets overlap and if you carefully tailor products you can reach more than 100 per cent of that market. Take portable personal stereos, for instance. Sony produces not just the walkman, but the sport walkman, the outback walkman, the professional walkman, big bass walkman for the boom-box crowd; all essentially the same appliance with the same function but designed and packaged differently. (This is Sony alone. There are also many other products.) People, instead of being conceived and appealed to as individuals who may need or want or be capable of being talked into wanting a walkman, are being appealed to in their roles or functions. They need a walkman for their uptown job, one to go the gym with, one to take camping. People are not being appealed to at all, their roles are, turning lives into demographic fragments. This is one way to think of Baudrillard's notion of 'the end of the social' or the 'death of the real'. People do not exist in this arena at all except as disparate roles.

The fragmented social suited the purposes of business in its drive to sell more and more product, and it was also exactly what colleges and universities needed in their crisis: more consumers. Fragmentation delivered. Students now are not just 'all the college-aged kids', but so many demographic segments; middle-class undergraduates who want to go to law or business school, housewives who want to pick up a few liberal arts courses, working-class high school kids who want to trade up by going to an engineering college; whatever. They have become multiple consumers.

There are many ways the fragmented social can be used to produce demographic statistics of the 'four out of five doctors prefer' type. A large state urban university, one of North Urban's potential 'competitors', wanted to increase its rating with services like Barrons and Fiske. One way to do that was to accept only a higher-ranking pool of students; students with higher SAT scores and better grades. But if they did do that across the board that they wouldn't have enough students. So they raised the requirements for regular daytime admission, and then with rejection notices they included a letter saying the student had been rejected by the daytime college but could reapply to the continuing education school, where they would be accepted. The potential student was assured s/he could take daytime classes, that costs were the same and the degree was the same. No future employer would ever know they came to the university through the less prestigious evening college. The administrators knew that Barrons and Fiske use the daytime college statistics for their ratings. Raising daytime requirements and funneling the lower-end applicants into the university college made it possible for the university to increase its rating without changing its overall population, and the new rating not only enhanced the prestige of the university but gave it a new pool of potential applicants, since better students would be encouraged to apply as a result of the superior rating of the school. Fragmentation takes many forms, making the social nothing more than statistical manipulation. It's no longer a matter of lying with statistics — that would imply a 'real' to lie about — it has become simply a matter of producing the desired social effects. Baudrillard would say the map goes before the real.

Planning and Social Control

The establishment of the Carnegie Commission on Higher Education in 1967 was part of efforts to plan and control the development of higher education and the social movements within higher education. On the national level, the Nixon administration began attempting to manage and control the democratic movement in education as well. There was a clear federal policy of replacing education that produced thinking citizens to take their place in a democracy, with education aimed at careerism (Shor, 1986, pp. 4–5). If there hadn't been any other changes in the economy and society, the Nixon repression of education might not have been very successful. There were, however, many other important changes. 1969 saw the first big economic recession since World War II and this was just the beginning of a series of recessions and economic problems. In such an environment, management in the form of 'instrumental reasoning' was quite an effective means of social control. A generation of children grew up thinking, not of their place in a democracy whose course they could steer, but of how they could survive in hard times. The message they took to heart was that survival depended on buying an education that would buy you a job in the marketplace.

Democratization of education was subverted to the interests of those in power, and in a very particular way, by carefully designing social control to take the appearance of democracy. Students got 'freedom of choice', that is to say, they were offered choices among prepackaged educational goods. This gave them the illusion of freedom, but the days when they had a real hand in changing existing systems of inequality, by opening admissions, getting rid of grades and making decisions about the directions and meaning of education, were over. Democracy had been subverted to commodification.

Nowadays the liberal arts colleges can advertise sub-disciplines like women's studies, African-American studies, semiotics, Marxism; all relatively new areas of study opened in the 1960s when the curriculum was democratized. Political consciousness (of students and others in the population) became one of the first new 'products' sold in the marketplace of commodified culture. What had begun as a democratic political movement was successfully taken over by the semiotic of commercialization. As these ideas became products they were changed by market forces, while education itself was becoming a market-driven arena. Faculty members not only respond to market forces in the kinds of courses they offer to students, they do the same thing with regard to the kind of scholarly work they pursue. Fashions move through academic disciplines at an accelerating rate and it's necessary to keep up with the latest 'images' being sold in the market of intellectual capital. Deconstruction, post-structuralism, practice, postmodernity — all these were once ideas but are now merely product, changing moment by moment in response to market pressures. Commodification masquerading as democracy serves an economic need and makes social control possible as well, using the instrumental reasoning of the marketplace. It offers people the hope, if not the reality, of good jobs after school. It does not encourage the production of knowledge or discussion about where we ought to go as a nation, what should we do about the environmental crisis, how could we have sustainable economic development that would be good for people and not just transnational corporations.

The crisis-ridden seventies conjured an administrative army of people to create new programs, advertise them, make sure there were faculty to teach them, recruit specialized students, create new colleges, so on. During this decade, administration jobs grew two to three times as rapidly as the faculty. The production of the image, (the packaging) of education was, and is, demonstrably more important than the education itself. This is the clearest indication of education's commodity status — institutions care very little about the use value of the education they offer. The image, on the other hand, is of utmost importance because the image is what produces exchange value. Image became more important then content (Haug, 1986, pp. 40–1).

And the images being sold in the in the 1980s as a result of this new administrative army of curriculum developers was no longer fashionable political movements but a course in real estate, hotel management, physical therapy, healthcare administration etc. These are the new service economy technocratic positions. They open the hope of an area of job growth but may fall short of their promise. I spoke with a student who, after finishing his business degree in the early 1980s returned to night school to get a nursing degree. He had been working in a bank in a job that was going nowhere at a time when business was glutted with business degrees. At the time that he started the nursing program, there was a shortage of nurses and salaries were twice what he was earning in the bank. Half-way through his BSN, the professional literature was predicting a glut on the market of nurses. All of this was well before the recent closing of hospitals and downsizing of healthcare. The product offered looks good, people go for it but then it turns out to be not what they needed. Career professionals don't see a bit of irony in this, they say with authority that the average worker will have to retool five times in the modern world; it's just the nature of a fast moving economy.

An administration class growing by leaps and bounds also shifted the balance of power within the university. As we have seen, corporate management has been taking behind-the-scenes control of the university since the beginning of this century. But by the mid-seventies universities were visibly dominated by administrators, if for no other reason than that there were so many of them, and as chapter 9 will show, this has begun to have an negative impact on curriculum and course content. Administrative culture is not inculcated in the academic values and practices it seeks to regulate in the name of institutional effectiveness. The faculty can no longer say 'we are the university' because they are so clearly only a very small part of this image-producing machine. The need to produce more product and bring in more consumers, directly linked to the rationalization of the productive sector, and seeing universities and colleges in market terms makes the movement of the faculty toward worker status inevitable. It is no accident that faculties have responded by attempting to unionize.

The issue of who controls the university has been unmasked. Universities, while they still pretending to believe in the tradition of faculty control because it harks back to a great university tradition in the past, and such an image is a useful marketing tool, are in fact being run by salespeople and marketers. Ivy-covered tradition simply has no substance in the present. Faculty members are glorified in the brochure's advertising pages only to be completely squeezed out of all actual decision-making in the university. The contradiction is very clear to the faculty.

This new market orientation of education normalizes crisis. When schools first began using marketing technologies to bring in students they had no idea how successful they would be. During the early eighties at many North eastern schools they very successful indeed. It was not uncommon to see a newspaper article about the declining secondary school population side-by-side with one about local college enrollments going up. Most colleges saw this as a good thing and worried only about doing it again next year.

Advertising does work but how well? Are there absolute limits to how much the market can expand? Where these are major concerns a flexible work-force is essential. It enables the administration to expand or contract the faculty depending on the number of students who do respond to the advertising. The flexible work force also offers the advantage of keeping productive costs down. Schools, by keeping a large portion of the work force temporary and/or part-time, get flexibility and cheap labor at the same time. This keeps faculty members on their toes, not to say on edge. What will enrollment be? Will I be able to teach my research area or just basic courses? Will my course run? Will there be release time? For part-timers the questions are even harder. Will I have a job? How much will I work? How many institutions will I have to work at? What new hoops do I have to jump through to get jobs?

Market technologies were clearly the response to the enrollment crises of the seventies and eighties. What is less clear to all involved is how advertising changes relationships: faculty to workers, students to consumers, administrators to business people. The many contradictions this process produces for workers, students and for the culture have made it difficult to know what education is. Marketing and advertising are undeniably technologies of social control. We tend to see them, are encouraged to see them, as simply ways to help the market along but that model is wholly inaccurate. These technologies redefine the market, the product and the people involved and impose their definitions willy-nilly on the world. This apparatus of power is itself producing new contradictions as it wields its power to name, classify, define. Workers resist, consumers get bored, and the product is criticized for lacking substance. Education in America today is coming under increasing attack for not being what it is imagined to be.

Running through all of this is the confusion between democratization of education, which is a political activity, and commodification, which is not. Thanks to policies of the Federal government and the university's own administrative responses in the 1960s and 1970s, commodification has become the dominant force. There are still many educators who understand that the issues of access to education and the right to question the status of knowledge are political questions and ones which moreover need to be addressed by a democratic society. There is ideological hegemony; the model of the marketplace and the influence of instrumental reasoning, but there is also conflict and contestation as well.

Notes

1   This is not surprising. Barrow (1990) shows that the dominant force on the Board of Trustees of America's colleges and universities in 1870 was the clergy (p. 47). The university was never a medieval guild in the US but it had close ties to the image of the church and monastic orders. The common way of referring to college as being not the 'real' world probably came from this religious image.
2   In the 1980s when Barnes and Noble, an indirect subsidiary of Exxon, took over a university bookstore they filled it with petroleum by-products: plastics, polyester tee-shirts and sweatsuits that advertised the school, CDs, tapes; all petroleum based goods. It is a nice isomorphism. The retailer is indirectly owned by an oil company and fills the bookstore with indirect oil products.
3   J. Peterman is an up-scale mail order clothing business whose specializes in a dazzling array of tongue-in-cheek bourgeois fantasies.

Chapter 8

Symbolic Struggles

When I began my research into the commodification of higher education, the notion of commodification was a new one. In the years since then, commodification of culture has come to be widely recognized as a ubiquitous process with profound implications for all aspects of life. In the 1990s it is being cited by both major political parties in Washington as the solution to our social ills. The marketplace is increasingly the crucible in which decisions are made, so (the reasoning goes) let EVERYTHING compete willy-nilly in the marketplace — including government policies concerning public services, welfare, health, and education.

The commodification of education has to be seen against a shifting landscape which is both transformed by and transforming education, politics and life in general. The market is seen as a panacea, but it opens up many contradictions. First, the market rhetoric is often the sign of an institution in crisis.[1] Higher education has had to manage declines in enrollment over the last two decades and declines in government funds. These fiscal crises have opened the way for a commodifying discourse. But further, as a state institution or state funded institution, higher education has had to deal with the decline of the vision of the welfare state in the United States. This crisis of legitimacy is part of the overall political landscape in the US where the state is expected to manage on less and less. I will argue that this fiscal climate and the climate of economic decline for average Americans is the backdrop for the controversies around political correctness and multiculturalism.

The idea of political correctness — PC — has undergone an amazing metamorphosis during this period. At first it was a joke lefties liked to tell each other, a kind of shorthand reference to agreed-upon values almost invariably at odds with those of the ideological right. Paul Berman (1992) suggests that PC began[2] as an approving phrase of 'Leninist left' and then took on a more ironic tone within the left as a critique of a humanist position (p. 5). Berman sees the complexity of the term as having a lot to do with what he sees as the two moments of radicalism in the 1960s.

> The first phase was an uprising on behalf of the ideals of liberal humanism
> — an uprising on behalf of the freedom of the individual against a soulless
> system. The second phase was the opposite, as least philosophically. It was
> a revolt *against* liberal humanism. (*ibid.*, p. 6)

Berman goes on to point out that this critique was theoretically very sophisticated especially in France and grew into the post-structuralist ideas that attacked not only capitalism but the oppressive nature of liberal social systems in general.

One response to the extreme left has been to turn PC into an epithet the right invokes against the entire spectrum of the left, 'correct' coming ironically to denote INcorrect. In this move the extreme leftism of the Tel Quel and Maoist groups of the 1970s is conflated with mainstream liberalism to invoke an image of an all-pervasive communist phantom oppressing young minds on college campuses. The following quote comes from a 1991 article in *The Chronicle of Higher Education* on Donald Kagen, Dean of the College at Yale University. The sub-heading of the section of the article I will quote is titled 'Fighting left-wing orthodoxy'.

Mr. Kagen, who is also professor of history and classics and author of a highly acclaimed four-volume work on the Pelopponnesian Wars, has held the job (dean) for two years now. (He's planning on three more.) But only recently has he emerged as a national figure, an ally of traditionalist scholars who contend that higher education has become dominated by a left-wing orthodoxy.[3]

Most recently, PC has come to mean — and not just for the right — a new way for 'them' to cheat 'us' in the debates around multiculturalism. In a global economy where more of us are competing for less — jobs, university admissions, goods, etc. The tendency to see members of other groups as the enemy, and to see those other groups as organized conspiracies is becoming more common. Below are two quotes, the first from D'Souza where he articulates the 'culture wars' as an unqualified 'them' against a qualified 'us' where excellence is lost in the exchange. What is further interesting about D'Souza discourse is that he is part of what I would call a new strategy of representation on the part of the political right. He is an 'other' person from non-Western culture who has converted to the greatness of the West.[4] The second quote from Todd Gitlin suggest that the controversy is not about loss of a great tradition but maybe just an increase of minority representation.

But hardly anyone predicted the possibility of a tyranny of the minority, or more precisely, tyranny in the name of minority victims. Marching under the banner of equality, the new race and gender scholarship seems in reality to promote principles of inequality-minority sentiments, placed on a pedestal while majority sentiments are placed on trial. Those who challenge this intellectual framework are accused of collaborating in the historic crimes perpetrated against minorities. (D'Souza, 1991, pp. 214–5)

Let's face it: some of the controversy over the canon and the new multiculturalism has to do with the fact that the complexion of the United States — on its campuses and in the country as a whole — is getting darker. In 1960, 94 per cent of college students were white. Today almost 20 per cent are non-white or Hispanic and about 55 per cent are women. (Gitlin, 1992, pp. 185–6)

In this chapter I will argue that the attacks on multiculturalism and political correctness are a form of terrorism the discourse of which emanates from the extreme right and is then taken up by different state institutions like universities, federal agencies, the Congress, etc. and large profit-making media institutions, television, radio and especially national magazines and newspapers. The political motivations of these groups are often very different but are interlocked in a complex system of representation requiring both a forgetting of the past and a fetishized imagination of the present. This process takes place in a landscape continually transformed by capitalist relations. The particular forgetting of the past involves a forgetting of the history of education and its role in US society. Forgetting the history of groups and the discourses of the past allow us to imagine a product — the canon — which is being threatened today.

David Harvey (1989) has argued that 'capitalism is a process and not a thing' (p. 343) and as such is constantly transforming social life:

> Precisely because capitalism is expansionary and imperialistic, cultural life in more and more areas gets brought within the grasp of the cash nexus and the logic of capital accumulation. To be sure, this has sparked reactions varying from anger and resistance to compliance and appreciation (and there is nothing predictable about that either). But the widening and deepening of capitalist social relations with time is, surely, one of the most singular and indisputable facts of recent historical geography. (*ibid.*, p. 344)

The process of reimagination I have discussed in the preceding paragraph is one of the ways higher education is being drawn into what Harvey calls 'the cash nexus and the logic of capital accumulation'. The transformation of social life that this process of capitalist expansion brings about has helped to produce a number of new social conflicts around the imagination of identity and the politics of knowledge.

Speech Codes: University of Wisconsin

PC and multiculturalism are very hot topics in and around educational institutions. Two recent examples of the ways in which the discourse has played out are instructive. The first story comes from the University of Wisconsin by way of the *New Republic* (Emerson, 1991). A fraternity held a mock slave auction, where students in black face (pledges) were offered for 'sale' to the audience. Not surprisingly, the performance offended African-American students. They filed a complaint, and when the Student Disciplinary Committee ruled that the auction was constitutionally protected free speech, they occupied the administration building in protest. Then university Chancellor, Donna Shalala, and the university administration responded to this situation by creating a rule (UWS, 17) that forbade speech 'demeaning to individuals'. As the *New Republic* article quoted the rule:

> Students may be disciplined for 'racist or discriminatory comments, epithets or other expressive behavior directed at an individual or on separate

occasions at different individuals' if these 'intentionally demean the race, sex, religion, color, creed, disability, sexual orientation, National Origin, ancestry, or age of the individual or individuals; and create an intimidating, hostile, or demeaning environment for education, university-related work, or other university-authorized activity.' (*ibid.*, p. 18)

It is instructive that the concern of the university in this was less the slave auction — no disciplinary action was taken against the fraternity or its members — than that the student demonstration might result in negative press and that might bring outside pressure on the university from civil rights groups, so it acted to forestall this. This was straightforward, if lamentable, but when the university was then taken to court by the ACLU because the code violated First Amendment rights, the media then responded to this as an example of the way political correctness threatens our personal liberties. The article quoted above is part of a larger set of *New Republic* articles about the problems of political correctness on campus, the special section is titled 'The derisory tower'. This special section of the articles on different examples of PC on college campuses in the *New Republic* is introduced with a warning of the loss of freedom on America's campuses.

There are several interesting things to be noted about this example. As so often when political correctness is at issue, there is a collapsing of various groups and lines of force into a monolithic Other. Often the Other is the so-called left wing radical. Now, wake somebody up in the middle of the night and ask them what a left-wing radical is, and nine times out of ten you'll hear . . . someone who grew up in the sixties, carried one of Mao's little red books and believes in cultural revolution and the indoctrination of citizens through a controlling totalitarian discourse. Or words to that effect, evoking an imaginary reality, a product of dreams and television rhetoric.

The PC position in this instance is not a Mao-spouting longhair, but a university administration, a bureaucracy which sees its legitimacy in the management of factions which must be satisfied or silenced; parents, students, the political left and right, faculty and the ACLU. That this patently contradictory and impossible task is something a university administration is expected to perform is one of the contradictions of modern bureaucracy. And it was from this impossible set of requirements that the Other was constructed by the media. This Other is constructed out of a collapsing of the different lines of force and the different interests in the situation; i.e., the university administration, conservative journalists, students and families involved, the faculty, etc.

The author of the *New Republic* article points out that the University of Wisconsin code was carefully written to deal with individuals and not hate speech in general because more general university regulations have been struck down by the court. He further goes on to point out that while the code may be legal it would not have been able to stop the slave auction because the action was not directed at individuals. He quotes the administration as saying that the code is a 'welcome mat to minority students and their parents' (*ibid.*, pp. 18–19).

I suggest that in its effort to manage the crises of legitimacy produced by a globalizing economy and transnational movements of labor, capital and information, the university administration imagines the subject[5] as a product of an imaginary homogeneous, internally coherent culture. The doctrine of cultural relativism encourages us to protect indigenous cultures from ethnocentric slandering. This imagination is a form of nostalgia for the other of the colonial era, (Koptiuch, 1991; Dominguez, 1992; Clifford, 1988) invoking not only the homogeneous other but the imperial self. It takes place, however, in a fragmented late twentieth century landscape where different groups seek their interests through the educational apparatus, and institutions of higher education seek financial solvency and institutional legitimacy through hegemony over the production and dissemination of knowledge. In their role as both the arbiters of culture and the arena where greater employment opportunities can be gained through education credentials universities seek to protect their preeminence in defining what is legitimate social knowledge, while at the same time providing equality of access to that education for diverse groups. Part of this process involves the university in defining who the groups are that they serve as well as telling them what their history is.

There is also fear associated with notions of multiculturalism and political correctness. In a 1991 article from the *New Republic* one author states:

> The more closely we look at the relationship between multiculturalism and its host culture, the more peculiar it becomes. Multiculturalism is not just about equivalence of world cultures; it is also about their equivalences *within* Western culture. The tremendous energy of multiculturalism, which now reigns in universities, on public television stations, and in arts organizations, comes not from its noisy enthusiasm for other cultures, but from a frightened response to, and animus against, the West. (Rothstein, 1991, p. 32)

Even for *New Republic*, which often publishes attacks on multiculturalism, there is an odd tone in this quote. First, the use of the term 'host culture', implying that multiculturalism is a guest, and not a very good guest either. It is a guest who when invited to talk about 'equivalence of world cultures' (benevolent patriarch that the host culture is), instead attacks the host. Frightened response? Animus against? Talking about my next-door neighbor in these terms would mark me as anti-social at best, and probably paranoid.

The Water Buffalo Case

The second case is the so-called water buffalo case at the University of Pennsylvania. A group of Black women students participating in a sorority initiation were reported to have been making very loud noises near midnight outside a dorm. A number of students yelled at them to shut up, and one yelled, 'Shut up you water buffaloes; if you want to stomp go to the zoo.' The girls complained to the university. The police went from room to room asking the students if they had yelled at the girls. All students denied yelling except the one who made the water buffalo comments. Penn at the time had a speech code and speech monitors were used to see if disturbing hateful language was being used to hurt people or groups, so the complaint was taken up by the university judicial system. The subsequent hearing was to be closed but the student being investigated talked to the press. The story first came out in a small upstate New York newspaper and was later picked up by the *Wall Street Journal* and hit the media big time. The student claimed on the evening news that in his culture 'water buffalo' is not a racist remark and he was not guilty of anything, but just another example of a person being victimized by the politically correct. The university was very slow to act at first. Eventually the speech code was eliminated and the university is now finishing a new code that includes first amendment protection.

Once again, there is a bureaucratic administration conflated with a radical left agenda; a collapsing of lines of force into an imagined other. What is interesting about the Penn case is the way it became media spectacle. Newspapers and magazines routinely and dutifully carry the statistics of the increasing numbers of sexual assaults on campus, hate crimes, and abuses to members of minority groups, but these lived social relations, ways in which people interact with people in large numbers even when motivated by grander forces; are all presented as things — statistics, cold facts empty and devoid of emotion, human life . . . or death. They're easy to miss, carried as they are on back pages with the weather and the stock prices. But the student oppressed by the forces of PC was picked up by the national media. Even an issue of *Firing Line* was taped on Penn's campus to underscore the national attention to the 'water buffalo' incident.

Further, the issue became one of national political interest as the Clinton administration nominated then University President Sheldon Hackney to head the NEH as the quote below from the *Philadelphia Inquirer* indicates:

> When University of Pennsylvania President Sheldon Hackney recently (a) expressed compassion for frustrated black students who trashed one day's press run of the *Daily Pennsylvanian*; (b) declined to suspend Penn's 'hate speech' code when it was enforced against a white student who called noisy black women students 'water buffaloes'; and (c) was nominated by President Clinton to head the National Endowment for the Humanities, the *Wall Street Journal* thought it had discovered an editorial writer's dream: a symbol of all that's wrong with politically correct American colleges and its politically correct government, wrapped up in a single mealy-mouthed academic. (Rottenberg, 1993, p. A09)

In no way do I wish to belittle the conflicts of race, gender, and class on today's college campuses. They are a current struggle over the issues of power and representation that one would necessarily expect to find in the institutions where knowledge is produced. At issue are the basic questions of what constitutes knowledge and who has the authority to say so. But I would suggest that there is a fetishism of the contradiction and crises on America's campus. The mass media fetishize aspects of the crises to make commodities — commodities that are themselves without substance — the images and stories of a beleaguered liberal democracy fighting the foe of tyranny. Here is a marker of the new political economy of information or what Derrida (1994) has called the 'media tele-technology, economy, and power' (p. 39) The stories serve the profit interests of the new fortune 500 companies, the newspaper, a magazine, television info/entertainment industries, while serving an ideological function as well. In the processes of fetishizing the events on campus the subtlety of the positions that people inhabit is lost.

The simple opposition of PC/multicultural/anti-humanist versus the voices of freedom and tolerance is a symbol that not only has sold well on television and in newspapers, but it is a symbol that allows us to make simple ideological choices about good and evil, something that American like in the movies and their lives. It has been the stuff of special issues of *The New Republic* and *The Atlantic*, as well as being in national newspapers and on television. It disguises the variety of interests we have been trying to spell out. The bureaucratic hierarchy of the universities have a different set of interests from those of the mass media. One is trying to produce a great deal of profit the other is often trying to manage crisis and secure a minimal profit or manage debt. A university administration sees its job as providing education for a broad spectrum of the American public, while at times having to seek actively paying students, private donations, and grant monies to stay out of the red. These contradictions of the university administration are often the pressures for politically correct acts. Left-wing professors are often imagined as dangerous powers by the media in these events, but more often than not they are relatively powerless. Conservative pundits often imagine themselves disenfranchized by a powerful political left, but they are often connected to large economic and political institutions. And so we have a spectacle presented to the public where little is what it seems and an imagination of power is seen as threat to our democratic values when in fact the real powers (the media and big business) have little concern for those values.

Of course, all this is not to say that university administrations don't have contradictory motivations or even that they are often in the wrong. It is also not to say that there aren't real cultural conflicts, perhaps irreconcilable ones. But cases involving PC and multiculturalism, as represented by these two examples, often have a hysterical quality to them, an unspoken fear of regulation by an other who remains nameless. All of this is happening at the historical moment when forces on the right argue vehemently that the welfare system, together with non-traditional morality of sexual preference groups, feminists and minorities; are conspiring to threaten the moral fabric of the country. That the right speaks so loudly to these issues tends (perhaps this is intended) to obscure its influence in rolling back the rights of women, minorities and others in an supposed effort to reclaim some imaginary good old era. The right dislikes, so they tell us, regulation by government, although it would seem to be not regulation per se that is targeted; only certain forms of regulation imagined to be issuing from the 'Spectre of Marxism', to use Derrida's phrase.

Representation and Control

It is very important to have a good story, one which speaks to the public's experience, while at the same time involving complex chains of signification that create
an imaginary. For example, Camille Paglia and Katie Roiphe have acquired a kind
of celebrity beyond what one would expect of a university professor and a graduate
student. These two are white women telling us that there are no crimes against
women, only machinations of the evil PC. So to fear rape or be concerned with
sexual harassment is a sign of weakness. In the ideological climate produced by
Paglia and Roiphe, the route to success for women is not to complain but to assume
the mantle of machismo. While these voices grab front page news, we are being
encouraged to forget the ongoing real crimes against women and minorities, but we
are also implicitly being urged to forget the history of struggle against the powerful.
(Aronowitz and Giroux, 1993; Herman and Chomsky, 1988). Defining who is the
other and what they have done is an exercise of symbolic power. In this way Paglia
and Roiphe are taken to represent all women — because they, and the media, say
they are; and if they are not victims then by extension no one is.

Henry Giroux (1993) in discussing the politics of literacy points out that where
the representation of others is produced through textual borders, difference is produced discursively (p. 368). If we are to maintain our hegemonic relation to them,
we cannot accept cultures and gender groups as existing in the world. Such a positivist notion makes these groups devoid of process and means that membership
and affiliation is a simple matter. Rather the mechanism to control and subjugate
groups has happened through text, as has their struggle against subjugation (Apple,
1993, pp. 206–7). As Edward Herman and Gerry O'Sullivan (1989) point out in
The Terrorism Industry, there is a complex mechanism whereby government interests and media interests are complicit in representing the acts of some groups as
terrorists, while acts of our government (or its allies) are not terrorism even when
the atrocities are greater on our side. This was certainly the case in Vietnam, where
the enemy was imagined as a band of thugs (the Vietcong) who were threatening
the good people of Vietnam. The US presented itself as the fighters for freedom.
The reality was much more complex and recently we in the US have acknowledged
our own terrorist acts against the Vietnamese. The process of imagining the other
as a source of terror has domestic implications as well.

Domestically, one much-used mechanism in the construction of subaltern groups
is the metonymic convention of part for whole. The Willie Horton ads were an
example of this. Horton was clearly used by the Bush campaign as a sign of the
group, Black men, and the ads were widely criticized for representing all Black
men as violent criminals. It hardly needs to be pointed out how rampant this
tendency is in the media. It is no less than a dominant code for the representation
of minority groups. Of course, the part-for-whole mechanism is not always used in
a negative way. Often it shows groups as sexy, having a sense of style, and other
more or less desirable attributes.

The mechanism of representation used in the debates around political correctness and multiculturalism are part of a process Herman and Chomsky have called

turing consent'. They involve the complex relationship between govern-
versities and corporate interests and the ways these interests get expressed
ss culture. The process is not an active conspiracy. The net effect of
government and corporate interests, all of them clearly invested in the maintenance of power and control of an increasingly more plural and complex society, is
far more overwhelmingly powerful than any possible conspiracy. These mechanisms of control ironically fuel both the contradictions being seen on America's
campuses and the conflicts that become the events that universities feel they have
to manage, and they also dictate the actions universities will take in that regard.
More and more students grow up amidst packaged images of minority groups in the
mass media and come to college with calculatedly prepackaged ideas about who the
other is. Many white college students assume African-Americans are there because
of affirmative action. They assume that affirmative action means less-qualified people
taking things that belong to them, because they have been shown in the media that
this is so. The environment produced by these predispositions is not only conducive
to hate speech and violent acts, it works to subvert the basic aims of affirmative
action, which are to redress patterns of inequity and level the playing field.

Of course there has been a liberal reaction to these representations that abhors
the ways minority groups have been treated. Many policies and court decisions
have attempted to rectify the ways minority groups have been treated by this
powerful set of forces. This is fine as far as it goes, which is not far enough. What
that liberal reaction has not looked at is the ways in which the dominant discourse
has constructed the Other. Not only is there a conservative discourse, hysterical
in tone and rife with expressions of fear toward the Other; there is also a liberal
discourse, which self-consciously seeks reconciliation with the Other. The liberal
discourse also produces difference in this complex semiotic. The Other is seen as
a homogeneous cultural whole. The nineteenth century anthropological notions of
culture and cultural relativism have helped to produce a reification of the Other
which is *also* a product of imagination. I will call this tendency as liberal multiculturalism and I see it as different from a more critical multiculturalism (Aronowitz
and Giroux, 1993, pp. 205–8; Turner, 1993, p. 414) Liberal multiculturalism involves
two levels of symbolic collapse, or processes of condensation. First, the diversity
of interests, orientations, class background are ignored in favor of a more internally
homogeneous imagination of the minority group. Further, the struggle over access
and control of knowledge and power, the interests of intellectuals, university professors, activists, university administrators and politicians and particularly the profit
interests of large mass media organizations are collapsed into the PC versus those
who are against PC.

Education as Product

While these issues have broad interest, it is worthwhile to digress and think for a
moment about the commodification of education. What is interesting about the
discussions around education today is the way that education is talked about as a

thing or, as Taussig (1992) says, having both thingness and spectrality (p. 4). It is an object, but a special kind of object; an object that has power to do things for us and to us. On a local radio-talk show there was a discussion of core curriculum and multiculturalism. At the beginning of the program, a local professor of English said that parents would like to know that there is a 'solid product at the core of under-graduate education'. Here in the language we hear people use daily is the vision of education — a product sold to parents for their children, that has some real substance.

Throughout this book I argue that it was in the early twentieth century that higher education took on its current form as it adapted to, and was influenced by, the developing industrial infrastructure (Veysey, 1965; Levine, 1986; Barrow, 1990; Noble, 1977) Other theorists have discussed the ways in which higher education became structured along corporate lines as it took on more market roles of provid-ing skilled technicians, R&D labs and later state funding (Apple, 1982a; Noble, 1977 and 1989; Cowan, 1990). This period also saw the establishment of the under-graduate curriculum, that canon of what is to be learned. Interestingly, in order for the canon to become such it had to be reimagined. It is now no longer books and ideas that people read and share and teach about, education has become a thing to package and distribute to consumers. In a sense it has become a commodity, one of the many new commodities that young people must line up for in their quest for a better social position. In this way, mass-culture, upward mobility, the reification of cultural capital, and the commodification of education can be seen as inter-linking processes. In a real way the production of education and the production of mass-market commodities are both linked to the same processes of expanding industrial commodity production and are both driven by the politics of a liberal, market-exchange polity.

Our current imagination of higher education and scholarship often involves a forgetting of this historical process. We seem to think the curriculums of Princeton, or Harvard or Chicago simply exist. They are things which have a facticity the status of which seems never to be questioned. But they in fact came into being as an object, through the process of reflection, itself stimulated by the developing industrial structure. Before the canon, there is knowledge and teaching and schol-arship — the practices which remained to be imagined as a thing — a canon. Therefore current efforts to question the canon or question modes of interaction and scholarship are viewed as attacks on things — rather than as part of the pro-cesses of knowledge production which run counter to the dominant commodity form developed over the twentieth century, and as such, an integral part of know-ledge production itself.

Further, we doubly forget the past by imagining culture and society as a bounded entity sharing language, culture and history. This has always been con-tested. The very industrial infrastructure grew up in the era of colonialism and neo-colonialism. Our relationship to other groups has always been one of a powerful nation with imperialistic interests. Individuals and groups as representatives of those who fall out of this shared liberal rational polity have been disciplined both corporeally and discursively. Herman and O'Sullivan (1989) point out that we used to call those we now call terrorists, bandits or savages (pp. 5–7). The histories of oppressed people of the Caribbean, Central America, Africa have always been represented in the dominant press as homogeneous groups seeking to steal from us. Their history is not seen as a valid one but one that deserved forgetting. In the recent past, this list tended to include the Irish, Italians and other immigrant Catholic groups who were also seen as an other who attempted to survive at our expense. The current canon was born of ideological domination and has to be maintained with continual symbolic and physical violence.

Derrida's Irony

There is an irony here forcing us to read the current debates around political correctness and multiculturalism symptomatically. Derrida points out in his recent work on Marx that the economic and political liberalism of the West has been established more or less globally. Never before has Western culture enjoyed greater world influence at precisely the moment when many all sides of the political spectrum fear the threat to the Western Liberal tradition from multiculturalists and others advocating the supposed 'tyranny' of political correctness. The question is why would such a large powerful worldwide movement fears such an object as political correctness — a phantom itself created by the apologists for the liberal democratic Western market-oriented tradition? Or to put it differently, in what ways is assuming a mantle of the dispossessed useful in the maintenance of power? The question it seems to me needs to be pursued in the history of popular culture, higher education, global transformations of capitalism, the shifting space-time continuum of global accumulation and the still extant contradictions Marx identified at the heart of capitalist accumulation.

Herman and O'Sullivan (1989) have shown thinking about the United States and its position in the global economy that maintaining global political and economic dominance involves a good bit of repression and that repression produces its own violent reactions. An important part of the symbolic effort is to see our acts of aggression as 'justice' and the Other's acts of violence as 'terror'. There are political and economic forces then that produce fear, because it is in their own interests in maintain global economic domination. These interests are presented to the domestic public as a dangerous enemy outside who uses terror to try and take away our freedom.

But there are other interests in the global economy as well, the interest of markets and trade across cultures. At the very moment that one locus of power is pumping out images of the fearful other, other loci are promoting a liberal view of multiculturalism, perhaps the other who is different on the outside but a self-maximizing individual on the inside. This other is useful in the global marketplace where future economic growth is essential. In this view we see the other as exactly like us. Especially in the post-communist era, the other is a rationally enlightened self-maximizing consumer. If we reach out to him/her, and learn their culture, we can open new markets to our products and expand our economic horizons.

We saw this contradictory set of images recently where during the NAFTA debate Mexicans were the market-oriented Other who would be good partners, and then later during the politics of Proposition 187 they were the conniving Other taking our jobs. Behind these images is a complex movement of contradictory economic forces involving the movement of capital labor and products. Both the conservative view and the liberal view of the Other miss the realities of people, their histories and their struggles; because neither view is tied to the experiences of people. Each is tied to ideological instrumentalism of institutions attempting to direct the contradictory process of capital accumulation to its own advantage. Each view is a 'conservative' one, in the broader sense, trying to manage the contradictions of global capitalism. When these forces are criticized or even pointed to by intellectuals, those intellectuals are imagined as an evil which will overpower the society, corrupt the young and destroy all that the liberal state has been about.

The Factory of Knowledge

Part of the social movements of the 1960s, which were themselves motivated by a reaction to the new state apparatus Kerr termed the multiversity, the war machine, and the globalizing capitalist economy, was to lay claim to the production of knowledge. Knowledge, it was argued, was the product of human social activity, particularly the struggles of ordinary people to claim their own lives, fight the tyranny of power and define their own futures. People, it was reasoned, produced knowledge and that knowledge should be recognized. In the 1960s women, minorities, gays, workers and other groups not only demanded access to higher education but demanded full share in the production of knowledge an decisions about where that knowledge was going. In the 1960 Jean-Paul Sartre wrote and essay titled 'A plea for intellectuals'. Sartre's article comes against this backdrop of changes in the university in the 1960–70s. While in some ways university reform went much further in France, Sartre (1974) was very aware of the contradictory role of intellectuals (pp. 228–30). He suggested that whenever intellectuals challenge the status quo they are demonized as the cause of everything that has gone wrong.

These new groups of intellectuals generated a growing awareness that knowledge production was being dominated by what was called at the time the military industrial complex. When the early 1970s leftists began to ask, who owns the universities? The answer was clearly, 'government and big business'. The new student groups began to challenge the right of these groups to control knowledge and the products of the universities. Growing tensions on America's campuses, coupled with the resistance to the Vietnam war, produced a serious crisis for the State, and this created the space for an imagination of terror, the slide of civilization in barbarism.

While much of the struggle during this period of time was about a real contest over the control and definition of knowledge, and questions were being asked anew about who controlled the university and what kinds of knowledge should be pursued; conservative forces attempted to show that there was evidence that these non-traditional pursuits were in fact producing a slide into barbarism. The hysteria associated with the changes in the composition of college students has been with us since the seventies. Newspaper articles and scholarly research constantly points to the decline in SAT scores of the new freshman class of students. This decline looks as if American students are getting dumber but in fact, as many critics have pointed out, it only indicates there is a more plural college audience some of who are not as skilled at taking the SAT exam — an exam which was designed in the first place to test dominant values and linguistic skills as well as to measure college performance (Shor, 1986, p. 74).

Shor provides an interesting analysis of the development of the meritocratic system in higher education in *Culture Wars*. The Nixon administration, alarmed by the level of political activity on America's campuses, moved to defuse it by maneuvering education toward a career-oriented curriculum. The administration was also encouraged in this direction by the recessions of the seventies and the way business responded to these recessions. More and more manufacturing work moved offshore in the seventies, leaving only low paying service jobs and some high paying service jobs for the college educated (Harrison and Bluestone, 1988, p. 25). In this new environment many are going to college to compete for these few high paying jobs. This introduced an era of degree inflation, as discussed before. The BA became only part of what was needed to succeed; you then needed an MBA as well.

The meritocratic emphasis initiated in this period was itself as much a product of the commodifying process as it was the response to the perceived crisis. In the sixties, students were concerned not only about education, but about power as well. They were concerned about access to education, who controlled the curriculum, the purpose of grades. It is no accident that during this period disciplines like sociology experienced tremendous growth in enrollment. Students quickly saw that they needed an understanding of the institutional and power structures in order to have a say in the future of those institutions.

Nixon policies worked to take that power away. The Department of Education bombarded students with the meritocratic images, the FBI and the CIA harassed them, and the National Guard shot them. For the most part, repression worked and the grass-roots critique was silenced. Left in its place was a continual flow of media analyses of higher education. Popular understanding of the politics of education was reduced to a Time-Life/Warner Communications perspective. What students lost during this period was their claim to the production of knowledge. The student of the late seventies and eighties became a consumer, to be managed by a discourse of consumer rights and consumer control. The thingness of education had become a pawn in a struggle for hegemony. That thingness needed to be solid and powerful, seen as a diploma or certificate that could be bought and then turned first into cultural capital and then into cash on the job market.

As the 1960s political struggle faded in the background issues of WASP male hegemony resurfaced. Allan Bloom, a man imprisoned by the Black Panthers at Cornell in the sixties, returned in the eighties to write a runaway best seller called *The Closing of the American Mind*. Bloom's book represents the flip side of the nostalgia for the past that was overtaking the country; he expresses both the hysteria at the loss of hegemonic control by the WASP elite (at the very moment that hegemony has been most clearly reestablished), and fear that the educational sign has lost value. In the marketplace, cultural capital having been reduced to technical rational expertise, the idea of great civilization seems to be hollow. Bloom, in his overtly racist book collapses the emptiness of the educational sign onto the slide into barbarism. The American mind is in decline because (he says) students are read Chinua Achebe instead of Shakespeare and Plato. In other words, multiculturalism is the external enemy upon whom we can blame the devaluation of our capital, and not (as one might postulate) the internal bankruptcy of the system of signification.

The hysteria in higher education about the loss of control of white Anglo-Saxon supremacy is paralleled in the general culture by the nostalgia for earlier decades in the twentieth century. In advertising, images of the colonial are popular as fantasy themes around which the goods are presented. Kristin Koptiuch, (1991) in her vision of the 'third worlding' of America sees both the revival of categories of cultural other and liberal cultural relativism as ways to manage immigrant groups, social strife and new crises of control.

Careening over the Landscape

The revolution in information technologies and the new political economy of information, coupled with continued globalization of the world capitalist economy has led to completely new crises that are just beginning to be felt. Social scientists are beginning to use terms like transnationalism, Roger Rouse (1995) has recently stated:

> More corporations operating in the United States are foreign-based, more US corporations are involved in other countries and more migrants are caught in a chronic state of divided orientation and allegiance.
>
> In these circumstances, it is, I think, vital to approach the contemporary United States from a transnational perspective, to see it not as a clearly bounded and internally coherent national space or as global epicenter of determining transformations but as fluid, contested and constantly restructured site in which different and divergent circuits of internationally organized capital, labor and communications collide with one another as much as with the increasingly tattered remnants of 'local' ways of life . . . (p. 368)

Rouse cautions us to not see this in itself as a new state of being or as the corporations eclipsing the power of the state but as a dialectical process where 'the national and multinational has been giving way to one between the national and the transnational'. (*ibid.*, p. 368) In this transformation of the accumulation of capital, boundaries are being reworked, labor, capital, materials, goods, images and information are establishing new patterns of flow and with those new flows come new contradictions. As global unemployment reaches frightening levels and a new crisis of overproduction is on the horizon, the spectre of Marxism looms. As Derrida says, not the old Marxism of essentialized teleologies and groups, but a new Marxism made up of the growing disenfranchisement of the world's working populations, the polluted unemployed and underemployed poor, minorities, women; the subaltern who are now found everywhere in the world; no longer united by geographic space but by a new spatialization — of the global constrictions of commodity production and consumption.

Their stories, their knowledge, their losses and victories are a powerful critical voice that brings the whole global Western liberal democratic market-based political economy into question. The failure of the new world order is huge, but it is spatially dispersed. Aronowitz and Giroux (1993) in *Education Still Under Siege* state:

A critical multiculturalism represents an ideology and set of pedagogical practices that offer a powerful critique and challenge to the racist, patriarchal, and sexist principles embedded in American society and schooling. Within this discourse, the curriculum is viewed as a hierarchical and representational system that selectively produces knowledge, identities, desires and values. The notion that the curriculum represents knowledge that is objective, value free, and beneficial to all students is forcefully challenged as it becomes clear that those who benefit from public schooling are generally white, middle-class students whose histories, experiences, language, and knowledge largely conform to dominant cultural codes and practices. (p. 203)

Part of the global flows of the new world order are all the dispossessed laborers, who find themselves in American ghettos united by the fact that their languages, histories and experiences do not conform to the dominant order. In this new context the powerful groups of the nation face new challenges to hegemonic control and a critical multicultural literacy becomes a threat.

It is no accident that there is an ideological war being waged over the term *multiculturalism* in education. It is certainly no accident that a phantom 'politically correct' has been fabricated. The tools of the hegemonic discourse are an imaginary memory of the past, a time when the Other was part of homogeneous cultures and ethnic and racial boundaries were clear (this is the content of Gingrich's tele-course on American civilization) and an equally imaginary present haunted by PC ghosts plotting to take our freedom away. These are tools for subjugating a growing number of disenfranchised people, whose numbers are beginning to approach those of the dominant group, for whom a critical education might mean the power to resist the new regimes of capital accumulation.

Taussig in his discussion of terrorism in *The Nervous System* talks about giving a talk at a university where the colleague who invited him was happy to discuss incidents of terror abroad; almost as if multiplying the examples assuaged the unspoken, nervous fear that we too might be participating in a system of terror. Taussig (1992) says:

> But it is well known that some twenty-five years back this particular university, for instance, had applied relentless financial pressure on the surrounding ghetto-dwellers and that during that time there were many strange fires burning buildings down and black people out. There was hate. There was violence. Nobody forgot the dead white professor found strung up on the school fence. (p. 14)

Taussig goes on to talk about the university developing the third-largest police force in the state to push the residents out and ultimately transforming the public space around the university into a sort of fortress. He continues:

> It became unlawful to post certain sorts of flyers on university notice boards, thus preventing certain sorts of people from having any good reason for being in the vicinity. Thus, in time, while preserving the semblance of democratic openness, the university came to reconstruct the ghetto into a middle class, largely white, fortress within an invisible *cordon sanitaire*. Terror as usual, the middle class way, justified by the appeal to higher education, to the preservation of civilization itself, played out right there in the fear-ridden blocks of lofty spires, the fiery figures of burning buildings, and the calm spotlights of policemen with their watchful dogs. We remember Walter Benjamin: 'no document of civilization which is not at the same time a document of barbarism'.

The attacks on multiculturalism and political correctness are part of 'terrorism the middle class way' that Taussig describes. They are attacks that an older model of liberalism with its notions of cultural relativism and homogeneous bounded cultures is at best powerless to defend against. At worst, liberalism is forced to become part of the way in which less powerful groups are cordoned off and silenced. As the new lines of force develop out of the transformation of the system of capital accumulation to national/transnational, there will be new fissures, more chaos produced by global unemployment and more alienation from a system of empty signification. Terror is a byproduct of these new lines of force, often organized but sometimes not, as it masquerades as the ideals of a unified liberal democratic nation.

As higher education itself becomes more of an industry providing product to a student market, it becomes the center of these controversies. The institutions of higher education are dominated by a liberal multiculturalism. That liberal discourse sees minority groups as homogenous and sees them as reified entities rather than as a heterogeneous groups of people, with differing amounts of social power, engaged in a struggle with the institutions of power and knowledge. The view of the bounded whole, the minority group as homogeneous, is one the college tries to maintain and protect and it does this with ethics codes and speech regulation. This liberal view is one of the ways university administrations deny their contradictory positions in a society that promises equal opportunity while managing inequality. The university sees its mission as having representatives of different groups on campus as their way of protecting equality of opportunity. But the liberal model of culture is not just one that is part of the institutions of higher learning, it is also part of commodity producing corporations, their marketing departments and national business as they attempt to communicate cross-culturally in the global market. It is a model with force behind it. The economics of the consumer society drives the lip service to different cultures, tastes and interests.

Further, as different groups come to get different things from the university, as they see themselves as consumers of education, the politics of confrontation becomes one of consumers' rights and not people trying to piece together the process of history and the constitution of knowledge. There is no room at the university for such a process, once arguably the only process appropriate to the setting as the university manages the conflicting demands of its various consumers. The school must be (seen to be) a safe comfortable place where all can come and consume knowledge.

Against these pressures are those coming from the political right. As managing the global political economy becomes more contradictory both at home and abroad, the discourse of fear proliferates, and the contradictions on campus become exaggerated. What is needed is a critical multiculturalism that requires people to produce knowledge out their own struggles, and the communities and groups they form. We need to discuss how particular lines of force were created, where the boundaries came from and how they have moved. In short, the viability of the university is tied to the members of that community powerfully resisting the model of consumer of knowledge and taking its own responsibility for the production of knowledge.

Notes

1 Recently the Head of the CIA, talking to the national press club, used market imagery to talk about the new role of the CIA. He refered to internal and external clients of intelligence services in the new post cold war era. Certainly part of what is going on is the CIA looking for a new logic to legitimate its existence. They now sell intelligence services. External clients would be people who apply for the services and internal clients would be the arms of the government itself like the White House.

2 See also Ruth Perry's article 'A short history of the term politically correct,' in *Beyond PC: Toward a Politics of Understanding*, edited with an introduction by Patricia Auderheide (1992) Greyworf Press. Here she also argues that PC has always been an ironic term. She sees it as the left's tendency to crticize itself.

3 The article quoted is titled 'Activist Dean at Yale brings controversy to his post with strong views on study of Western civilization' by Carolyn J. Mooney in *The Chronicle of Higher Education*, (pp. A11, A12) 19 June 1991. See also 'Tenured radicals: How politics has corrupted our higher education' by Roger Kimball (1990) New York, Harper & Row.

4   There is a complex set of representational moves happening in conservative circles where Western culture and civilizations greatness is further underscored by members of minority communities. The subaltern is now a convert to western culture and values and is amazed that there are white males are part of a conspiracy to undermine Western culture by suggesting that other traditions might be equally valuable.

5   Here I am thinking of Althusser's notion that the school in the modern era is an ideological state apparatus, with the goal of imagining the subject as its chief ideological function.

Chapter 9

Real Struggles

Part-time faculty are designated by myriad titles and are classified by a confusing variety of appointments and salary terms, so that comparison among them is difficult. They are called 'adjuncts', 'special lecturers', 'acting faculty', 'wage-section faculty', 'hourly', 'short-term', 'emergency' and 'temporary' employees — despite the obvious potential for abuse latent in these appellations. Their salaries are usually but a fraction of those of full-time tenure-stream faculty of equal qualifications. While often hired year after year, they are commonly appointed for one term only, paid by the course or credit hour and denied benefits and regular increments. While usually held to workloads below those of full-time faculty, many nontenure-stream part-time instructors carry teaching loads equal to or greater than those of full-time faculty. (From 'Higher education's exploitation problem', the AFT's statement on part-time faculty employment, *On Campus*, April 1996)

Introduction

This chapter will focus on some of the contemporary problems that faculty members face in the university today; problems generated by the political and economic forces discussed throughout. I will focus on the part-time and temporary work which is the centerpiece of the new flexible accumulation in higher education. But we will all be feeling the effects of flexible accumulation in the coming days and so I will move on to ways the professoriate in general might be threatened. Finally I'd like to suggest some of the ways these problems impact on students as they deal with the commodification of knowledge. That commodifying process contributes to the delegitimation of that knowledge and foretells a total collapse of legitimacy in higher education.

Two of North Urban's graduates who have taught at a number of institutions in the area ended up teaching at River College, a small liberal arts college. River, like many small colleges particularly in the East, has moved in the last ten years away from a general liberal arts curriculum to specialize in the professions. It has a large education program with a good reputation in the area for training teachers and a physical therapy program which many students and faculty consider a major draw for students coming to the college. Enrollments have been very good, the college is at full capacity and building dorms to house more students. Ned Harris and Sam Phillips work in the Sociology Department. Sociology is not a big program but the Department does have about fifteen major and many more minors; and so it is not an irrelevant program. Ned is a full-time faculty member and Sam is part-time; with four full-time positions and three to four part-time positions in the department, in all. These numbers are not unusual. There might be some concern about the high percentage of part-timers in the department but this could be chalked up to the size of the school and the department. There are many more full-time faculty in other programs, especially education, and physical therapy.

But beneath the official statistics and their attendant rationales (the line that things are not as bad as they could be) lies another story. Of the full-time faculty members, one is emeritus, one shortly retiring and the two remaining full-time faculty members are temporary positions; the chair (who is on a temporary contract) and Ned, who is on a three-year temporary contract created by making him the Director of the Core Curriculum — an administrative job — in addition to teaching. The part-time faculty teach very different amounts. Sam teaches three courses a semester and is teaching about as much as the full-time faculty. Other part-time faculty teach less. The Department's voice in the College is limited by these structural facts and is considered by most at River a service department in a college primarily engaged in technical training. Tellingly, the Sociology Department's vision of the route to greater prominence within the College has been to come up with more professional training programs such as a Bachelor of Social Work program. Under the mantle of the liberal arts college River is a technical institute.

Ned's position was created by the Dean of the College, but his professional standing in the college is tenuous and filled with ambiguities. In a meeting the Dean once slipped and referred to Ned as a part-time faculty. The Dean immediately realized his mistake and they were both embarrassed. Shortly after that episode, Ned attended an honors convocation and his academic robe was too small. As he was walking with other faculty, and feeling embarrassed about the shortness of his sleeves, an economist walking with him said 'well you don't have your PhD do you? Maybe the sleeves are *supposed* to be shorter.' Ned, shocked, replied that of course he had his PhD but the economist had turned without hearing him. For Ned this incident encapsulates his situation; a job that doesn't quite fit — a combination of administrative and teaching responsibilities, pieced together by the Dean to hire Ned (an academic with administrative skills) — that makes him look awkward in the eyes of his colleagues and fails provide legitimacy.

Ned's situation is instructive. In the last decade administrative jobs have grown much more rapidly than teaching jobs. While faculty have increased by about 22 per cent administration has increased by about 80 per cent over the last decade.[1] These statistics are experienced by younger faculty in very personal ways. One Assistant Dean of an evening program I spoke with had a PhD in history. She said she hadn't been able to get an academic job so she went into administration; shortly after we talked she was hired by another college to head their evening division. It was very clear to her that while an academic job was no longer possible, administration was the way to realize one's personal career goals. The increase in administration is partly bureaucratic expansion but it is also a response to the new conditions of flexible accumulation. Schools are attempting to market new programs, reach new markets and manage a faculty which is more mobile and less committed to the institution. All of this control requires an apparatus to exact it.

If we look at the careers of Ned and Sam over time we see another aspect of this story. Ned and Sam are part of a network of about a dozen or so colleagues who have been helping each other find work for several years now. Each has worked at a number of institutions, in temporary full-time jobs, part-time jobs of a single course in a program and part-time jobs where they taught three to four courses a semester and came to be seen as a significant part of the Department by students; sometimes by faculty as well. They recommend each other to jobs they hear about and sometimes take a direct hand in helping to hire each other. They have not, as yet, been associated with a single institution seeking to lay claim to all of their considerable energies and talents as teachers and researchers, so have been by their consciousness and their actions an entrepreneurial workforce.

Statistics comparing full- to part-time employment, often used as a measure of how the profession is doing, are not an accurate way to see the changes taking place in higher education, at the center of which is 'flexible specialization'. Flexibility refers to both of the range of possible courses the faculty member can teach and the institution's ability to expand or contract that faculty member's role. If someone is needed to teach many courses over a period of time s/he may be given a more enhanced contract. If the institution is threatened with the loss of a teacher they need they may even offer a one-year (or more) full-time contract. Central to both survival in the role as flexible worker and the way they are exploited is the expectation of marginality and invisibility. In an ironic way university workers in the United States are in a similar position to foragers in places like Indonesia, where modernization and land development policies require erasure of the indigenous people who inhabit the land (Tsing, 1994).

Invisibility

Part-time faculty, and sometimes temporary full-time faculty as well, are invisible. No one knows them; they often don't even know each other. (At one institution where Sam has worked for several years some other part-time faculty know him only by reputation; they've heard about him and know that he teaches there but they never see him.) Often, part-time faculty are not listed in the university catalog or even the phone directory. They don't participate in commencement, convocations or holiday gatherings. They don't go to lunch with full-time faculty, they don't have a voice in department meetings, faculty senates, or other committees. There is no space which they occupy.

Since there are structural biases against the part-timers, as well as the obvious constraints of time and geography, part-time faculty who work in different places must make strategic choices about where they invest in their visibility. This will often be where there is more, or more regular, work or the carrot of full-time work.

Choices may be made to work only in the evening in one institution, day-time in others. Many people must make these choices and they result in unusual patterns of collegial interaction. Part-time faculty see some colleagues frequently if their teaching routes happen to converge, but others are invisible to each other, even if they teach in the same department. Collegial networks like Sam and Ned and their friends grow up around people who know each other socially or from graduate school, much less commonly from working together, because most part-time faculty do not know the full-time or part-time members of other departments. There are almost no activities that include part-timers as a group, either by themselves or with the other faculty.

Invisibility is sometimes billed as advantage. Full-time colleagues will say to part-time colleagues they like, 'be glad you don't have to go to committee meetings', or 'my whole life is wasted in meetings, at least you don't have to deal with that'. While it is true that the freedom from the formal side of the bureaucracy looks appealing, it also results in the part-timers' input on departmental and university business being minimal. In this and many other ways part-timers' standing and professional power is carefully circumscribed. They are expected to provide teaching labor, not influence the direction of the department. This belies the undeniable fact that part-time labor is the backbone of university teaching. Many Eastern universities use part-timers to teach up to 50 per cent of their classes. In teaching institutions where there is less concern over symbolic status, such as community colleges, willingness to use part-timers knows no bounds — one community college where I work hopes to move to a 100 per cent part-time labor pool.

The use of part-time faculty is only one facet of the growing proletarianization of faculty. State universities have started to track their faculty into teaching and research faculty. This is done by rewarding articles and grants with leaves and course release time. Increased teaching loads make it difficult to publish or write grant proposals without leave or release time, creating a competitive environment which pits workers against each other to compete for scarce resources. Some win, many more lose.

Full-time, but temporary and untenured, faculty are often let go at the end of their contracts. This strategy is commonly used at more prestigious universities and colleges where heavy use of part-timers would be too damaging to their reputation. Young faculty are hired in full-time positions with the hope of a tenure-track position dangling at the end of the one-, two- or three-year contract, but the contract is not renewed. Academic departments in this setting, where image is of paramount importance, are divided between a few highly-paid faculty of repute and a large group of under-paid, never-to-reach-tenure teachers. Departments hire a few expensive faculty stars to create a desired image and then use a large number of lower-paid faculty to do most of the work. The lower-paid include the temporary full-time and part-timers.

Part-time faculty are the bottom of the system of faculty stratification, the top is high-prestige full professors, (important because of their political position in relationship to the university administration or because of academic status in the world at large). Immediately below the heavy hitters are tenured faculty, the tenure-track (people hired in expectation of being considered for tenure at the end of several years), one-year appointees, visiting lecturers and finally the part-time. In this hierarchy, teaching load is often a marker of low status. Faculty have status in inverse proportion to their teaching requirements, and part-timers have the lowest status because all they do is teach,. Of course, many schools do value teaching, but there is structural pressure to see teaching as low status. Often the administration's efforts to raise the discourse around good teaching is an attempt to compensate for this structural dilemma.

Different kinds of part-time employees tend to break down by field. Bourdieu (1984) shows that cultural capital has a tendency to be inversely related to financial capital. Business people and engineers, because of a greater orientation to the accumulation of capital, often hold full-time jobs and teach on the side. In the humanities and social sciences where capital is largely educational and cultural, the part-time employees are more likely to seek full-time academic employment and therefore need to support themselves with a number of part-time jobs. Even within the social sciences there are differences. Psychologists and economists are more often full-time employees elsewhere, teaching for extra money or their own personal enrichment; while anthropologists and sociologists are usually gypsy academics. All of these groups of part-time faculty are important, and certainly their professional lives are all shaped by the imperatives of the flexible workforce, but I will limit my discussion to those part-time faculty who are working to support themselves with part-time academic jobs while looking for permanent, full-time, tenure track academic employment. This group is the bottom of the academic underclass; the migrant workers of higher education.

If we look at the campus in cost-profit terms, as corporate mentality is wont to do, in an era of diminishing returns it makes sense that universities should strategies their use of teaching staff the way that they do. The well-known faculty earn their high salaries in advertising value, while the lower-paid do most of the work. The tenure system makes it difficult for institutions to adjust their work forces to the enrollment or the financial situation of the moment. Tenured faculty are difficult to fire.[2] It is even difficult to fire tenure-track people; after all the whole purpose of tenure is to provide stability and security for academic scholars and teachers. When a university has financial problems, as many do; and if they try to fire new hires in tenure-track positions, the administration has to face a very angry faculty. Tenured faculty and their positions are a department's institutional power. Loss of any tenured position represents not only a larger share of the workload for those remaining, but a threat to the viability of the department, not to mention a threat to personal security. Part-timers, on the other hand, can be fired with impunity. (Many full-time faculty are sensitive to the plight of the part-timers but they rarely do anything about it for fear of the political implications.) Part-timers don't even have to be actually fired, they can simply fail to be rehired. They are the university's flexible work force. If enrollment is high more part-timers can be hired. If money is tight, the part-timers are not rehired.

The function of invisibility has very specific time-space implications for the part-time worker. First, there are many kinds of part-time faculty (Leslie, *et al.*,

1982; Abel, 1984) and this fact is another of the reasons for their invisibility. Many institutions are quick to point out that many of their part-time faculty are professionals elsewhere, or are young mothers, who of course could be working full-time if they didn't actually prefer the flexibility of part-time. And of course these things are sometimes true. In their drive to replace a stable teaching staff with a flexible work force colleges and universities use all kinds of temporary employees.

Many part-timers do have their primary status and roles elsewhere, so they put no energy into developing a place for themselves in the university setting, and the university responds in kind. Part-timers are paid almost what might be considered a courtesy honorarium. Because they are considered flexible employees they are not listed in the phone books or on the rosters. They often don't know their teaching assignments until the last minute. Many departments don't have desk space, phones or office support for part-time faculty. The full-time faculty respond to this invisibility in the expected way, by not seeing their co-workers. Many full-time faculty do not know the part-timers in their own departments, they certainly do not invite them to colloquia, and they rarely realize these people are scholars with interests similar to their own. In recent years there has been a growing awareness of this problem, together with efforts to make university facilities available to 'independent scholars' and to recognize part-time contributions to a department. But the issue is tricky and the visibility of the part-time faculty member must always be carefully managed.

Most universities and colleges do not have a part-timers union. In the universities and colleges that are unionized part-timers are often included with the full-time group and their interests and needs (very different from most full-time faculty members) ignored though they pay the same dues. One of the mechanisms that allow the full-time faculty to do this is part-time invisibility. In a unionized school where Sam worked he complained to a tenured faculty member who was a union representative about having to pay union dues although there was no representation of his (Sam's) interests. The union representative's straight-faced response was that Sam was 'unique', and because there weren't that many part-time faculty at the school it was understandable the union hadn't evolved any ways of representing their interests. To the anthropologist's ear, this rationale sounds oddly like what elites in places from Indonesia to Latin America say when asked why their countries don't have policies protecting native populations from outrageous exploitation. It's very common to hear that there are no indigenous people or that they have all been assimilated into the mainstream; simply, that there is no problem. They don't exist. Of course often the same American academics who are very concerned about the representation of indigenous peoples abroad don't see the marginalization and invisibility in their departments. The union representative Sam talked to admitted 'it was true the English department was mostly part-time people'. They were invisible.

Part-timers are complicit in this invisibility; some because they have other full-time investments, others because they move around so much. The gypsy academic, the person seeking full-time academic employment who experiences the brutality of being discounted and made invisible on a daily basis, can come to internalize this oppression. Part-time faculty exclude themselves voluntarily by not attending faculty meetings, commencements and the other social functions of academia. This is partly explained by a reluctance to do anything not being paid for; part-timers get paid, after all, very little, and even if they are willing to spend time gratis, they are kept busy hustling from place to place just earning a living. And unsurprisingly they usually have little emotional investment in the institutions for which they work, so it is understandable that not many part-timers show up at faculty meetings and the like, but the fact is by not participating at all part-timers collude in their invisibility and do nothing to gain a voice. In cases where part-time faculty do participate in the day-to-day academic politics, full-time faculty and deans and even presidents can become sensitized to their issues. Participation can help part-timers join the network of jobs and research opportunities, while self-exclusion limits mobility.

Part-time faculty are also complicit in their invisibility because they are embarrassed by their positions, having often internalized their position in this complex political economy as personal failure. This internalization of failure happens even to social scientists with objective knowledge of the forces that have landed them where they are. Double-think allows intellectuals who are often very clear in their critique of meritocracy (in other arenas) to believe implicitly in meritocracy in the academic arena. Social scientists with a very sophisticated understanding of the structural and cultural mechanisms of inequality and of the way meritocratic belief disguises the individualism implicit in that meritocratic idea; hence disguising the structural mechanism of inequality, often fail to bring that knowledge to their own practice in the university. It is a paradox that in order to critique meritocratic ideologies in other arenas academics feel the need to believe in free scholarship and the meritocratic ideal that the best ideas will rise to the top, at least in their departments. In this way scholarship is deeply complicit in the relationships of power and the structure of inequality in the United States. This faith in the meritocratic ideal in higher education is often shared by part-timer and full-timer alike though their experience of academic life contradicts that belief.

While part-timers and temporary faculty internalize their failure and cooperate in their own invisibility, their full-time tenured colleagues engage in another kind of doublethink about their career successes. In my field, anthropology, many of our mentors tell stories of returning from the field in 1968–70 and finding jobs lined up for them before they've unpacked. These stories have become apocryphal, part of the mythology of the discipline. This same generation of senior scholars, looking at a job candidate who has been on the job market for a number of years, with no full-time job experience, will exclude her/him assuming there must be something wrong with this person for failing in the system so miserably. I will expand on these ideas in the last chapter. Social scientists, especially anthropologists and sociologists, who have been admonished by C. Wright Mills to engage in the 'sociological imagination' still as a group fail to see the larger external forces that have gone into producing either their academic success or their place in the academic 'underclass'.

The gypsy academics, both full and part-time temporary workers, are the bottom of the university pile. Abused by a system of power that barely acknowledges their existence, many of them are deeply discouraged. They know they will probably never be offered a full-time job at any place they teach part-time and so they are likely to be stuck in this low status position for a long time. This lowest part of the work force is also subject to the most empty-headed bureaucratic control and the worst abuses of the system.

We can look at the gypsy academic along two lines of analysis. First, we will think about the twin forces of selection and exclusion, (Bourdieu, 1984 and 1988; Willis, 1981). How do adjunct faculty allow themselves to be at the bottom of the pile? How do they help choose their own fate? Second, what macro-structural forces are there that select against certain individuals? What are the features of these larger force of exclusion? How do they change? Finally, I will also look at how perceptions of space-time enter into the analysis of selection and exclusion, (Harvey, 1989; Fabian, 1983).

Exclusion

Time has always been a primary mechanism of academic exclusion. Slow progress on PhD dissertations or publications tend to be seen as a sign of laziness or lack of genius; in either case, failure. This has not changed, as the academic job market becomes more difficult, 'slow' is still a way to label failures; a way people can blame themselves for their failure. The main official exclusionary mechanism for adjunct faculty is still the PhD. Academics pursuing a career as an academic are usually working on the PhD. Only a small percentage of adjuncts have completed their PhDs., and it's not hard to see why. Under the best of circumstances, the degree can take a very long time. The gypsy academic often works, perforce, in two to four colleges at a time. (It is not uncommon to teach six to eight courses a term. With the pay averaging between $1500–3000 a course, it's possible to have more work than is humanly possible to do and still not be making enough money.) Teaching is the main obstacle to rapid finishing of the PhD, which leads directly to the second mechanism of exclusion. There is an assumption in any field that speed is associated with intelligence. The young 24-year-old with a doctorate will be perceived as brighter and better than the 34-year-old who has only just finished. (Of course, the 24-year-old will also be cheaper to hire in most instances, requiring less money to live on and having relatively little job experience.)

Further, finishing a PhD in a soft economic market is a double-edged sword symbolically. On one hand finishing in a timely fashion lends credibility to personal character and the quality of work. On the other hand, having the degree gives a faculty member more trouble justifying being part-time. Part-timer status for the PhD candidate can be a plus, it indicates teaching experience and being good enough to hire even before the degree. It allows the full-time faculty and the part-time faculty to imagine the PhD candidate's future as promising success; 'it's a harsh market out there but you'll get a job'. But actually having a degree interrupts that imaginative process with the harsh reality that the possibility that the person is not going anywhere. Ned Harris complaining about being asked about how his dissertation was going by full-time colleagues who had hired him and knew he was finished is a case in point. For some older tenured faculty it is important to imagine a hopeful future for younger faculty even if they have to forget and distort facts to do it.

Cary Nelson (1995) has recently written about the difficulty of this process for younger faculty and the double edge of publishing. For Nelson the same contradictions and issues of imagination come up for young scholars after they finish their degree and face the dilemma of to publish or not. Publishing indicates that you are a serious scholar and are not a hack, but at the same time publications can limit you in the job market because the faculty who might hire you will have more trouble imagining you in their own ways. Nelson makes a very interesting argument that consensus and the future of academic programs are imaginative processes going on in the minds of the tenured faculty, projected in the form of hopes onto younger scholars. If a younger scholar has an extensive publishing record, the faculty cannot imagine him in the ways they may like or need. The reality is always less, more restricted than the promise and so publications may actually hurt chances for a job.

One of Sam Phillips' colleagues is Oliver Olsen. Oliver also moved from a variety of full-time and part-time jobs after finishing his PhD at North Urban. At interviews, Oliver, who has been a very diligent and well-published scholar, often faces the further embarrassment of having more publications and papers given at scholarly meetings than many of the people who interview him. The cracks in the meritocratic system become very apparent and are detrimental to the applicant. Oliver says that this puts members of the hiring faculty on the defensive and certainly does not work to his benefit in interviews.

As we moved from the sixties, a time when there was a great need for university professors and other college graduates as well, to the late seventies, when the supply far outstripped the demand, there was something Bourdieu calls degree inflation. Credentials are not worth as much as they used to be. As mentioned above, many anthropologists of the last generation have told me stories about coming home from fieldwork to jobs waiting for them. In that generation of the late sixties in many fields, completing the dissertation was often the requirement to move up to associate professor. In the present market even among those who have completed their PhDs there is the often a need to publish articles (some publish books) before getting their first job. Publication is yet another mechanism of exclusion for adjuncts. It is just as hard to develop a long list of publications while teaching a number of courses as it is to write a dissertation, further extending the time it takes to come to a point of being a marketable commodity. And publishing is a double bind — publishing a lot proves you're not a hack academic but it may exclude you from potential jobs.

Another important issue of the current job climate for young professors is the status of the institution granting the PhD, the intellectual cachet to degrees from prominent institutions. This is another aspect of the meritocratic ideology — if you are a serious student and have done good work you will have gone to a good school. But this meritocratic belief forgets the critique of meritocracy and elitism that was part of the 1960s and 1970s. The 1960s and 70s produced a political climate where the rejection of the status educational system was a respectable decision. In the novel *Nice Work* by David Lodge the heroine, Robin Penrose, chooses to go to university at Sussex rather than Oxford or Cambridge. In the English context this was a choice of high quality, non-elite education; something also important in the States on the public university campuses. Many young intellectuals were concerned with education, its political position and the role it plays in democracy and mobility. The concern is a valid one. Obviously education is an important gatekeeper in Western democracies (Willis, 1981, Bourdieu, 1988). Then too, the Nixon administration in the United States worked to erode the emphasis on education for a democratic citizenry and encourage education for career mobility (Shor, 1986). Lodge shows a parallel movement in Great Britain when Robin's mentor in the novel tells her to leave Sussex and do her PhD at Cambridge. The sixties are over, he tells her.

Embedded here are some important points. 'Fashionable downward mobility', such as the democratic student movement, was not only a way to democratize education but it worked to democratize the work place. As that era came to an end, pedigree again became an important issue. By the 1980s it had become absurd; most major magazines were devoting a special issue annually to the prestige ranking of colleges and universities; almost as a hot seller as the swimsuit issue.

Many young intellectuals who chose less prestigious institutions in 1972 for political reasons found themselves completely frozen out of the academic marketplace by 1979, creating a 'lost generation' which has been the subject of much media attention. This is symptomatic of the Bourdieu's degree inflation. Not just the media but faculty and deans too are looking everywhere for prestigious degrees. The ranking of one's university and department have become very important issues, although this is not always consciously acknowledged. Many have internalized the status system without reflecting on it. From childhood we have seen ourselves defined by grades, college board scores; then universities attended and worked at. Many professors working at institutions of so-called lower status feel as if the low status of their university is a measure of their failure.

Selection

Much of this work has looked at the political-economic and historical forces that go into the structure of exclusion and its transformations. My emphasis has been on this because we have failed to seriously account for these forces affecting our academic production. But in any set of given conditions social actors choose from a limited set of strategies available to them (Bourdieu, 1990c, p. 63). These strategies are not be completely constrained by rules though they are limited by the objective forces. (A PhD from State U in 1979 is not restricted to one avenue of achieving academic employment, but s/he will probably be more limited in choices than a graduate from Ivy U.) Further, social actors have differential knowledge of their situations. That differential knowledge sometimes helps to achieve their goals but it also often works toward exclusion. And the actors are often complicit in the exclusionary process. This is what I will call the subjective mechanism of exclusion. These subjective mechanisms themselves are not self-generated, but like advertising, arise from a technology of consumption. They are produced.

Internalized mechanisms of exclusion are important in Western society. Willis (1981) suggests, in his study of a working class high school, that the economic inequality intrinsic to capitalism and the democratic ideals of Western democracies are in fact contradictory forces. In England (and in the US) people have been convinced to choose their own inequality. If they wouldn't do this do this it would be necessary to use external force and then there would no longer be the illusion of democracy. These internal mechanisms of exclusion are part of the active personal strategies of individuals, strategies that limit them as often as they improve their conditions. As strategies, they are subject to patterns but they are not all alike and they do change. The very words I write about these things is part of the process of change.

One of the most successful mechanisms of control is internalization of failure. This gets broad support in American society and indeed is a major mechanism of social control in society at large. The dark side of the myth of the individual is the myth of the individual as locus of failure. The power of this myth is hinted at by the fact that social scientists who so clearly understand structural forces in other areas fall prey to this myth themselves. Faculty at less prestigious universities, as observed, often feel bad about themselves. They take this feeling of inferiority out on their students, by telling them how bad they are, how incapable doing the work that is done at 'better' universities. This feeling of failure is one of the ways professors pass on the inculcation of class position to their students. Students at prestigious universities are assumed to do good work; the attitude will be inculcated in the students, they often come from backgrounds where this cultural capital is already presumed and they will perform well. There will be a few 'Cs' and no 'D' or 'F' grades. The attitude at state universities and less prestigious colleges is quite different. There it is assumed most students are not worthy and will get 'Cs' and many will get 'Ds'. Only a few are considered able to get 'A', 'B' (or 'F') grades. (A teacher attempting to go against this system, particularly if an adjunct, will quickly learn the limits of academic freedom, but more on this later. Full-time faculty also experience the pressure to grade students down.) I observed a conversation between two tenured faculty at a non-elite state university, one a tenured professor and reputed to be one of the hardest graders in the department, being chastized by the other for giving more than 10 per cent 'A' grades in a required course. The entire process of meritocracy becomes internalized and people not only feel bad about themselves but view other faculty and students through the lens of perceived failure to climb the social status ladder.

The internalization of the history discussed in previous chapters as personal failure is part of what has happened to adjunct faculty. It is one of the reasons they are complicit in their invisibility. They don't want to be seen, embarrassed as they are by what they are. Few part-time faculty members of the academic underclass see themselves as part of a particular set of economic situations and political decisions. One day Sam Phillips, speaking with Ned Harris, mentioned his latest strategy to get a 'real' job, meaning a full-time tenure-track academic job. Ned said, 'maybe you already have a real job'. He elaborated; 'What if the job you have now, working in a semi-permanent arrangement, part-time, at several institutions, *is* a real job for our generation? What if this is it?'

For many part-time and temporary faculty the late 1980s was a sort of watershed. The job situation didn't get much better and it wasn't just North Urban PhDs who were having trouble finding permanent arrangements. Graduates of Ivy League and more elite institutions were starting to have the same troubles. (Last year the graduate students at Yale university made the news when they refused to turn in their grades to protest their position as an exploited teaching workforce with a large prominent university.) Naturally, when these issues start to reach the most prestigious universities in the country they began to be reported in the national media, and the word was the job crisis in higher education was here to stay. It was starting to become clear that the flexible workforce was a permanently structured reality. Finally, as other middle class professionals started being forced out of their secure jobs and into part-time and flexible work, many began to realize that the problems in higher education are part of the larger global economic problems.

Bourdieu in *Homo Academicus* (1988) talks about how as academic jobs became scarcer in France, professors would string their underlings along, always promoting the hope that when a more prestigious position opened they would have it, without promising anyone the next position because of course it was necessary to keep up the hopes of several people with the same potential job. Back in the United States, the ideology that we are all waiting for our shot at a 'real job' is used to keep us from any political activity. We are all docile day-laborers failing to see strength in our numbers, vaguely embarrassed by the idea of collective action. Embarrassments are everywhere, some part-time faculty are embarrassed to cash their paychecks because the amount is so low. Like many low status workers adjunct faculty become defensive, fail to participate in the academic life of the institutions in which they work and neglect networks of colleagues there in front of them; further reinforcing notions of failure.

There is also another level of importance in seeing part-time positions as real jobs. Part-timers subsidize the lives of the full-time faculty. At the several institutions I know part-time faculty teach three to four courses a term, no full-time faculty teach that much. Most teach two or three courses; on occasion only one. The difference is that full-timers are paid for their research when not teaching, while the part-time person is not. The part-time faculty member has the option of not going to faculty meetings or getting involved in university business but there is a double edge to that freedom. If I exercise that freedom I reinforce my invisibility and I have no voice. Part-timers subsidize the faculty, and many times the tenured full-time faculty are insulated from the changes and failures in the university by that subsidy. It is not their fault, of course, but a problem of the system, but they are complicit in that system. Many of them feel guilt about the dedicated part-timers, and some of the part-timers misrepresent that guilt as a form of power. In fact it is a small form of power. Rather like Genovese's notion of resistance and accommodation, the guilt can be used to get travel money out of a benevolent chairperson or other such small perks; nothing more significant. Pushed too far, it will be denied. Sometimes the ideology of quality is used by the tenured to avoid this reality; in that discourse the part-timer is of inferior quality as a scholar, which is why s/he is in this position. This discourse requires much forgetting of past history in order to be articulated.

Part-time and temporary faculty are not unique in the US economy. It is clear that one of the new strategies developed by industries and corporations to deal with fluctuating profit s is to use part-time labor. They are much cheaper. (fewer benefits, lower wages and they are most often not unionized). Many workers in America today work sixty or more hours a week, not for one employer, but two or three (Davis, 1986). As Shor suggests for the general culture, the democratic movement which produced an active student public participating in the shaping of their education and created interest in people becoming educated and representing themselves, was turned into education for career mobility; the meritocratic system. Graduate education went through the same crisis. The once proud politically active graduate student body became the most careerist of generations. That sudden and tremendous shift toward careerism, together with very little analysis by social scientists has left the academic underclass bereft of any explanation of their situation other than personal failure.

Academic Freedom, Academic Power

Most part-time faculty have very little academic freedom. If you consider that in some universities 50 per cent or more of the classes are being taught by part-time faculty, the inescapable conclusion is that there is a great deal of administrative control over the process of teaching and education. Often administrations are not that interested in content. (Although I am personally familiar with a dean's directing part-time faculty not to teach Marxism). Administrations are more interested in subtler aspects of the process of education; the kind of discursive control along the lines of Foucault's (1979) notion of the *panopticon*. What is important is the requirement to take a role, there is pressure to report students who are not performing well to the administration. Faculty teach in a certain time-space. Temporary faculty are told by many institutions how to grade. ('You are giving too many high grades or you are giving too many low grades'.) While on the surface these things may seem less important than content issues, I believe they are crucial.

Further, as there are so many part-time faculty now, the administrative mechanisms of control are beginning to reach the content of the classroom as well. Oliver Olsen was teaching at a small college with many affluent international students. The college is very concerned about what gets taught in the classroom on two levels — they do not want complaints from parents about what the students are taught and they want to make sure there is a minimum competence, by a standard of education that is measurable. Oliver was hired to teach a course on international development. The first time he taught the course he was in charge of the class though he was first told what books had been ordered for the course. But in the middle of the following semester, the dean of the evening school made a decision to change the process of examination for the students. Halfway through the course he was told that the dean would be giving the students additional quizzes that would count toward their grade. He demanded a meeting with the deans and when he met with them they explained their concern for the students well-being. Oliver complained that this was excessive micro management and let them know he was uncomfortable in the process they had created. The college did not rehire him the following semester though he had worked there for nearly three years. While there may be a place for administration taking part in the setting of a standardized curriculum, this story demonstrates both the face of power, and the fact that the flexible workforce makes it easy to get rid of difficult elements.

Research in the sociology of education show that process is as important as content. Basil Bernstein *et al.*, in the four volumes of *Class, Codes and Control*, has shown that the way in which students are spoken to and interacted with as children greatly affect school performance. While there are many valid criticisms of Bernstein's work, the general thesis, that forms of discourse affect how people respond in the world, is well taken. Greater educational surveillance shapes students to work in job settings with greater surveillance. More lower income jobs have mechanisms of worker surveillance than high income jobs. So we are training workers for low income jobs and how to respond to the system of surveillance. The part-time faculty member, a victim of such surveillance, has little opportunity to resist this process. If s/he does, there just won't be a job the following term. In some situations, receiving a final paycheck is contingent upon participating in the particular administrative task required. These sorts of control and injustice go on with little full-time faculty awareness. The full-time faculty don't know what is going on and the part-time faculty don't tell them, occupying, as they do, a different social space.

There is a growing awareness of these issues among part-time faculty members. In many institutions part-time faculty are organizing to combat these problems. Unionization is one important step. Two of the institutions in the North Urban area I have worked at have set up part-time bargaining units; one is at a community college which has met with a great deal of success; the other at a state university with so far less success. The state university has been successfully ignoring the part-timers and pretending the unit doesn't exist, because they have a large body of graduate students to draw on as teachers, making it easier for them to marginalize the part-timers.

In many settings part-time faculty even without unions are attempting to gain their voice. They are spending more time with full-time faculty, working against their invisibility and attempting not to participate in the exclusion process. This is not a big movement yet but as more people write about the part-time faculty, more awareness of these issues will follow. While they don't always agree with each other many full-time faculty and their unions are creating alliances with the part-timers against the growing instrumental control of the administration. Because even with tenure the faculty, as we have seen, are also slated to become the factory workers of higher education, a transformation we should all be resisting far more strenuously. Further, as many full-time faculty become more aware of the part-time situation they become more sensitive to putting the part-time issues on the agenda. These positive changes come in harsh economic times, with many schools finding it necessary to scale back. The first group to go is naturally the flexible workers. It remains to be seen what will happen.

With the loss of the 'community of scholars' in the modern university, many administrations are seeking new means to wield administrative control of the departments. Older notions of the community are giving way to technologies of surveillance and control under the gun of fiscal crisis, and these new mechanisms of control are beginning to give full-time, part-time, permanent and temporary faculty common ground.

At North Urban the university has brought something they call Responsibility Centered Management to the colleges and ultimately the goal is to bring it to the departments. (The way this works is income and expense will be measured at the department level. Not only should the university be financially solvent but each department should be as well. The number of majors and students taking courses should produce more revenue than the faculty, employees, photocopying and other resources used by the department. If the resources used by the department are greater, even if the university is fiscally in good shape, the department must either increase its share of the students or reduce its costs.) We've seen in chapter 7 that the competition between universities for students is potentially destructive in that it reduces higher education to a set of advertising signs where the image of the university is more important than the substance. The intra-university competition for students promises to be even more destructive in its impact on the university. Faculty will be increasingly pressured by administrative policies to draw students to majors and courses that can be advertised; the rule of marketplace will be the state of the university; what sells is right. To say the least, this will threaten curriculum and the pursuit of knowledge established by a scholarly community will cease to exist.

Even more profoundly, many states entertain the downsizing of university systems by directly firing tenured professors and terminating departments. In New York the SUNY and the CUNY systems are both under the these pressures and many other states are beginning to make similar decisions. These changes are coming at a time when the public sees the increased need for higher education and so will be pressuring for the preservation of at least technical programs. The changes begun under the Nixon administration to move away from a liberal education where a democratic public engages in a dialogue to make decisions about its collective future and toward a career education, a technical education are coming to a point where the idea of a liberal education will be threatened for all but the most affluent or privileged individuals. These changes not only affect faculty but raise profound questions for the future of a democratic society and a public culture. Further, these changes are for the first time making full-time tenured faculty aware of the scope of the changes that began in the 1980s with the part-time and temporary labor market.

Finally, the system has created a situation of student disaffection. Students, increasingly courted as paying customers but unclear about their roles in a future society and unsure that the credentials they are getting are going to help them, are more and more alienated from the process of education. They are not given much say in their education, do not get a chance to exercise ideas and discuss issues but they do get a smorgasbord of educational choices. These educational choices are the commodities offered by the educational marketplace to help the student achieve greater opportunities in the future. But, in the history of education in the United States, curriculum choice has often been used as a mechanism to curtail the student's aspiration for a more prestigious position (Spring, 1972). Choice becomes one of the ways that an institution can offer vocational choices and encourage students in that direction.

Interestingly, in the nineteenth century, students and their families would have resisted vocational choices. They were aware that these choices took them away from the cultural training that the elites had and they did not. Of course it can be argued that this is still the case. The kinds of cognitive and linguistic skills offered by a liberal arts education, which still available to only a minority of people in the elite schools, are the kinds of skills one really needs for both a political place in a democracy and a meaningful position in the economy. But what is different from the nineteenth century is that in the late twentieth century the commodity form has been so successful that it is the main way in which people think themselves. Identity has been equated with labels, commodity signs and the signs of Levi-Strauss, Gucci, Lexus, to mention a few names, define who we are in the modern world. In this world dominated by the commodity form, the choice of practical training is what many students seek, in order to buy a credential that says they are an expert in something. They hope this sign can be parlayed into a job. In the last chapter I will argue that social scientists must take into consideration their own positions within the university, where increasingly faculty, especially the flexible workforce, are being disciplined to teach more. What they are teaching is being marketed as a commodity, a product that will hopefully give the buyer the necessary credentials to get a job in the global economy. This alienated commodity process produces a two-tiered faculty with an alienated workforce and a growing administrative apparatus and disaffected students. As we begin to imagine a reengineered higher education without people directly involved in the process we glimpse a small part of the larger problem of global capitalism, a system that serves the needs of that system, but threatens the life-world of human interaction.

Notes

1   Statistics from the US Department of Education for 1975–1993; National undergraduate enrollment grew 28 per cent, faculties increased by 22 per cent and non-teaching administration grew by 83 per cent (reported in *The Philadelphia Inquirer*, 31 March 1996).
2   Though not impossible. CUNY recently fired twenty-nine tenured faculty, mostly by eliminating their departments, and declared a state of 'fiscal exigency' that will enable the university to lay off tenured professors with twelve months notice (reported in *The New York Times*, 26 March 1996).

Chapter 10

Conclusion

This book grew out a personal political desire to use the tools of cultural anthropology and ethnography to think through the ways American capitalism is to transforming the university and hence the production of knowledge. In a sense the project is a reflexive one that attempts to bridge the divide between self and other. In this effort I have been strongly influenced by the work of Pierre Bourdieu who examined the ethnographic, together with the macro sociological, positions of the social scientist relative to the object of social study. It seemed to me these oppositions needed to be joined in concrete ways, and that only when we are able to see that research on capitalist penetration in the rainforest is not separate from the commodification of education, will social science be in a position to see the particular limitations to this knowledge, and to glimpse the dangerous cultural forces operating to constrain discourse and human freedom.

Structure and Practice

Throughout this book I have moved from the experience of faculty, particularly part-time faculty, in the university of the late twentieth century, and my own position as a marginalized intellectual, to the larger political and economic forces producing the history of the late twentieth century American university. My position allows me to produce certain knowledge. Said (1983a, pp. 5–9) recalls the story of Erich Auerbach (1968, p. 557) and his marginalization within European society during World War II. It was thanks to the distance marginalization maintained that Auerbach could reflect on broader contours of representation in Western literature. Said's Auerbach, like other members of marginalized groups, occupied positions that engender certain habits, and allow a practice and a way of looking at the world (Bourdieu, 1977, p. 72).

But there is weakness in this perspective as well. Like the anthropologist who is outsider to a culture s/he studies, I am outside certain relations of power and social interactions in the university. I do not, for instance, go to meetings or play racquetball with university presidents or members of administration. My access to their world, which consists of reading publications, going to conferences and asking them questions, is all voyeuristic, from the outside. The same could be said about my relationship to full-time tenured faculty. Issues of position and its relationship to the data produced by the anthropologist are part of an ongoing contemporary discussion in anthropology.

I observed in the introduction the trend in anthropology away from a traditional scientific discourse where the scientist produces a model of social reality and uses that model to construct an ethnography (Ortner, 1984; Clifford, 1988; Stoller, 1989, p. 26). The move toward ethnography as a form of literature and in practice has been very fruitful. Paul Stoller (1989) sums up some of the work on ethnography as a form of literature (Clifford and Marcus, 1986; Marcus and Fischer, 1986; Clifford, 1988). Ethnography changed in form in the late nineteenth and early twentieth centuries from travel accounts by individuals with deep knowledge of a culture to the realist scientific treatise (Clifford, 1988, p. 26–7). In Stoller's (1989) view, following Marcus and Cushman (1982), the structure of the ethnography took on many of the characteristics of realism which was a new fashion in literature at the time. One important aspect of realism is that it disguises the author's relationship to the text and the peoples being described. Clifford (1988) takes this idea further, looking at the transformation of ethnography after Boas and Malinowski. The work of Boas and Malinowski around the turn of the century made an uneasy compromise between the traditional deep description of a culture based on years of involvement with a group and new scientific models. The scientism of the next generation, notably Margaret Mead and Evans-Pritchard in the forties and fifties, suggests among other things that learning the language is not necessary and neither are years of study; it is possible instead to focus on specific aspects of the culture, do a quick, thorough analysis with new scientific tools and come away in a year or so with a meaningful understanding of the people involved (*ibid.*, p. 30).

Unmentioned in this analysis is that anthropology has become a middle class profession in twentieth-century society. People like Margaret Mead and E.E. Evans-Pritchard could not afford to spend decades in the field; they needed to be at home managing their careers and their positions in the power nexus of university and society. This contradiction remains. It takes years to do fieldwork; many years to thoroughly understand a way of life and a group of people. But there are pressures at home. The job market is tight, you need to get in it and move up. There are other professional issues needing to be addressed as well: involvement in the broader university and intellectual life, for example. These pressures cause most anthropologists to limit their fieldwork, but this aspect of the politics of ethnographic fieldwork and the production of texts about cultures and groups of people remains unarticulated. The place where the real lines of force are drawn, the constraints on the production of knowledge operating on us all, is repressed, silent. To talk about it would be to unmask the ways power operates. Anthropologists and sociologists carefully study the ways people are constrained by societies and cultures, but equally carefully present their own scholarly discourse as if it were free of constraint. This is one implication of what Bourdieu calls the 'scholastic view' — we don't submit ourselves and our works to the same analysis as the other. In this way the other serves to disguise power relations in our own culture.

Contemporary ethnographers no longer believe in the superiority of our methodological tools, unlike the generations of the 1930s and the 1950s. Bourdieu (1977) sums up the feeling of the next generation of anthropologists — my own — by proclaiming we have taken as our objective models our 'methodological objectivism' and made a virtue out of weakness (pp. 72–7). For many American anthropologists, the breakup of the realist paradigm, the questioning of the superiority of Western objective science and the ethnocentrism of this cluster (Said, 1979) led to a new level of relativism. If there is no truth, and nothing can be said with any authority, all discourse becomes a creative act (Rorty, 1979). This is one aspect of the crisis of modernism leading to the development of post-modernism, (McCarthy, 1990a and 1990b; Rorty, 1990) not the post-modernism of Harvey and Lash who look at the transformation of the capitalist infrastructure, but the post-modern response to the failure of realism to produce a true science as well as fear of the implicit racism imbedded in that realist science. This post-modernism, instead of offering us a critique of our own culture and system of power relations, offers radical relativism. More on this later.

On some level Clifford, Marcus, Stoller and especially Bourdieu are searching for something else, seeking to escape this move to radical relativism. Stoller, the most relativist of the three, is deeply skeptical of all objectivizing models. He attempts to embed his knowledge in ethnographic practice and a phenomenology of the body; a kind of unapologetic Malinowskian preoccupation with the ethnographic, rejecting anthropological theory and the literary tradition of realism. Stoller's texts are in some sense experimental. They use varying narrative techniques and self-consciously focus on the bodily presence of the anthropologist in the culture with details about meals, bodily needs and functions.

Clifford (1988) suggests that Bakhtin's (1981) concept of heteroglossia may help us to understand the breakup of ethnographic authority and the plurality of new theoretical images to become part of the anthropologists 'toolkit' (a term he borrows from Foucault, 1977 and 1980) to be used in a 'bricoleur' fashion (p. 23). Marcus, attempting to situate the problem of ethnography in the context of a changing world capitalism, suggests there are new models or experimental techniques in ethnography already being pursued. He discusses the development of new models of ethnographic research which attempt to deal with the globalization of capitalism. Marcus (1986, pp. 171–3) finds two new models of ethnography interesting to him. In one, researchers look at multiple sites and discuss their interconnections and at another, a site is embedded in the large political/economic context. These models are literary experiments that attempt to map the relationships between culture, society and the larger political/economic context. Not realist, they do not give in to radical relativism either. For Marcus, at the time Paul Willis's (1981) *Learning to Labor* was an excellent example of the second approach, a placing of the local ethnographic context into the larger political/economic framework. (Jean Comaroff's (1985) *Body of Power, Spirit of Resistance*, and James Scott's (1985) *Weapons of the Weak*) are other excellent examples of this trend in ethnography.) Willis' lads find themselves at the bottom of the socioeconomic ladder because of their resistance to the system of domination (the school system) and Willis shows that their habitus and their practice are central to their exclusion. Willis is not saying that the conformist kids will do better in life because of their strategy; most likely they will not. But the lads strategy is the result of a partial penetration of the system of ideological domination, (Willis, 1981, pp. 119–23). They understand that this is class domination though they do not see how their resistance, while strategic and successful on a small scale (Scott, 1985), fails to help them and in fact condemns them to a life of poverty and marginal employment. Lois Weis' (1990) analysis of Freeway Girls makes a parallel case. In it we see that due to the forces of deindustrialization and the interruption of the traditional roles men and women play in the working class household, the consciousness of working-class high school girls partially penetrates the patriarchal system.

One question that has motivated my work is how to think about the consciousness of university professors and the political and economic context out of which that consciousness has grown. Further, how has that political and economic context developed through history. Bourdieu (1977) suggests that rather than turning to the structural rules, as is typical of the scientific anthropology, we need to create a probabilistic social science (p. 77). This probabilistic theory is a probability of objective constraint and of strategy intervention. I think the allusion to physics is intentional. Physicists, having faced the crisis of realism and relativism in the early part of this century, have now moved beyond a science composed of mechanical laws to one which accounts for the position of the scientist, the probability of certain effects given a set of causes and the means of measuring. Bourdieu seeks this kind of science for sociology. While he has not said as much, Bourdieu's sociology clearly attempts to move past the limits of sociocultural anthropology and sociology to create a new science looking at the probability of a given set of practices within a structured social field. The structured field being itself a product of the position of the analyst and the historical forces, previous struggles have gone into producing a particular set of arrangements. In this way Bourdieu holds on to the hope of a kind of relatively totalizing vision for sociology, holding onto the modernist goal of knowledge.

Bourdieu is unquestionably one of the most important thinkers for me. But while his model of practice and probability of certain actions within a given field attempt to move beyond the subject/object dichotomy, his analysis of the historical structuring of objective arenas or social fields is often limited. It is for this reason that some have criticized the reproductionism of Bourdieu, seeing it potentially ahistorical or functionalist (Garnham and Williams, 1986; Thompson, 1984; Lash, 1990; Apple, 1982a and 1982b). If we look at a recent work like *Homo Academicus* (1988), it's possible to see that there is indeed concern for the effect of history on the structure of the field of faculty and university relations but is somewhat limited. Bourdieu rarely looks in detail at the effects of the larger economy or political system on the structure of the university.

My analysis has attempted to present a detailed look at the political economic and historical conditions of the formation of an objective field, which are absolutely essential to understanding what kinds of interactions are taking place within the universities of the United States today, while attempting to include the revolutionary insight of Bourdieu, the notion of a set of calculated practices being enacted with a particular social field. Jean Comaroff (1985), in *Body of Power, Spirit of Resistance*, has worked out more thoroughly the project Bourdieu initiates when he admonishes that social science needs to move beyond the objectivizing moment and find 'the dialectic of the internalization of externality and the externalization of internality' (Bourdieu, 1977, p. 72). Comaroff, in her research among the Tshidi, looks very carefully at the relationship of events, the strategies and practices producing those events and their relationship to the larger macrostructure of South Africa. That macrostructure is itself produced by a dynamic history of the strategies of people and institutions in South Africa as it moves from the precolonial to colonial to capitalism and apartheid. My research is in very different setting, but it is possible to see that a similar research design provides a perspective on higher education in the United States capable of explaining social reality at a number of different levels. Allowing us to see how such isomorphisms as the split in the Supreme Court over Yeshiva, the contradiction faculty experience over their status as either workers/professionals, are produced. The consciousness of individuals as they engage in their daily practice, whether a landmark court decision, a faculty strike or an administrative 'rationalization', is in fact a complex product of the history going on before as well as the habitus of individuals and groups they are engaging in the struggle within this domain of activity.

But there is yet another dimension to my analysis, because unlike Comaroff and other anthropologists, who model objective historical systems not their own and then think about the consciousness of actors produced within, I have attempted to subject the site of our own knowledge production to the same analysis.

Beyond Self and Other

In the same breath that Bourdieu encouraged movement beyond subjectivism and objectivism he suggested that social science research needs to move past an 'anthropological model of practice' to seek a 'scientific theory of probabilities'. Unlike the natural sciences, such a theory of probabilities require researchers to understand '. . . a whole body of wisdom, sayings, commonplaces, ethical precepts. and, at a deeper level, the unconscious principles of the ethos' (*ibid.*, p. 77). Bourdieu is suggesting here what Stoller (1989) also reaffirms: that to be outside a culture is weakness and it is necessary to have a deep understanding of the subjectivities of individual such as can only be acquired by such a model as habitus where we see how such subjectivities are produced.

Further, Bourdieu is suggesting that social scientists stop denying coevalness (Fabian, 1983). We share space-time with individuals in other places involved in a complex set of interactions with their own 'event history' and structure (Comaroff, 1985). While many anthropologists embrace these ideas, much anthropological discourse remains tied to a working through of a philosophy of the Other. The concern with otherness takes anthropology to issues like nationalism and the nation state, imagined communities, issues of identity and belonging, and the representation of subaltern and non-Western groups. Such concerns in, and of, themselves are not necessarily problematic though they can be, and often are, used to deny coevalness and resurrect the objectification of the other.[1]

Much of the ethnographic research in education has reproduced this form of othering, where the other is not an exotic tribesman or third-world peasant, but the member of a class, race, ethnic, religious or gender minority group. These others are often the victims of power and much of the ethnographic literature has looked at the ways schools reproduce power relations or, in effect, keep less powerful groups from becoming powerful whether through the member's own agency or larger structural force. Obviously I don't mean to suggest this work is not important or valuable, but it does suffer from the 'scholastic view'. We put the other, 'lads', 'hallway hangers', 'brothers', 'jocks', 'burnouts' or 'vatos' (to name a few), under the scholarly lens to reflect upon the ways institutions constrain people and the ways individuals creatively respond to those constraints. But the actors' motivation, in these situations, remain obscured to us because we see them through the lens of objective scholarship. We cannot see their practical strategies because we do not reflect upon our own.

There is also a denial of political practice. In 1987, at the American Anthropological Association annual meeting in Chicago, the American Ethnological Society invited Edward Said to speak as one of anthropology's interlocutors. The panel was organized such that Said could lecture for an hour and then allow several prominent anthropologists to respond to his talk. The program for the meeting suggested that Said's *Orientalism* had had a profound effect on anthropologists and Said would come and talk about the discipline, the new interpretive (representation) schools and their place in the counter-hegemonic discourse of East and West.

Said discussed a number of important issues but his main point was a critique of academic anthropology's lack of political engagement. With all the changes in the world like the destruction of rain forests, relocation of peoples and genocide (among other things); anthropologists have remained silent about these issues and have only discussed philosophical issues of representation. Said accused anthropology of conservatism. One can see in interpretive and post-modern orientations in anthropology a voyeurism and failure to engage politically with these changes. Said himself has been very politically active in Palestinian movements, seeking a larger, more generalized audience and engaging political struggle.

After Said finished his discussion Renato Rosaldo, Paul Rabinow, Richard Fox and Ann Stoler responded. Of all the respondents only Stoler was not a typical representative of the so-called new interpretive orientation in anthropology. Her response to Said was also the most interesting. She said politically active anthropologists do exist but that the discipline does not give them much voice. There has been a long tradition of involvement with people and dedicated political activity and to suggest that there hasn't been, as Said did, is to further alienate their voice because it denies it ever existed. Stoler suggests, with some justice, that hegemony works in the anthropological discourse in subtle ways; and by officially authorizing an important political activist to come and speak about anthropology's failure to be politically active, denies the very existence of the work of politically committed and active anthropologists.

This is a complex issue because there are many politically active, progressive individuals working within the discipline of anthropology and education. One question we need to ask is, how is hegemonic control produced and/or maintained in a context where there is a great deal of struggle? One of the dangers of this discourse around representing the other is that one never gets to the political issues at hand, remaining trapped in an idealistic discourse rather than engaging in research that has its own political practice. I see my current work as addressing some of the dilemmas raised by ethnographic work in anthropology and education. By looking at the lines of force and the ways in which the university is being restructured along flexible lines we can see how our own discourse is marginalized or commodified or valorized.

For instance, the celebrated return of the public intellectual, only a few years after Russell Jacoby mourned the death of such a one, raises interesting questions. I don't think we should naively embrace this as a new social movement but instead should recognize that within the commodified university there are pressures to legitimate it and its functions to an increasingly preoccupied and cynical public. Those pressures encourage academics to write to a broader audience, give public lectures and go on radio and TV talk shows.

There is one final implication of the ideology of otherness. I have encountered many colleagues engaged in political practice in other countries, not just anthropologists but sociologists, political scientists, historians, who engage in an interesting form of self-censorship. Discussions of this self-censorship yield a coherent ideology which is certainly part of the academic thinking on the left. The line goes, if we criticize the university they (the administration) may make it even harder to work and engage in a progressive political praxis in other countries. These colleagues suggest that issues like the lack of freedom of speech (and other problems) are more important in third world countries than at home in their university. They sacrifice critique at home in order to be able to speak out about what's going on abroad.

This pattern of self-censorship is also part of the denial of coevalness (Fabian, 1983; Said, 1979; Clifford, 1988) suggesting as it does that the expert has more to say about the other than others do themselves, and therefore sacrifice of freedom of speech at home is justified. But really if there is no real academic freedom at home how much influence can the academic have in the third world? Sure s/he protects their ability to discuss the Third World with students and to the media and might even go and do work in the country. But denial of freedom of speech issues at the university adds up to political non-participation in larger US politics, which means no real changes at the level of US policy which are often important issues facing many third world countries. Said makes some similar points when he suggests that the retreat of the literary Marxists into deep reading of texts is in fact a sign of the inability of that group of leftists to make any real impact on the US political scene and is the real triumph of Reaganism (Said, 1983b).

This pattern of the ideology of the other is only part of the contemporary struggle on American campuses. Many intellectuals do fight freedom-of-speech battles at home and in their communities. Noam Chomsky travels regularly around the country speaking to college students about transformations of global capitalism and its impact; but Chomsky is an interesting exception. I suggest that there is a danger in the discourse of the other and the university and other institutions should be of central concern around issues of democracy, freedom of speech and equality, at home or abroad.

Management and Control

The expansion and development of higher education in the United States has been part of a complex set of forces. As we have seen, it has developed out of the need to satisfy American desires for greater educational and economic opportunities. At various junctures, like the post-war period and the 1960s, rapid expansion of the educational system were produced. Higher education in the US, like many other American institutions, is decentralized and diverse. There is real strength in a system of higher education so broad and diverse, catching as it does the interest of a lot of people. It has been one of our society's great achievements. Students who do not fit into the more narrowly cast systems of higher education in their own countries can find a place in an American university. The result of this is a system admired by the world, one that has provided educational opportunities for many Americans. If part of the commodification process has been tied to the expansion of an institution imagined as a booming industry then we must grant that commodification is not just a process to be demonized but perhaps one that has served many people very well.

But that boom industry serves the global economic order and will be in crisis for the foreseeable future. With economic crisis the reality of the state and the institutions of higher education, how we respond to these crises is crucial. Economic metaphors may not be enough; it is incumbent upon us all to develop ways of responding to the crisis of higher education creatively. This issue is that is central to higher education and our democratic culture in general. In an era of declining corporate profit the response on the part of the huge transnational corporations has been one of increasing control over the movement of capital, people, goods, services and information. Lean production is a way to attempt to preserve profit in an era of slow economic growth, but this requires tight control over people. This is why Gamble (1988) refers to the 'free economy and the strong state'. There must be great flexibility in the economy to move capital, labor and goods but a strong state is necessary for coercive force (*ibid.*, p. 31).

That disciplinary force, as it has been exerted within universities, has had several faces. Corporations have used universities as research facilities, and with changes in the patent law, benefited from State-sponsored research. Government, attempting to pass part of the cost of the excesses of the 1980s on to consumers, is reducing student aid and funding to higher education. University administrations have responded to these new crises by going into high gear managing consumers, funding and workers. All these forces have been documented here. The result is that the university has become a disciplinary system where workers and students alike are managed for maximal efficiency, to minimize the contradictions and legitimacy crises that threaten to the whole system with crisis.

I conclude with a story from West Urban Tech. It is a story about the technocratic drive to manage the university space, and the way that drive produces apathy. West Tech had a series of racial incidents a couple of years ago, and a group of students from the Black Students' Union suggested to the President of the University that the University sponsor a diversity week with workshops, and teach-ins and other chances for people to talk about racial attitudes, to begin to create a forum where these problems could be discussed. The University thought this was a great idea and unveiled a program the next fall. Diversity Week had become Diversity Day, scheduled to coincide with the University's Convocation. Maggie Kuhn, then-Leader of the Grey Panthers, came to speak at the Convocation about diversity. After the Convocation a Professional Diversity Manager was hired to lead a group discussion on diversity, not a sociologist or anthropologist or African-American scholar, a businessman who goes to major corporations and helps their Black/White, Christian/Jewish and female/male management work with each other.

After his discussion, the people who remained in the auditorium, (not many), broke into smaller groups and continued the sensitivity training. When the day was over, the faculty was indignant, the Black students felt ripped off and the White students thought it had been boring and stupid. Two nights later there was a major racial incident in which a group of fraternity students beat up a Black student for allegedly throwing eggs at their house. This incident is still the focus of much campus attention and the racial hatred is greater than ever.

Almost everyone involved was surprised that the University did not use their own resources. The University has a number of African and African-American faculty who deal in their work with issues of minorities, social stratification and cultural studies. Further, there are a large number of social scientists, sociologists, historians, political scientists and anthropologists working on these issues as well.

The students expected a week of activities with democratic participation, in-cluding the planning of the event, but what they got instead was something rather like a TV game show. The audience participation was of a rather passive type. The administration had put together something they genuinely thought might begin to address these problems. When they were asked by the students for a diversity week, nothing seemed more natural than to turn to professional diversity managers and hire a consulting firm. This is 'instrumental reasoning'. From the point of view of an administration trained in a management school of thought, they did the reason-able thing.

The student response was by and large that of disgruntled consumers. They were either bored with the product or dismayed that it was so flimsy. The Black Students' Union went back to the drawing table and (after the next racial incident that came a few days later) made a new set of demands on the administration. They were the only group on campus that did not respond in televisual terms. They were the subject of many editorial attacks run by the student newspaper with impunity. These editorials by White students responded in shock to the Black Students' Union's attempt to empower itself ('who do they think they are, making demands?').

And the faculty responded like workers ignored by management. Many of them left during the event, visibly grumbling or shaking their heads. Many lashed out at the administration while talking to each other later in the halls or over coffee or lunch, but no one approached the administration to ask why they hadn't been included. (In fact they could have asked before the event but no one did.) Of course there were a few faculty members who worked with the administration on the diversity day project. But these faculty were people looking for raises and/or positions in administration and in order to achieve these ends took on the administrative point of view.

The images of the marketplace and the economy influenced all of us in how we saw this situation. The management model is so deeply in-grained in university administration that it probably seemed more professional to them to turn over to a management consulting team than leave it in the hands of their own faculty. These are the models this administration has to deal with a problem, and they thought they were doing the right thing. I might also say here this is a non-prestige private university. Other universities might have used their own faculty to save money if they were small or poor or, if it were a prestigious institution, they might parade a nationally-prominent faculty before the community; a sort of free advertising. How a university or college responds to commodifying influences is very much influenced by where they are in the hierarchy of universities and colleges.

The faculty and the students each made what seemed to them an appropriate response. The faculty have become middle-class workers and they don't like their position but they don't want to rock the boat. Their only response to this situation was to grumble privately, not complain publicly (an example of weak resistance [Scott, 1985]). The students also respond to the market image. They are buying a product. It's a special kind of product, one they don't have a lot of control over the content of, but it's something they want and perceive they need to have. In that respect it's a lot like television, which encourages a passive bored response (but no matter how bored and hostile you become you're always bodily there).

Habitus affects how one responds to this institution, (Bourdieu, 1977, 1984 and 1988). We can see that the exceptional response of the Black Students' Union, making active demands, shows there is contestation here. However, regardless of habitus the arena or field is structured by images of commodification and the managed institution. We not only need a model for this commodifying process and notions of the practices of individuals around this commodification, we also need to think about power and the structuring influence that uses of power have on the social arena (Comaroff, 1985; Bourdieu, 1977 and 1984; Scott, 1985).

The story of West Tech's racial problems and the way the administration sought to respond to them is at the heart of what is happening in universities. A sterile administrative culture, concerned only with managing problems and controlling people, not only exacts control but produces alienation in its wake. West Tech faces a crisis of legitimacy typical of many universities. Administration, with a debt crisis, feels it must micro manage all situations to provide the best result. Faculty feel overworked, part-timers are exploited, students feel alienated and just there to get the credential; learning, knowledge and political participation are not much on anyone's mind.

Commodification begins to come to the university at the moment in capitalism when the factory or Fordist system is on the rise. Because of that particular history the model of the university being structured like industry is taken up. The vision of the university came in with the bankers, lawyers and businessmen who began to populate the Board of Directors and with the growing professional class of administrators. That commodification went through transformations, the university taking on new importance when capitalism shifted to a flexible mode of accumulation. Flexible accumulation is a form of capitalism where factories are still used but they are no longer the dominant image. The image of the computer network, the web which brings factory workers in Mexico and Brazil together with pieceworkers in rural India and rural Iowa together with managers in Detroit; this is the dominant image, the spider web moving around the globe (as nicely illustrated in US Sprint commercials).

This model is coming to the university as well, as scholars work on and solve problems at a rapid rate over the Internet, and administrators become excited about new ways to efficiently disseminate college curriculum, like distance learning. Perhaps the image to come is one of faculty as pieceworkers in an international system of knowledge and technologies. If that is the case maybe the part-time and temporary faculty are the leading edge of this new movement; one that is coming to many other industries and people throughout the United States.

As social scientists scramble to understand these forces, they need to look at ways in which the site from which the knowledge is produced, is structured. This reflexive political practice is necessary in order to effectively raise a voice against the dominant movement in American capitalism. Currently we favor the survival of systems, corporations and bureaucratic institutions over the well-being and lives of people. If we are to survive the coming century we will need to humanize these forces and prioritize people over things. Universities need to reinvigorate the quest for knowledge; knowledge that serves the interests of people, brings healing and benefit to the planet and reestablishes a concern for human values. This will only happen if university intellectuals become aware of the institutions in which they work and the global pressures on those institutions.

Note

1   A case in point, I submitted a paper for an American Ethnological Society meeting on the Imagination of the Supreme Court in Yeshiva. The meeting's title was 'Nations and Peoples: Aspects and Implications of Identity'. I received a call from the organizer who told me he thought my paper sounded interesting and he wanted to include it in the meeting but he was having trouble justifying its inclusion because it was off the meeting theme. While dealing with issues of interest to those dealing with the meeting theme, it was about *us* and not *them*. Of course meetings get crowded, papers have to be eliminated but the logic was interesting to me. It is a logic which has become commonplace in anthropology. Now we no longer write about the other, we critique writing about the other while continuing to engage in writing about the other. This is still a denial of coevalness.

References

ABEL, E.K. (1984) *Terminal Degrees: The Job Crisis in Higher Education*, New York, Praeger Publishers.

AGGER, B. (1989) *Fast Capitalism: A Critical Theory of Significance*, Urbana, IL, University of Illinois Press.

AGLIETTA, M. (1979) *A Theory of Capitalist Regulation: The US Experience*, London, New Left Books.

ALTBACH, P.G. and BERDAHL, R.O. (1981) *Higher Education in American Society*, Buffalo, NY, Prometheus Books.

ALTHUSSER, L. (1971) 'Ideology and ideological state apparatuses' *Lenin and Philosophy and Other Essays*, London, New Left Books.

AMARIGLIO, J. and CALLARI, A. (1989) 'Marxian value theory and the problem of the subject: the role of commodity fetishism', *Rethinking Marxism*, **2**, 3, pp. 31–60.

ANDERSON, B. (1991) *Imagined Communities: Reflections on the Origin and Spread of Nationalism*, (rev edn) London and New York, Verso.

ANYON, J. (1980) 'Social class and the hidden curriculum of work', *Journal of Education*, **162**, pp. 67–92.

APPADURAI, A. (1988) 'Introduction: Commodities and the politics of value' in APPADURAI, A. (ed.) *The Social Life of Things: Commodities in Cultural Perspective*, Cambridge, Cambridge University Press.

APPADURAI, A. (1990) 'Disjuncture and difference in the global cultural economy', *Public Culture*, **2**, 2, pp. 1–24.

APPLE, M.W. (1982a) *Education and Power*, London, Routledge and Kegan Paul.

APPLE, M.W. (ed.) (1982b) *Cultural and Economic Reproduction in Education*, London, Routledge and Kegan Paul.

APPLE, M.W. (1993) 'Between moral regulation and democracy: The cultural contradictions of the text', in LANKSHEAR, C. and McLAREN, P. (eds) *Critical Literacy: Politics, Praxis and the Postmodern*, Albany, NY, SUNY Press.

ARAC, J. (1986) 'Introduction', in ARAC, J. (ed.) *Postmodernism and Politics*, (Theory and History of Literature, Volume 28), Minneapolis, MN, University of Minnesota Press.

ARNOVE, R.F. (1980) 'Foundations and the transfer of knowledge' in ARNOVE, R.F. (ed.) *Philanthropy and Cultural Imperialism: The Foundations at Home and Abroad*, Boston, MA, G.K. Hall and Company.

ARONOWITZ, S. and GIROUX, H.A. (1985) *Education Under Siege*. South Hadley, MA, Bergin and Garvey.

ARONOWITZ, S. and GIROUX, H.A. (1993) *Education Still Under Siege: Second Edition*, Westport, CT, Bergin and Garvey.

ASAD, T. (ed.) (1973) *Anthropology and the Colonial Encounter*, London, Ithaca Press.

AUERBACH, E. (1968) *Mimesis: The Representation of Reality in Western Literature*, (paperback edition) Princeton, NJ, Princeton University Press.

BAKHTIN, M.M. (1981) *The Dialogic Imagination*, Austin, TX, University of Texas Press.

BARROW, C.W. (1990) *Universities and the Capitalist State*, Madison, WI, University of Wisconsin Press.

BARROW, C.W. (1995) 'Beyond the multiversity: Fiscal crisis and the changing structure of academic labor' in SMYTH, J. (ed.) *Academic Work*, Milton Keynes, Open University Press.

BARSAMIAN, D. (1990) 'Alexander Cockburn: Amazonia and justice', interview with Alexander Cockburn in *Z Magazine*, **3**, 5, pp. 46–51.

BAUDRILLARD, J. (1975) *The Mirror of Production*, St. Louis, MO, Telos Press.

BAUDRILLARD, J. (1981) *For a Critique of the Political Economy of the Sign*, St. Louis, MO, Telos Press.

BAUDRILLARD, J. (1983) *Simulations*, New York, Semiotext(e).

BAUDRILLARD, J. (1988) 'Consumer society', in POSTER, M. (ed.) *Selected Writings*, Stanford, CA, Stanford University Press.

BAUDRILLARD, J. (1988) 'The system of objects', in POSTER, M. (ed.) *Selected Writings*, Stanford, CA, Stanford University Press.

BAUMAN, Z. (1992) 'On the state and the intellectuals, and the state of the intellectuals', *Thesis Eleven*, **31**, pp. 81–104.

BENJAMIN, W. (1969) 'The work of art in the age of mechanical reproduction', in ARENDT, H. (ed.) *Illuminations*, New York, Schocken Books.

BERGER, J. (1969) 'The moment of cubism', in BERGER, J. (ed.) *The Moment of Cubism and Other Essays*, New York, Pantheon Books.

BERGER, J. (1977) *Ways of Seeing*, London, British Broadcasting Corporation and Penguin Books.

BERMAN, P. (ed.) (1992) *Debating PC: The Controversy Over Political Correctness on College Campuses*, New York, Dell.

BERNSTEIN, B. (1971) *Class, Codes and Control*, London, Routledge and Kegan Paul.

BERNSTEIN, B. (1982) in APPLE, M.W. (ed.) *Cultural and Economic Reproduction in Education: Essays on Class, Ideology, and The State*, London and Boston, Routledge and Kegan Paul.

BLEDSTEIN, B.J. (ed.) (1976) *The Culture of Professionalism: The Middle Class and The Development of Higher Education in America*, New York, Norton.

BLOOM, A. (1987) *The Closing of the American Mind*, New York, Simon and Schuster.

BLUESTONE, B. and HARRISON, B. (1982) *The Deindustrialization of America*, New York, Basic Books.

BODLEY, J.H. (1996) *Anthropology and Contemporary Human Problems* (3rd edn), Mountainview, CA, Mayfield Publishing Co.

BOK, D. (1982) *Beyond the Ivory Tower*, Cambridge, MA, Harvard University Press.

BOURDIEU, P. (1973) 'Cultural reproduction and social reproduction', in BROWN, R. (ed.) *Knowledge, Education and Cultural Change*, London, Tavistock.

BOURDIEU, P. (1977) *Outline of a Theory of Practice*, Cambridge, Cambridge University Press.

BOURDIEU, P. (1984) *Distinction: A Social Critique of the Judgment of Taste*, Cambridge, MA, Harvard University Press.

BOURDIEU, P. (1985) 'The social space and the genesis of groups', *Theory And Society*, **14**, 6, pp. 723–44.

BOURDIEU, P. (1988) *Homo Academicus*, Stanford, CA, Stanford University Press.

BOURDIEU, P. (1990a) *The Logic of Practice*, Stanford, CA, Stanford University Press.

BOURDIEU, P. (1990b) 'The scholastic point of view', *Cultural Anthropology*, **5**, 4, pp. 380–91.

BOURDIEU, P. (1990c) *In Other Words: Essays Towards a Reflexive Sociology*, Stanford, CA, Stanford University Press.

BOURDIEU, P. and BOLTANSKI, L. (1978) 'Changes in social structure and changes in the demand for education', in GINER, S. and ARCHER, M.S. (eds) *Contemporary Europe: Social Structures and Cultural Patterns*, London, Routledge and Kegan Paul.

BOURDIEU, P. and PASSERON, J.-C. (1977) *Reproduction in Education, Society and Culture*, London, Sage Publications.

BOURDIEU, P. and PASSERON, J.-C. (1979) *The Inheritors: French Students and their Relation to Culture*, Chicago, IL, University of Chicago Press.

BOWEN, H.R. and DOUGLASS, G.K. (1971) *Efficiency in Liberal Education*, Macalester Foundation Report issued by Carnegie Commission on Higher Education, New York, McGraw-Hill Book Company.

BOWEN, H.R. and SCHUSTER, J.H. (1986) *American Professors: A National Resource Imperiled*, Oxford, Oxford University Press.

BOWLES, S. and GINTIS, H. (1987) *Democracy and Capitalism: Property, Community, and The Contradictions of Modern Social Thought*, New York, Basic Books.

BOYD, W.L. and KERCHNER, C.T. (1988) *The Politics of Excellence and Choice in Education* (1987 Yearbook of the Politics of Education Association), London, Falmer Press.

BOYER, E.L. (1988) *College: The Undergraduate Experience in America*, Carnegie Foundation for the Advancement of Teaching, New York, Harper and Row.

BRENEMAN, D.W. and YOUN, T.I.K. (eds) (1988) *Academic Labor Markets and Careers*, London, Falmer Press.

BRINT, S. and KARABEL, J. (1989) *The Diverted Dream: Community Colleges and the Promise of Educational Opportunity in America, 1900–1985*, New York, Oxford University Press.

BRUNER, E.M. (1990) 'The scientist vs the humanist', *Anthropology Newsletter*, **31**, 2.

BUCHANAN, A. (1990) '150 years of white domination in New Zealand', *Race and Class*, **31**, 4, pp. 73–80.

References

Bureau of National Affairs (1947) *The Taft-Hartley Act: After One Year*, Washington, DC, Bureau of National Affairs Inc.

Burris, B.H. and Heyderbrand, W.V. (1984) 'Technocratic administration and educational control', in Fischer, F. and Sirianni, C. (eds) *Critical Studies in Organization and Bureaucracy*, Philadelphia, Temple University Press.

Capra, D. (1989) *Soundings in Critical Theory*, Ithaca, NY, Cornell University Press.

Caret, R.L., Dumont, R.G. and Myrant, M.-A. (1987) 'Developing a strategic academic staffing plan based upon a rationale of institutional reduction', *Planning for Higher Education*, **16**, 2, pp. 61–9.

Carlson, D. (1992) *Teachers and Crisis: Urban School Reform and Teachers' Work Culture*, New York, Routledge.

Carnegie Commission on Higher Education (1971) *Dissent and Disruption*, New York, McGraw-Hill Book Company.

Carnegie Commission on Higher Education (1972) *The More Effective Use of Resources*, New York, McGraw-Hill Book Company.

Carnegie Commission on Higher Education (1973a) *Governance of Higher Education: Six Priority Problems*, New York, McGraw-Hill Book Company.

Carnegie Commission on Higher Education (1973b) *Priorities for Action: Final Report of the Carnegie Commission*, New York, McGraw-Hill Book Company.

Carnegie Council on Policy Studies in Higher Education (1975) *The Federal Role in Postsecondary Education: Unfinished Business 1975–1980*, San Francisco, CA, Jossey-Bass.

Carnegie Foundation for the Advancement of Teaching (1975) *More Than Just Survival: Prospects for Higher Education in a Period of Uncertainty*, San Francisco, CA, Jossey-Bass.

Carnoy, M. and Levin, H.M. (1985) *Schooling and Work in the Democratic State*, Stanford, CA, Stanford University Press.

de Certeau, M. (1984) *The Practice of Everyday Life*, Berkeley, CA, University of California Press.

de Certeau, M. (1988) *The Writing of History*, New York, Columbia University Press.

Clammer, J. (1973) 'Colonialism and the perception of tradition in Fiji', in Asad, T. (ed.) *Anthropology and the Colonial Encounter*, London, Ithaca Press.

Clark, B.R. (1987) 'Planning for excellence: The condition of the professoriate', *Planning for Higher Education*, **16**, 1, pp. 1–8.

Clifford, J. (1988) *The Predicament of Culture*, Cambridge, MA, Harvard University Press.

Clifford, J. and Marcus, G.E. (eds) (1986) *Writing Culture: The Poetics and Politics of Ethnography*, Berkeley, CA, University of California Press.

Collins, H. (1982) *Marxism and Law*, Oxford, Oxford University Press.

Collins, R. *et al.*, (eds) (1986) *Media, Culture & Society: A Critical Reader*, Beverly Hills, CA, Sage Publications.

Comaroff, J. (1985) *Body of Power, Spirit of Resistance*, Chicago, IL, University of Chicago Press.

COMAROFF, J. and COMAROFF, J.L. (1987) 'The madman and the migrant: Work and labor in the historical consciousness of a South African people', *American Ethnologist*, **14**, 2, pp. 191–209.

COMAROFF, J. and COMAROFF, J.L. (1990) 'Goodly beasts, beastly goods: Cattle and commodities in a South African context', in *American Ethnologist*, **17**, 2, pp. 195–216.

COUGHLIN, E.K. (1990) 'Years of adversity, decade of growth change face of university publishing', *The Chronicle of Higher Education*, 27, June.

COWAN, R. (1990) 'Academia un-incorporated', *Z Magazine*, February.

CREMIN, L.A. (1989) *Popular Education and Its Discontents*, New York, Harper and Row.

DANIELS, L.A. (1989) 'Some top universities in squeeze between research and academics', *The New York Times*, 10 May.

DARKNELL, F.A. (1980) 'The Carnegie philanthropy and private corporate influence on higher education', in ARNOVE, R.F. (ed.) *Philanthropy and Cultural Imperialism: The Foundations at Home and Abroad*, Boston, MA, G.K. Hall and Company.

DAVIS, M. (1986) *Prisoners of the American Dream*, London, Verso.

DELAMONT, S. (ed.) (1992) *Fieldwork in Educational Settings: Methods, Pitfalls, and Perspectives*, London, Falmer Press.

DELEUZE, G. and GUATTARI, F. (1977) *Anti-Oedipus: Capitalism and Schizophrenia*, New York, Viking Press.

DERRIDA, J. (1994) *Specters of Marx: The State of the Debt, the Work of Mourning and the New International*, New York, Routledge.

DOMHOFF, G.W. (1967) *Who Rules America?*, Englewood Cliffs, NJ, Prentice-Hall.

DOMINGUEZ, V.R. (1992) 'Invoking culture: The messy side of "cultural politics"', *The South Atlantic Quarterly*, **91**, 1, pp. 19–42.

DOUGHERTY, K. (1987) 'The effects of community colleges: Aid or hindrance to socioeconomic attainment?', *Sociology of Education*, **60**, 2, pp. 86–103.

DOUGLAS, J.M. (ed.) (1981) 'The Legal and Economic Status of Collective Bargaining in Higher Education: Proceedings, Ninth Annual Conference', New York, National Center for the Study of Collective Bargaining in Higher Education, Baruch College-CUNY.

DOUGLAS, J.M. (ed.) (1982) 'Campus Bargaining at the Crossroads: Proceedings, Tenth Annual Conference', New York, National Center for the Study of Collective Bargaining in Higher Education, Baruch College-CUNY.

DOUGLAS, J.M. (ed.) (1985) 'Unionization and Academic Excellence: Proceedings, Thirteenth Annual Conference', New York, National Center for the Study of Collective Bargaining in Higher Education, Baruch College-CUNY.

DOUGLAS, J.M. (ed.) (1989) 'Power Relationships on the Unionized Campus: Proceedings, Seventeenth Annual Conference', New York, National Center for the Study of Collective Bargaining in Higher Education, Baruch College-CUNY.

D'SOUZA, D. (1991) *Illiberal Education: The Politics of Race and Sex on Campus*, New York, Free Press.

ECO, U. (1989) *Foucault's Pendulum*, New York, Harcourt, Brace and Jovanovich.

EDELMAN, B. (1979) *Ownership of the Image: Elements for a Marxist Theory of Law*, London, Routledge and Kegan Paul.

EMERSON, K. (1991) 'Only correct', *The New Republic*, 18, February.

ESPING-ANDERSEN, G. (1990) *The Three Worlds of Welfare Capitalism*, Princeton, New Jersey, Princeton University Press.

EWEN, S. and EWEN, E. (1982) *Channels of Desire: Mass Images and the Shaping of American Consciousness*, New York, McGraw-Hill Book Company.

EYERMAN, R. *et al.* (eds) (1987) *Intellectuals, Universities, and the State in Western Modern Societies*, Berkeley, CA, University of California Press.

FABIAN, J. (1983) *Time and the Other*, New York, Columbia University Press.

FABIAN, J. (1990) 'Presence and representation: The other and anthropological writing', *Critical Inquiry*, **16**, 4, pp. 753–72.

FAY, M.A. and WEINTRAUB, J.A. (1973) *Political Ideologies of Graduate Students*, Berkeley, CA, Carnegie Commission on Higher Education.

FEATHERSTONE, M. (ed.) (1990) *Global Culture: Nationalism, Globalization, and Modernity: A Theory, Culture & Society Special Issue*, London, Sage Publications.

FINKELSTEIN, M.J. (1984) *The American Academic Profession*, Columbus, OH, State University Press.

FOLEY, D.E. (1990) *Learning Capitalist Culture: Deep in the Heart of Teas*, Philadelphia, PA, University of Pennsylvania Press.

FOSTER, H. (ed.) (1983) *The Anti-aesthetic: Essays on Postmodern Culture*, Port Townsend, Washington, Bay Press.

FOUCAULT, M. (1973) *Madness and Civilization*, New York, Vintage Books.

FOUCAULT, M. (1977) 'Nietzsche, genealogy, history', *Language, Countermemory, Practice*, pp. 139–64.

FOUCAULT, M. (1979) *Discipline and Punish: The Birth of the Prison*, New York, Vintage Books.

FOUCAULT, M. (1980) *Power/Knowledge*, New York, Pantheon Books.

FOWLER, R. *et al.* (1979) *Language and Control*, London, Routledge and Kegan Paul.

FREELAND, R.M. (1992) *Academia's Golden Age: Universities in Massachusetts, 1945–1970*, New York, Oxford University Press.

FREEMAN, C. (1993) 'Designing women: Corporate discipline and Barbados's offshore pink collar sector', *Cultural Anthropology*, **8**, 2, May, pp. 169–86.

FREIRE, P. (1970) *Pedagogy of the Oppressed*, New York, Seabury Press.

GAGNON, A.G. (ed.) (1987) *Intellectuals in Liberal Democracies*, New York, Praeger.

GAMBLE, A. (1988) *The Free Economy and the Strong State: The Politics of Thatcherism*, Durham, Duke University Press.

GARNHAM, N. and WILLIAMS, R. (1986) 'Pierre Bourdieu and the sociology of culture: An introduction', in COLLINS, R. *et al.* (eds) *Media, Culture & Society: A Critical Reader*, Beverly Hills, CA, Sage Publications.

GERAS, N. (1987) 'Post-Marxism?', *New Left Review*, **163**, pp. 40–82.

GIROUX, H.A. (1983) *Theory and Resistance in Education*, South Hadley, MA, Bergin and Garvey.

GIROUX, H.A. (1992) *Border Crossings: Cultural Workers and the Politics of Education*, New York, Routledge.

GIROUX, H.A. (1993) 'Literacy and the politics of difference', in LANKSHEAR, C. and McLAREN, P.L. (eds) *Critical Literacy: Politics, Praxis and the Postmodern*, Albany, NY, SUNY Press.

GITLIN, T. (1992) 'On the virtues of a loose canon', in AUFDERHEIDE, P. (ed.) *Beyond PC: Toward a Politics of Understanding*, Saint Paul, MN, Greywolf Press.

GOFFMAN, E. (1959) *The Presentation of Self in Everyday Life*, Garden City, NY, Doubleday.

GORDON, D. (1988) 'The global economy: New edifice or crumbling foundations?', *New Left Review*, **168**, pp. 24–64.

GOULDNER, A.W. (1979) *The Future of Intellectuals and the Rise of the New Class: A Frame of Reference, Theses, Conjectures, Arguments, and an Historical Perspective on the Role of Intellectuals and Intelligentsia in the International Class Contest of the Modern Era*, New York, Seabury Press.

GRAFF, G. (1987) *Professing Literature*, Chicago, IL, University of Chicago Press.

GRAMSCI, A. (1971) *Selections from the Prison Notebooks of Gramsci* (edited and translated by Quintin Hoare and Geoffrey Nowell Smith), New York, International Publishers.

GRASSMUCK, K. (1990) 'Big increases in academic-support staffs prompt growing concerns on campuses', *The Chronicle of Higher Education*, 28, March.

GREGORY, C.A. (1982) *Gifts and Commodities*, London, Academic Press.

GROSS, D. (1987) 'Hope among the ruins', review of Russell Jacoby's *The Last Intellectuals, Telos*, **73**, pp. 167–72.

GROSSMAN, R.J. (1988) 'The great debate over institutional accountability', *The College Board Review*, **147**, Spring.

HABERMAS, J. (1971) *Toward a Rational Society*, Boston, MA, Beacon Press.

HABERMAS, J. (1987) 'The idea of the university', *New German Critique*, **41**, pp. 3–22.

HABERMAS, J. (1989) *The Structural Transformation of the Public Sphere*, Cambridge, MA, MIT Press.

HABERMAS, J. (1992) 'Further reflections on the public sphere', in CALHOUN, C. (ed.) *Habermas and the Public Sphere*, Cambridge, MA, The MIT Press.

HALL, S. (1986) 'Popular culture and the state', in BENNETT, T. *et al.* (eds) *Popular Culture and Social Relations*, Milton Keynes, Open University Press.

HARAWAY, D. (1989) *Primate Visions: Gender, Race and Nature in the World of Modern Science*, London, Routledge, Chapman and Hall.

HARDY, C. (1987) 'Turnaround strategies in universities', *Planning for Higher Education*, **16**, 1, pp. 9–23.

HARRISON, B. and BLUESTONE, B. (1988) *The Great U-Turn*, New York, Basic Books.

HARTNETT, R.T. (1987) 'Has there been a graduate student "brain drain" in the arts and sciences?', *The Journal of Higher Education*, **58**, 5, pp. 562–85.

HARVEY, D. (1989) *The Condition of Postmodernity*, Oxford, Basil Blackwell.

HAUG, W.F. (1986) *Critique of Commodity Aesthetics*, Minneapolis, MN, University of Minnesota Press.

HEAD, S. (1996) 'The new ruthless economy', *The New York Review of Books*, 29, February, pp. 47–52.

HEBDIGE, D. (1979) *Subculture: The Meaning of Style*, London, Methuen and Company.

HEBDIGE, D. (1988) *Hiding in the Light: On Images and Things*, London, New York, Routledge.

HERMAN, E.S. and CHOMSKY, N. (1988) *Manufacturing Consent: The Political Economy of the Mass Media*, New York, Pantheon Books.

HERMAN, E. and O'SULLIVAN, G. (1989) *The Terrorism Industry: The Experts and Institutions That Shape Our View of Terror*, New York, Pantheon Books.

HIRSCH, E.D. Jr (1988) *Cultural Literacy*, New York, Vintage Books.

HOBSBAWM, E. and RANGER, T. (1983) *The Invention of Tradition*, Cambridge, Cambridge University Press.

HOOVER, K. and PLANT, R. (1989) *Conservative Capitalism in Britain and the United States: A Critical Appraisal*, London, Routledge.

HOROWITZ, H.L. (1987) *Campus Life: Undergraduate Cultures From the End of the Eighteenth Century to the Present*, New York, A.A. Knopf.

HUGHES, J.F. (ed.) (1975) *Education and the State*, Washington, DC, American Council on Education.

JACOBY, R. (1987) *The Last Intellectuals*, New York, Basic Books.

JACOBY, R. (1994) *Dogmatic Wisdom: How the Culture Wars Divert Education and Distract America*, New York, Doubleday.

JAMESON, F. (1981) *The Political Unconscious*, Ithaca, NY, Cornell University Press.

JAMESON, F. (1989) 'Marxism and postmodernism', *New Left Review*, **176**, pp. 31–45.

JENCKS, C. and RIESMAN, D. (1968) *The Academic Revolution*, Chicago, IL, University of Chicago Press.

JOHNSON, B. (1988) 'Marketing is not everything', *The College Board Review*, **146**, winter 1987–88.

JOHNSON, R. (1987) 'What is cultural studies anyway?', *Social Text*, **6**, 1, pp. 38–80.

JOHNSTONE, R.L. (1981) *The Scope of Faculty Collective Bargaining*, Westport, CT, Greenwood Press.

KATZ, M.B. (1975) *Class, Bureaucracy, and Schools*, New York, Praeger.

KATZ, M.B. (1987) *Reconstructing American Education*, Cambridge, MA, Harvard University Press.

KAUFFMAN, J.F. (1993) 'Governing boards', in LEVINE, A. (ed.) *Higher Learning in America 1980–2000*, Baltimore, MD, Johns Hopkins University Press.

KELLER, G. (1983) *Academic Strategy: The Management Revolution in American Higher Education*, Baltimore, MD, Johns Hopkins University Press.

KELLNER, D. (1989) *Jean Baudrillard: From Marxism to Postmodernism and Beyond*, Stanford, CA, Stanford University Press.

KERR, C. (1982) *The Uses of the University*, Cambridge, MA, Harvard University Press.

KOPTIUCH, K. (1991) 'Third-worlding at home', *Social Text*, **9**, 3, pp. 87–99.

KOPYTOFF, I. (1988) 'The cultural biography of things: Commoditization as process', in APPADURAI, A. (ed.) *The Social Life of Things: Commodities in Cultural Perspective*, (paperback edition), Cambridge, Cambridge University Press.

LABAREE, D.F. (1988) *The Making of an American High School: The Credentials Market and the Central High School of Philadelphia, 1838–1939*, New Haven, Yale University Press.

LACLAU, E. and MOUFFE, C. (1985) *Hegemony and Socialist Strategy*, London, Verso Books.

LACLAU, E. and MOUFFE, C. (1987) 'Post-Marxism without apologies', *New Left Review*, **166**, pp. 79–106.

LADD, E.C. JR and LIPSET, S.M. (1973) 'Professors, Unions, and American Higher Education', prepared for the Carnegie Commission on Higher Education, Washington, DC, American Enterprise Institute for Public Policy Research.

LARSON, M.S. (1977) *The Rise of Professionalism: A Sociological Analysis*, Berkeley, CA, University of California Press.

LASCH, C. (1995) *The Revolt of the Elites: And the Betrayal of Democracy*, New York, W.W. Norton.

LASH, S. (1990) *Sociology of Postmodernism*, London, Routledge.

LASH, S. and URRY, J. (1987) *The End of Organized Capitalism*, Madison, WI, University of Wisconsin Press.

LASLETT, B. (1990) 'Structure, agency and gender: The social reproduction of a discipline', *Sociological Forum*, **5**, 1, pp. 135–41.

LEE, E.C. and BOWEN, F.M. (1971) *The Multicampus University: A Study of Academic Governance* (Carnegie Commission on Higher Education Report) New York, McGraw-Hill Book Company.

LEGOFF, J. (1992) *History and Memory*, New York, Columbia University Press.

LESLIE, D.W., KELLAMS, S.E. and GUNNE, G.M. (1982) *Part-Time Faculty in American Higher Education*, New York, Praeger.

LEVENSTEIN, A. (ed.) (1980) 'Campus Bargaining in the Eighties: A Retrospective and a Prospective Look. Proceedings, Eighth Annual Conference', New York, National Center for the Study of Collective Bargaining in Higher Education, Baruch College-CUNY.

LEVINE, D.O. (1986) *The American College and the Culture of Aspiration, 1915–1940*, Ithaca, NY, Cornell University Press.

LIVINGSTONE, D.W. and CONTRIBUTORS (1987) *Critical Pedagogy and Cultural Power*, South Hadley, MA, Bergin and Garvey Publishers.

LODGE, D. (1988) *Nice Work*, New York, Penguin Books.

LOWENTHAL, D. (1985) *The Past is a Foreign Country*, Cambridge, Cambridge University Press.

LUKE, T. *et al.* (1987) 'Roundtable on intellectuals and the academy', *Telos*, **71**, pp. 5–35.

MACHADO, D. and SHUMAR, W. (1996) 'The end of history or a new era of polymorphic liberal capitalism?', paper presented at the Eastern Sociological Society meeting, Boston, March.

MACLEOD, J. (1987) *Ain't No Makin' It: Leveled Aspirations in a Low-Income Neighborhood*, Boulder, CO, Westview Press.

MANDEL, E. (1975) *Late Capitalism*, London, New Left Books.

MARCUS, G.E. (1986) 'Contemporary problems of ethnography in the modern world system', in CLIFFORD, J. and MARCUS, G.E. (eds) *Writing Culture*, Berkeley, CA, University of California Press.

MARCUS, G.E. and CUSHMAN, D. (1982) 'Ethnographies as texts', *Annual Review of Anthropology*, **11**, pp. 25–69.

MARCUS, G.E. and FISCHER, M.M.J. (1986) *Anthropology as Cultural Critique*, Chicago, IL, University of Chicago Press.

MARX, K. (1963) *The Poverty of Philosophy*, New York, International Publishers.

MARX, K. (1967) *Capital, Volume 1*, New York, International Publishers.

MARX, K. (1973) *Grundrisse: Foundations of the Critique of Political Economy*, New York, Vintage Books.

MARX, K. and ENGELS, F. (1974) *The German Ideology*, Part 1, New York, International Publishers.

MCCARTHY, T. (1990a) 'Private irony and public decency: Richard Rorty's new pragmatism', *Critical Inquiry*, **16**, 2, pp. 355–70.

MCCARTHY, T. (1990b) 'Ironist theory as vocation: A response to Rorty's reply', *Critical Inquiry*, **16**, 3, pp. 644–55.

MCDONOUGH, P.M. (1994) 'Buying and selling higher education', *Journal of Higher Education*, **65**, 4, pp. 425–45.

MCLAREN, P.L. (1988) 'On ideology and education: Critical pedagogy and the politics of empowerment', *Social Text*, **19/20**.

MCROBBIE, A. (1978) 'Working class girls and the culture of femininity', in Birmingham English University Centre for Contemporary Cultural Studies, Women's Studies Group, *Women Take Issue* London, Hutchinson.

METZGER, W.P. (1987) 'The academic profession in the United States', in CLARK, B.R. *The Academic Profession*, Berkeley, CA, University of California Press.

MILLS, C.W. (1959) *The Sociological Imagination*, New York, Grove Press.

MINTZ, S. (1986) *Sweetness and Power*, New York, Penguin Books.

MITCHELL, W.J.T. (1986) *Iconology: Image, Text, Ideology*, Chicago, IL, University of Chicago Press.

MOOD, A.M. (1973) 'The Future of Higher Education', a report prepared for the Carnegie Commission on Higher Education, New York, McGraw-Hill Book Company.

MOONEY, C.J. (1990) 'Academics on corporate boards: Beneficial for universities or conflict of interest?', *The Chronicle of Higher Education*, January.

MOONEY, C.J. (1991) 'Activist dean at Yale brings controversy to his post with strong views on study of Western civilization', *The Chronicle of Higher Education*, 19, June.

NADER, L. (1972) 'Up the anthropologist-perspective gained from studying up', in HYMES, D. (ed.) *Reinventing Anthropology*, New York, Vintage Books.

NASAW, D. (1981) *Schooled to Order*, Oxford, Oxford University Press.

NASH, J. (1987) 'Devils, witches and sudden death', in WHITTEN, P. and HUNTER,

D.E.K. (eds) *Anthropology: Contemporary Perspectives*, (article reprinted from *Natural History Magazine*, March 1972), Boston, MA, Little, Brown and Company.

NATIONAL CENTER FOR EDUCATIONAL STATISTICS (1989) in BAKER, C.O. and ROGERS, G.T. (eds) *The Condition of Education 1989: Volume 2, Postsecondary Education*, Washington, DC, US Department of Education, Government Printing Office.

NELSON, C. (1995) 'Late capitalism arrives on campus', *Social Text*, **13**, 3, pp. 119–34.

NEWMAN, F. (1985) *Higher Education and the American Resurgence* (a Carnegie Foundation Special Report) Princeton, Carnegie Foundation for the Advancement of Teaching.

NISBET, R. (1971) *The Degradation of Academic Dogma: The University in America, 1945–1970*, New York, Basic Books.

NOBLE, D. (1977) *America by Design: Science, Technology and the Rise of Corporate Capitalism*, New York, Alfred A. Knopf.

NOBLE, D. (1989) 'The multinational multiversity', *Z Magazine*, April.

OHMANN, R. (1987) *Politics of Letters*, Middletown, CT, Wesleyan University Press.

ONG, (1987) *Spirits of Resistance and Capitalist Discipline: Factory Women in Malaysia*, Albany, NY, State University of New York.

ORTNER, S.B. (1984) 'Theory in anthropology since the sixties', *Comparative Studies in Society and History*, **26**, 1, pp. 126–66.

PARSONS, T. (1974) 'The life and work of Emile Durkheim', in DURKHEIM, E., *Sociology and Philosophy*, New York, The Free Press.

POSTER, M. (1984) *Foucault, Marxism and History*, Cambridge, Polity Press, (in association with Basil Blackwell, Oxford).

POSTMAN, N. (1993) *Technopoly: The Surrender of Culture to Technology*, New York, Knopf.

RAGAN, S.L. and MCMILLAN, J.J. (1989) 'The marketing of the liberal arts', *Journal of Higher Education*, **60**, 6, pp. 682–703.

RIDGEWAY, J. (1968) *The Closed Corporation*, New York, Random House.

RIESMAN, D. (1980) *On Higher Education: The Academic Enterprise in an Era of Rising Student Consumerism*, San Francisco, CA, Jossey-Bass.

RIGBY, P. (1985) *Persistent Pastoralists: Nomadic Societies in Transition*, London, Zed.

ROBBINS, B. (1990) 'Introduction', *Social Text*, **25/26**, pp. 3–7 (special issue on The Phantom Public Sphere).

RORTY, R. (1979) *Philosophy and the Mirror of Nature*, Princeton, NJ, Princeton University Press.

RORTY, R. (1990) 'Truth and freedom: A reply to Thomas McCarthy', *Critical Inquiry*, **16**, 3, pp. 633–43.

ROSALDO, R. (1989) *Culture & Truth: The Remaking of Social Analysis*, Boston, MA, Beacon Press.

ROSENBLUM, G. and ROSENBLUM, B.R. (1990) 'Segmented labor markets in institutions of higher learning', *Sociology of Education*, **63**, 3, pp. 151–64.

ROSENFELD, R.A. and JONES, J.A. (1987) 'Patterns and effects of geographic mobility for academic women and men', *Journal of Higher Education*, **58**, 5, pp. 493–515.

ROTHSTEIN, E. (1991) 'Roll over Beethoven', *The New Republic*, 4, February.

ROTTENBERG, D. (1993) quoted from 'Commentary', *The Philadelphia Inquirer*, 24, July.

ROUSE, R. (1995) 'Thinking through transnationalism: Notes on the cultural politics of class relations in the contemporary United States', *Public Culture*, **7**, pp. 353–402.

SAID, E.W. (1979) *Orientalism*, New York, Vintage Books.

SAID, E.W. (1983a) *The World the Text and the Critic*, Cambridge, MA, Harvard University Press.

SAID, E.W. (1983b) 'Opponents, audiences, constituencies and community', in FOSTER, H. (ed.) *The Anti-Aesthetic*, Port Townsend, WA, Bay Press.

SAID, E.W. (1989) 'Representing the colonized: Anthropology's interlocutors', *Critical Inquiry*, **15**, 2, pp. 205–25.

SALZMAN, P.C. (1988) 'Fads and fashions in anthropology', *Anthropology Newsletter*, **29**, 5, May.

SARTRE, J.-P. (1974) *Between Existentialism and Marxism* (translated from the French by John Mathews) New York, Pantheon Books.

SCOTT, J.C. (1985) *Weapons of the Weak*, New Haven, CT, Yale University Press.

SEYMOUR, D.T. (1988) 'Higher education as a corporate enterprise', *The College Board Review*, 147, spring.

SHOR, I. (1986) *Culture Wars: School and Society in the Conservative Restoration 1969–1984*, London, Routledge and Kegan Paul.

SHOR, I. (1987) *Critical Teaching and Everyday Life*, Chicago, IL, University of Chicago Press.

SHUMAR, W. (1995) 'Higher education and the state: The irony of Fordism in American universities' in SMYTH, J. (ed.) *Academic Work*, Milton Keynes, Open University Press.

SIMPSON, D. (1982) *Fetishism and Imagination: Dickens, Melville, Conrad*, Baltimore, MD, Johns Hopkins University Press.

SKLAIR, L. (1991) *Sociology of the Global System*, Baltimore, MD, Johns Hopkins University Press.

SLAUGHTER, S. (1990) *The Higher Learning and High Technology: Dynamics of Higher Education Policy Formation*, Albany, NY, State University of New York Press.

SMITH, D.N. (1974) *Who Rules the University: An Essay in Class Analysis*, New York, Monthly Review Press.

SMITH, G. (1991) 'Writing for real: Capitalist constructions and constructions of capitalism', *Critique of Anthropology*, **11**, 3, pp. 213–32.

SOLOMON, B.M. (1985) *In the Company of Educated Women*, New Haven, CT, Yale University Press.

SOLOMON, R.C. and SOLOMON, J. (1993) *Up the University: Recreating Higher Education in America*, Reading, MA, Addison-Wesley Publishing Co.

SPEAKS, M. (1989) 'Chaos, simulation and corporate culture', *Mississippi Review*, **49/50**, pp. 159–76.

SPIVAK, G.C. (1987) *In Other Worlds: Essays in Cultural Politics*, London, Methuen and Company.

SPIVAK, G.C. (1988) 'Can the subaltern speak?', in NELSON, C. and GROSSBERG, L. (eds) *Marxism and the Interpretation of Culture*, Urbana, IL, University of Illinois Press, pp. 271–313.

SPRING, J.H. (1972) *Education and the Rise of the Corporate State*, Boston, MA, Beacon Press.

STADTMAN, V.A. (1980) *Academic Adaptations: Higher Education Prepares for the 1980s and 1990s*, San Francisco, CA, Jossey-Bass.

STOCKING, G.W. JR (1968) *Race, Culture, and Evolution: Essays in the History of Anthropology*, New York, The Free Press.

STOLLER, P. (1989) *The Taste of Ethnographic Things*, Philadelphia, PA, University of Pennsylvania Press.

STRANGE, S. (1986) *Casino Capitalism*, Oxford, Blackwell.

SUMNER, C. (1979) *Reading Ideologies: An Investigation into the Marxist Theory of Ideology and Law*, London, Academic Press.

SUSSMAN, A. (1981) 'University governance through a rose-colored lens: NLRB v. Yeshiva', in KURLAND, P.B. and CASPER, G. (eds) (*1980*) *Supreme Court Review*, Chicago, IL, University of Chicago Press.

SYKES, C.J. (1988) *ProfScam: Professors and the Demise of Higher Education*, New York, St. Martin's Press.

TANNENBAUM, F. (ed.) (1965) *A Community of Scholars: The University Seminars at Columbia*, New York, Praeger.

TAUSSIG, M.T. (1980) *The Devil and Commodity Fetishism in South America*, Chapel Hill, University of North Carolina Press.

TAUSSIG, M. (1992) *The Nervous System*, New York, Routledge.

TAYLOR, F. (1911) *The Principles of Scientific Management*, New York, Harper Brothers.

THOMPSON, J.B. (1984) *Studies in the Theory of Ideology*, Berkeley, CA, University of California Press.

THUROW, L. (1996) *The Future of Capitalism: How Today's Economic Forces Shape Tomorrow's World*, New York, W. Morrow and Co.

TIERNEY, W.G. (1988) 'Organizational culture in higher education: Defining the essentials', *Journal of Higher Education*, **59**, 1, pp. 2–21.

TIERNEY, W.G. and RHOADS, R.A. (1995) 'The culture of assessment', in SMYTH, J. (ed.) *Academic Work*, Milton Keynes, Open University Press.

TSING, A.L. (1994) *In the Realm of the Diamond Queen: Marginality in an Out-of-the-Way Place*, Princeton, NJ, Princeton University Press.

TURNER, T. (1993) 'Anthropology and multiculturalism: What is anthropology that multiculturalists should be mindful of it?', *Cultural Anthropology*, **8**, 4, pp. 411–29.

UHL, N.P. (ed.) (1983) *Using Research for Strategic Planning*, San Francisco, CA, Jossey-Bass.

UNITED STATES CODE (1983) *United States Code*, (1982 ed) **12**, Title 29, Chapter 7, Labor-Management Relations, Washington, DC, United States Government Printing Office.

UNITED STATES REPORTS (1982) 'National Labor Relations Board v. Yeshiva', *United States Reports*, **444**. Washington, United States Government Printing Office, pp. 672–706.

VEBLEN, T. (1957) *The Higher Learning in America: A Memorandum on the Conduct of Universities by Businessmen*, New York, Sagamore Press.

VEYSEY, L.R. (1965) *The Emergence of the American University*, Chicago, IL, University of Chicago Press.

VIGODA, R. (1995) 'All's fair in love and war and a class on student revolt', *The Philadelphia Inquirer*, 15, March.

VOLOSINOV, V.N. (1973) *Marxism and the Philosophy of Language*, New York, Seminar Press.

WATERS, M. (1995) *Globalization*, London, Routledge.

WEILER, K. (1988) *Women Teaching for a Change: Gender, Class and Power*, New York, Bergin and Garvey.

WEIS, L. (1990) *Working Class Without Work: High School Students in a Deindustrializing Economy*, New York, Routledge.

WIEBE, R.H. (1967) *The Search for Order: 1877–1920*, New York, Hill and Wang.

WILKE, A.S. (ed.) (1979) *The Hidden Professoriate: Credentialism, Professionalism and the Tenure Crisis*, Westport, CT, Greenwood Press.

WILLIS, P. (1981) *Learning to Labor: How Working Class Kids Get Working Class Jobs*, New York, Columbia University Press.

WILLIS, P. with JONCE, S., CANNAN, J. and HURD, G. (1990) *Common Culture: Symbolic Work at Play in the Everyday Culture of the Young*, Boulder, CO, Westview Press.

WOLF, E.R. (1990) 'Facing power: Old insights, new questions', *American Anthropologist*, **92**, 3, pp. 586–96.

WOLFF, R.P. (1987) 'Review of The *Closing of the American Mind* by Allan Bloom', *Academe*, **73**, 5, pp. 64–5.

WOOD, E.M. (1986) *The Retreat from Class*, London, Verso.

WRIGHT, B.A. (1991) 'The rating game: How media affect college admission', *The College Board Review*, **158**, winter 1990–91.

ZEMSKY, R. and OEDEL, P. (1983) *The Structure of College Choice*, New York, College Entrance Examination Board.

ZINN, H. (1980) *A People's History of the United States*, New York, Harper and Row.

Index